OUR
REPUBLICAN
CONSTITUTION

ALSO BY RANDY E. BARNETT

Restoring the Lost Constitution

The Structure of Liberty

The Rights Retained by the People

OUR
REPUBLICAN
CONSTITUTION

Securing the Liberty and Sovereignty
of We the People

RANDY E.
BARNETT

BROADSIDE BOOKS
An Imprint of HarperCollins*Publishers*

HarperCollins books may be purchased for educational, business, or sales promotional use. For information, please e-mail the Special Markets Department at SPsales@harpercollins.com.

Broadside Books™ and the Broadside logo are trademarks of HarperCollins Publishers.

FIRST EDITION

Designed by Fritz Metsch

Library of Congress Cataloging-in-Publication Data has been applied for.

ISBN: 978-0-06-241228-7

16 17 18 19 20   OV/RRD   10 9 8 7 6 5 4 3 2 1

TO MY FATHER,

RONALD EVAN BARNETT

(1926–2015),

a true republican

CONTENTS

FOREWORD
by George F. Will

THIS BOOK, SLENDER and sharp as a stiletto, arrives at a moment when the nation's civic temperature is high, but not higher than the stakes of today's political argument. This volume is written by a law professor and lucidly takes readers into the thickets of jurisprudential controversies. It is not, however, merely, or even primarily, a book about American constitutional law. In fact, it demonstrates why any treatise on the major themes of constitutional law cannot help but be much more than that. It *must* be an encounter with the great issues of political philosophy—how to understand human nature, rights, freedom, equality, and justice. Or in Randy Barnett's formulation, "How should society be structured so that individuals can pursue happiness while living in close proximity to others?"

In the pages that follow, Barnett explains why the way we resolve two of today's interlocking arguments—about the Constitution's priorities and the judiciary's role in implementing them—will decide nothing less than the nature of the American regime.

Barnett is an eminent law professor and the prolific author of now eleven books and scores of law review articles pertaining to constitutional law. Also, through his engagement in public affairs—arguing in appellate courts and the Supreme Court, in the mass media and other public forums—he has become one of the nation's most prominent public intellectuals. Now however, in this book, he explicitly assumes a role implicit in his other roles, that of political philosopher.

His career, and this book, illustrate a profound truth about the American polity and its history, a truth sometimes missed by even the most accomplished students of American history. It is often said that ours is a nation indifferent, even averse, to political philosophy. And it is said that this disposition is a virtue and a sign of national health. The theory is that only unhappy nations are constantly engaged in arguing about fundamental things, and that the paucity—one should say the postulated paucity—of American political philosophy is evidence of a contented consensus about our polity's basic premises.

More than six decades ago, Daniel J. Boorstin, then a University of Chicago professor of American history and later librarian of Congress, published his own slender volume, *The Genius of American Politics*. It appeared in 1953, during America's postwar introspection about the nature and meaning of our nation's sudden global preeminence. Boorstin's argument, made with his characteristic verve and erudition, aimed to explain why our success was related to "our antipathy to political theory."

The genius of our democracy, said Boorstin, comes not from any geniuses of political thought comparable to Plato and Aristotle or Hobbes and Locke. Rather, it comes from "the unprecedented opportunities of this continent and from a peculiar and unrepeatable combination of historical circumstances." This explains "our inability to make a 'philosophy' of them," and why our nation has never produced a political philosopher of the stature of, say, Hobbes and Locke or "a systematic theoretical work to rank with theirs."

Well. Leave aside the fact that James Madison was a political philosopher of such stature. He was *because* he was a practicing politician. And leave aside the fact that, which it surely is, *The Federalist Papers*, although a compendium of newspaper columns written in haste to solve a practical problem (to secure ratification of the Constitution), is a theoretical work that ranks with Hobbes's *Leviathan* and Locke's *The Second Treatise on Civil Government*. Indeed, *The Federalist Papers* remains a recognizably major event in the Western political conversation begun by Plato.

Considered in the second decade of the twenty-first century, as we stand on the dark and bloody ground of today's political contentions, Boorstin's book remains interesting, but primarily as a period piece. It is a shard of America's now-shattered consensus. Or, more precisely, it is a document from the calm before the storm of the counterattack against progressivism's complacent assumption that its ascendancy was unchallenged and secure.

The theory that America is inhospitable to political philosophy is thoroughly wrong. The American argument about philosophic fundamentals is not only ongoing, it is thoroughly woven into the fabric of our public life. Far from being rare and of marginal importance in America, political philosophy is more central to our public life than to that of any other nation. It is implicated in almost all American policy debates of any consequence.

Indeed it is, like Edgar Allan Poe's purloined letter, hidden in plain sight. All American political arguments involve, at bottom, interpretations of the Declaration of Independence and of the Constitution, which was written to provide institutional architecture for governance according to the Declaration's precepts. So constitutional lawyers like Barnett are America's practitioners of political philosophy.

The Constitution, which Barnett calls "the law that governs those who govern us," is, he argues, properly read in the bright light cast by the great document that preceded it, the Declaration of Independence. The Constitution was written to provide the institutional architecture and the practices requisite for a national life lived in accordance with what Barnett calls Jefferson's "fifty-five compelling words":

We hold these truths to be self-evident, that all men are created equal, that they are endowed by their Creator with certain unalienable Rights, that among these are Life, Liberty and the pursuit of Happiness. That to secure these rights, Governments are instituted among Men, deriving their just powers *from the consent of the governed.*

Those fifty-five words are so familiar that the importance of two of them, a verb and an adjective, is insufficiently understood. Governments can derive many powers from the consent of the majority, but not all exercises of those powers are, simply because they flow from a majority, "just." And governments are instituted to "secure" our preexisting rights, not to bestow them. As Barnett insists, the great divide in America today is between those who do believe, as the founders did, that "first come rights and then comes government," and those who believe, as progressives do, that "first comes government and then come rights." The former are adherents of the Republican Constitution. The latter have given us the Democratic Constitution.

The debate between these cohorts is, Barnett believes, "about the meaning of the first three words of the Constitution: 'We the People.' Those who favor the Democratic Constitution view We the People as a group, as a body, as a collective entity. Those who favor the Republican Constitution view We the People as individuals." The choice between these two understandings has enormous consequences, especially concerning the proper meaning of popular sovereignty.

A Republican Constitution is a device for limiting government, including government's translation of majority desires into laws and policies when those conflict with government's business of securing the natural rights of individuals. Barnett adopts given/if/then reasoning: *given* the constancy and regularity of human nature, *if* our aim is the flourishing of individuals living in communities, *then* the following institutional arrangements are requisite for securing the rights of individuals.

A Democratic Constitution is a device for giving priority to the will of a collective, the majority. This Constitution expresses the desires of a majority of the people, allowing the majority's will to prevail. Hence, Barnett notes, any principle—or practice, such as judicial review—that impedes the will of the majority is presumptively illegitimate until proven otherwise. And "the only individual rights that are legally enforceable are a product of majoritarian will."

Barnett has elsewhere written that for decades now, American Lockeans have been losing ground to Hobbesians. Those who take their bearings from John Locke "are those for whom individual liberty is their first principle of social ordering." Those who are Thomas Hobbes's intellectual children "give the highest priority to government power to provide social order and to pursue social ends," even if the rights of individuals must be abridged.

Not all Hobbesians are progressives, but all progressives are Hobbesians because they say America is dedicated to a *process*—to majoritarian decision-making that legitimates the exercises of the government power that it endorses. Not all Lockeans are libertarians, but all libertarians are Lockeans because they say America is dedicated to a *condition*—liberty. Hobbesians say the core American principle is the right of the majority to have its way. Lockeans stress rigorous judicial protection of individual rights, especially those of private property and the freedom of contract, that define and protect the zone of sovereignty within which people are free to act as they please.

The 1896 *Plessy v. Ferguson* decision, in which the Supreme Court deferred to the right of the majority to codify racial segregation under the rubric of "separate but equal," was, Barnett argues, an example of the Democratic Constitution's majoritarianism. He says the 1954 *Brown v. Board of Education* decision, affirming the individual rights of individual school children against a majority's preference for segregated schools represented tardy fidelity to the Republican Constitution.

Barnett has become a leader of those who are reasserting the natural rights tradition that was overthrown during progressivism's long success in defining the nature of the Democratic Constitution and the judiciary's permissive role in construing the government's powers under it. But Barnett's challenge to progressives is also, and perhaps first, a challenge to conservatives. He is summoning them to reexamine the philosophic premises that have impelled them to celebrate judicial modesty, understood as deference to majoritarian institutions. Hence this book will be constructively discomforting, disturbing the dogmatic slumbers of people who occupy various positions along the political spectrum.

Barnett's readers will be convinced that political philosophy, far from somehow being an alien activity for Americans, is as American as apple pie. Margaret Thatcher, explaining why Europe and the United States are really not siblings, said: "Europe is a product of history. America is a product of philosophy." To read this book is to understand how right she was about America, and how right Randy Barnett is about the need for Americans to soberly consider how far their cumulative choices have taken their country from the founders' philosophy.

He has written not an agenda for action but a call to reflection. If his call is heeded, action will follow, and so, perhaps, will the restoration of the Republican Constitution.

OUR
REPUBLICAN
CONSTITUTION

TRIUMPH AND TRAGEDY

How the Obamacare Case Was Won . . . and Lost

NOVEMBER 12, 2009, was a fateful date for the Constitution. For it was on that day, in the foyer of Washington's landmark Mayflower Hotel, that the constitutional challenge to the Affordable Care Act—now known as Obamacare—was first conceived. I was at the Mayflower attending the Federalist Society for Law and Public Policy's annual National Lawyers Convention. Shortly after 10:15 a.m., I left a panel discussion in the ballroom to join a group of friends who had gathered near the coffee to chat.

By the time I joined the group, the topic had already turned to the so-called health care reform bill that was then bottled up in a committee of the Senate. While the House had already passed its version, the Senate's effort had been stymied by the need to get sixty senators on board so the bill could not be filibustered on the floor.

As I joined the group, my friend Todd Gaziano, who was then the director of the Center for Legal and Judicial Studies at the Heritage Foundation, turned to me and asked what I thought about the constitutionality of the pending bill. I replied that I hadn't given the matter much thought.[1]

In fact, back in September, I had read an op-ed in the *Wall Street Journal* questioning the constitutionality of the individual insurance "requirement" that was part of the bill. My disappointed reaction was, "Well, if this is the best argument against it, then the bill must be constitutional." A few days later, however, a debate over the op-ed erupted on the *Arena*, the now-defunct blog of *Politico* of which I was then a member.

The *Arena* editors posed the following question to the group: "Healthcare: Is 'mandatory insurance' unconstitutional?" Timothy Stoltzfus Jost, a health law professor at the Washington and Lee University School of Law, posted a caustic dismissal of any suggestion that the measure might be unconstitutional. "You are correct to invite your political experts to respond," he wrote, "because this is not a serious legal issue." In a lengthy post, he concluded by claiming that "a basic principle of our constitutional system for the last two centuries has been that the Supreme Court is the ultimate authority on the Constitution, and the Constitution the Court now recognizes would permit Congress to adopt health care reform."[2]

Although I had not been persuaded by the op-ed, Jost's smug dismissal of any constitutional argument based on the limits on Congress's power in the text of the Constitution provoked me to write a post that began: "OK, let's be old fashioned and start with what the Constitution says." I then proceeded to examine the text to find where it might authorize such an economic mandate. After finding no support for such a power in the original meaning of the Commerce Clause and the Necessary and Proper Clause, I turned to the Supreme Court's decisions, which Jost had claimed *was* the Constitution.

Professor Jost had relied heavily on the 2005 case of *Gonzales v. Raich*, in which the Court upheld the power of Congress to prohibit someone from growing marijuana in her backyard for her own medical use as authorized by state law. I was one of the lawyers who represented Angel Raich and Diane Monson in their challenge to this application of the Controlled Substances Act, and had argued the case before the Supreme Court in 2004. Although we lost, we did receive the votes of Chief Justice William Rehnquist and Justices Sandra Day O'Connor and Clarence

Thomas for our claim that this was beyond the power of Congress to enact.

After years of litigating the *Raich* case, I had become very well versed in the Supreme Court's Commerce Clause jurisprudence—an expertise that was to become extremely valuable when challenging Obamacare. And I strongly believed that Jost, like most law professors, was overreading that case, so I replied:

> As Angel Raich's lawyer, who argued the case in the Supreme Court, I think the Court erred (6–3) in reading the interstate commerce power broadly enough to allow Congress to prohibit you from growing a plant in your back yard for your own consumption. By all accounts, however, this is the most far reaching interpretation of the Commerce Power ever adopted by a majority, exceeding the reach of the past champion, *Wickard v. Filburn*. But even the six Justices in the majority did not say that Congress had the power to *mandate* you grow a plant in your back yard. Do you think a majority would find that power today?

I then suggested that "a bare majority [might] decide this matter by reviewing the text" of the Constitution and find no such power there. "Stranger things have happened," I observed. "After all, without any precedent standing in their way, a majority of the Supreme Court had recently decided to follow the original meaning of the text of the Second Amendment in *DC. v. Heller*."[3] A lively debate ensued, with my side joined by Roger Pilon of the Cato Institute and Northwestern University law professor Steve Calabresi in questioning the constitutionality of this claim of congressional power. We didn't progress very far, but the seed of an argument had been planted in my mind: if there was no Supreme Court precedent upholding a power to make you do business with a private company, then, as it had in 2006 with the right to keep and bear arms, a majority of the justices might feel free to rely on the original meaning of the text and find no such power exists.

So, when Todd Gaziano turned to me at the Mayflower and asked if I wanted to "do something" about the pending health care bill, I immediately answered yes. "Well, if we are going to do anything," Todd replied, "we have to do it soon," since the Senate bill was going to emerge from committee. I told him that I would need someone to do a first draft of a paper, but Todd already had someone in mind.

That someone was a young attorney named Nathaniel Stewart. Stewart's first draft was superb, but one particular discovery of his was crucial to how the debate unfolded: a 1994 report of the Congressional Budget Office—a nonpartisan arm of Congress—that said:

> A mandate requiring all individuals to purchase health in-
> surance would be an *unprecedented* form of federal action.
> The government has never required people to buy any good
> or service as a condition of lawful residence in the United
> States. An individual mandate would have two features
> that, in combination, would make it unique. First, it would
> impose a duty on individuals as members of society. Second,
> it would require people to purchase a specific service that
> would be heavily regulated by the federal government.[4]

I made that quote the epigraph of our paper, which I titled, "Why the Personal Mandate to Buy Health Insurance Is Unprecedented and Unconstitutional."[5] By making the "unprecedented" nature of the individual insurance mandate the centerpiece of our case, we immediately undercut claims such as the one made by Tim Jost that prior Supreme Court precedent clearly authorized such a mandate.

Four weeks later, on December 9, our paper was released, and the Heritage Foundation held a program to publicize it. Senator Orrin Hatch delivered an excellent keynote address supporting our theory, and I debated the merits of our argument with Professor Eugene Volokh of the UCLA School of Law. After the public program, we convened upstairs for a private briefing with congressional staffers.

Under Senate rules, senators may raise a point of order to object to the constitutionality of pending legislation. When they do, there must be a debate and vote on its constitutionality before the Senate may vote to pass the bill. Although senators supporting the bill will always vote that it is constitutional, in this case we thought holding such a debate could prove very useful.

We'd been told that Senate Republicans were not going to raise a point of order because their staffs could not think of a constitutional objection. Well, now we had such a theory, and a roomful of staffers was eager to hear the details.

As a result, the Senate Republicans did raise a point of order, and a debate on the constitutionality of the Senate bill was held on December 23. When the vote was taken, the entire Republican caucus voted that the bill was unconstitutional, while the Democrats were unanimous in opposition. With the failure of the point of order, the Senate was cleared to pass the bill on Christmas Eve.

Notwithstanding that the objection had failed, the debate proved to be a crucial event. Reporters started calling me to ask about our legal theory; conservative talk radio took up our argument and started publicizing it. In short, a very public buzz was starting to build.

In January I was contacted by Jim Ho, who was then solicitor general of Texas. Would I be willing, he asked, to speak with state attorney general Greg Abbott about the pending health care bill? Soon I was on the phone with Abbott, who wanted to know what, if anything, he could do to oppose the law as a state attorney general. After our call, Abbott and his staff began working with Florida attorney general Bill McCollum to organize other state attorneys general to challenge the law in court. This would prove to be a critical development.

The Senate bill to which we were objecting was never truly meant to become law. It had been devised behind closed doors to garner sixty votes mainly to get the measure out of the Senate and into a conference with the House, where the final measure would be drafted and sent back to both houses for final approval. However, with the death of Senator Edward Kennedy of Massachusetts in August 2009 and his replacement by Republican Scott Brown in a special election held on January 19, 2010, Senate Democrats no longer had a sixty-vote, filibuster-proof majority. If they wanted to enact something, their only option was for the House to accept the Senate bill, with all its faults, in its entirety. This some Democratic members of the House were reluctant to do, and so the process dragged on.

By the time the House finally passed the Senate bill on Sunday, March 22, 2010, thirteen state attorneys general, together with the National Federation of Independent Business (NFIB), were ready to file a lawsuit against the law the very next day in U.S. District Court for the Northern District of Florida. As additional states joined the lawsuit, and separate challenges were brought elsewhere by the attorneys general of Virginia and Oklahoma, eventually the number of states officially challenging the law would rise to twenty-eight, or more than half.

For the next year, with numerous lawsuits pending in lower courts around the country, I filed amicus briefs with Ilya Shapiro and Trevor Burrus of the Cato Institute, wrote op-eds for outlets such as the *Wall Street Journal*, and blogged regularly about the case on the *Volokh Conspiracy*, a law blog that was widely read by law students, law clerks, and even federal judges and justices. Other *Volokh* bloggers joined in.[6]

Like Professor Jost, the great majority of law professors continued to insist that our arguments so lacked merit they should be considered "frivolous." A few days after the NFIB and attorneys general filed their lawsuit, one professor went so far as to blog that any attorney who signed a pleading in the pending cases was at risk of sanctions for bringing a meritless complaint.

Then the tide began to turn. On August 2, 2010, federal judge Henry E. Hudson of the U.S. District Court for the Eastern District of Virginia became the first judge to hold that the individual insurance mandate was unconstitutional. The psychological effect of that ruling was enormous. Within moments of the decision, my good friend Yale law professor Jack Balkin sent me a single-sentence email: "Dear Randy: Your argument is officially not frivolous, per the E.D. Va."

With Judge Hudson's decision lending credibility to our theory, national attention now shifted to Florida, where the NFIB and attorneys general's challenge was pending before federal district court judge Roger Vinson. In December, I attended the oral argument in the packed Pensacola courtroom, as I would every court of appeals argument in the pending challenges. Washington attorney David Rivkin argued the case for the challengers to a courtroom packed with reporters.

In January 2011, in a lengthy and thorough opinion, Judge Vinson held that the individual insurance mandate was unconstitutional. And, because the mandate was an essential part of the entire scheme, he declared that it could not be severed from the rest of the law. As a result, he concluded, the entire Affordable Care Act (ACA) was unconstitutional.

Attempting to quash the now-growing credibility of the case, in February the Senate Judiciary Committee, chaired by Senator Richard Durbin, held a hearing on "The Constitutionality of the Affordable Care Act." The hearing was broadcast on C-SPAN. Along with former Reagan administration lawyer Michael

Carvin, I testified that the ACA was unconstitutional. Opposing us were former acting U.S. solicitor general Walter Dellinger III, Ohio attorney general Richard Cordray, and Harvard law professor Charles Fried, who had served as President Reagan's solicitor general and who was also my torts professor in law school.

The hearings did not have their intended effect. Carvin and I held our own under tough questioning by Democratic senators, and the Democrats' witnesses faced challenging questions from Republicans, especially freshman senator Mike Lee of Utah. If anything, the televised hearings increased our momentum.

In the wake of Judge Vinson's ruling, I was retained by the NFIB to help select a law firm to defend its victory against the government's appeal to the U.S. Court of Appeals for the Eleventh Circuit, in Atlanta. After a quiet competition among some of Washington's more elite firms, the NFIB selected the Jones Day team, headed by Mike Carvin and Greg Katsas, with me as cocounsel. The twenty-six attorneys general selected former U.S. solicitor general Paul Clement as their counsel. This meant we got to file two briefs rather than one in the court of appeals, and each advocate brought his own distinctive style to the case.

As it happened, as acting solicitor general, Paul Clement had been my opponent in the Supreme Court when I argued the *Raich* case. Back then he had defended the power of Congress to prohibit my clients from growing marijuana for themselves. Now, as my cocounsel rather than my adversary, he would contend that even the *Raich* case did not go so far as to authorize Congress to mandate economic activity.

To the chagrin of the ACA's supporters and most law professors, the Eleventh Circuit handed the government another defeat. Its two-to-one decision was authored by Judge Frank Hull, who, despite the misleading name, is a woman. Judge Hull, a Clinton nominee to the court of appeals, accepted our argument that the unprecedented insurance mandate was unconstitutional (though the panel also held, contrary to Judge Vinson, that it could be severed from the entire act).

The stage was now set for what would turn out to be a historic three days of oral argument in the Supreme Court beginning on Monday, March 26, 2012. (Supreme Court arguments, in even the most momentous of cases, normally last just sixty minutes.) Although you are never supposed to draw too many inferences from the tenor of oral argument, the first day seemed to go well for the challengers. But it was on Tuesday that the crucial issue of the constitutionality of the insurance mandate was to be argued.

Extra chairs had been added in the aisle next to the benches in the courtroom to help accommodate the intense demand for seating. Taking in the scene, I saw senators, congressmen, cabinet secretaries, and other prominent personalities being escorted to their seats. Even some of the justices' spouses were in attendance.

As the time for argument drew closer, the press filed into their box to the left of the justices' bench and started to crane their necks to identify personages in the audience for their stories. Reporters elbowed each other while pointing to and sharing the names of the dignitaries they spotted.

As the clock hand over the bench neared 10 a.m. and the lawyers and spectators grew silent, I was supremely grateful that it was Paul Clement and Mike Carvin who would be arguing the case and not me. After experiencing the pressure of the oral argument in *Raich*, never for a moment did I wish for that task. When veteran litigator and solicitor general Donald Verrilli stood to address the justices, he literally choked on a sip of water at the beginning of his argument.

Like everyone else in the courtroom, I was more interested in the justices' questions than the advocates' answers. That day, one question by Justice Anthony Kennedy jumped out as overwhelmingly significant:

I understand that we must presume laws are constitutional, but, even so, when you are changing the relation of the individual to the government in this, what we can stipulate is, I think, a unique way, do you not have a heavy burden of justification to show authorization under the Constitution?

This question was identical to a point I had made repeatedly in my many speeches, briefs, and articles.

Kennedy went on to say: "Here the government is saying that the federal government has a duty to tell the individual citizen that [he] must act, and that is different from what we have [upheld] in previous cases." That mandating conduct was "unprecedented" and, therefore, distinguishable from previous Supreme Court decisions was what I suggested in my *Arena* blog post, and it became the centerpiece of our Heritage Foundation paper.

In the old 1930s movies, when a big story breaks, reporters are shown running to a bank of telephone booths to file their stories. Had reporters been allowed to exit the courtroom during the argument—and if we still had phone booths—that is what would have happened next. On that day, however, as I left the courtroom and made my way to the row of television cameras for some prearranged interviews, I passed one reporter after another breathlessly relating to their viewers how it now looked like the challengers might well prevail. And they were right.

With the health care challenge, not one but two issues were on the table. The first was the survival of the Affordable Care Act, which in my view is an egregious public policy. The second was whether the Supreme Court would accept the expansive reading of congressional power that its supporters offered in its defense, which in my view threatened our constitutional scheme of limited and enumerated federal power. In the health care case, though we lost on the policy question, we won on the constitutional one. In short, the case was about saving the country from Obamacare and saving the Constitution for the country.

Before the decision, I figured it was all or nothing. If we lost on Obamacare, it would mean the government's (and law professors') reading of the Commerce and Necessary and Proper clauses would prevail. If we won, it would be because our contrasting theories had been affirmed by the Court.

As it happened, although we did not succeed in invalidating the ACA, our view of the Commerce and Necessary and Proper clauses was affirmed by five justices. And the reasons advanced by the government, by most law professors, and by the four liberal justices in Justice Ruth Bader Ginsburg's concurring opinion for upholding the ACA were rejected.

Indeed, with respect to constitutional law, the case has put us ahead of where we were before the ACA. Five justices of the Supreme Court have now definitively ruled that the Commerce Clause, the Necessary and Proper Clause, and spending power have limits; that the mandate to purchase private health insurance, as well as the threat to withhold Medicaid funding unless states agree to expand their coverage, exceeded these limits; and that the Court will enforce these limits. This was huge.

On the Commerce Clause, Chief Justice John G. Roberts Jr. and four dissenting justices accepted all of our side's arguments about why the insurance mandate exceeded Congress's power. "The individual mandate cannot be upheld as an exercise of Congress's power under the Commerce Clause," Roberts wrote. "That Clause authorizes Congress to regulate interstate commerce, not to order individuals to engage in it."[7]

Roberts adopted this view for the precise reason we advanced: granting Congress this power would gravely limit the liberties of the people. As he put it: "Allowing Congress to justify federal regulation by pointing to the effect of inaction on commerce would bring countless decisions an individual could *potentially* make within the scope of federal regulation, and—under the government's theory—empower Congress to make those decisions for him."[8]

Regarding the Necessary and Proper Clause, supporters of the health care overhaul had invoked the power of Congress "to make all laws which shall be necessary and proper for carrying into execution the foregoing powers," seeing it as a constitutional carte blanche to adopt any means to facilitate the regulation of insurance companies that did not violate an express constitutional prohibition. Roberts squarely rejected this argument: "Even if the individual mandate is 'necessary' to the Act's insurance reforms, such an expansion of federal power is not a 'proper' means for making those reforms effective."[9]

Tellingly, the chief justice soundly rejected the reasoning that, for two years, had been offered by the government and academic defenders of the insurance mandate:

Indeed, the Government's logic would justify a mandatory purchase to solve almost any problem. To consider a different example in the health care market, many Americans do not eat a balanced diet. That group makes up a larger percentage of the total population than those without health insurance. The failure of that group to have a healthy diet increases health care costs, to a greater extent than the failure of the uninsured to purchase insurance. Those increased costs are borne in part by other Americans who must pay more, just as the uninsured shift costs to the insured. Congress addressed the insurance problem by ordering everyone to buy insurance. Under the Government's theory, Congress could address the diet problem by ordering everyone to buy vegetables.[10]

He then continued:

> People, for reasons of their own, often fail to do things that would be good for them or good for society. Those failures—joined with the similar failures of others—can readily have a substantial effect on interstate commerce. Under the Government's logic, that authorizes Congress to use its commerce power to compel citizens to act as the Government would have them act.
>
> That is not the country the Framers of our Constitution envisioned. . . . Congress already enjoys vast power to regulate much of what we do. Accepting the Government's theory would give Congress the same license to regulate what we do not do, *fundamentally changing the relation between the citizen and the Federal Government.*[11]

For these reasons, the Court held that economic mandates are unconstitutional under both the Commerce and Necessary and Proper clauses.

As for the spending power, while the Court has previously invalidated statutes that exceeded the Commerce Clause, not since the New Deal had it rejected a law for exceeding the spending power of Congress—until *NFIB v. Sebelius*. The Court invalidated the part of the Affordable Care Act that empowered the U.S. Department of Health and Human Services to coerce the states by withholding Medicaid funding for existing programs unless the states accepted new coverage requirements.[12]

When the case was finally decided, against all odds five justices had completely accepted our claim that an individual insurance mandate was beyond the enumerated powers of Congress to impose on the people. All of this represented a fundamental departure from how most law professors viewed constitutional law before this decision. Under the holding of *NFIB*, economic mandates are unconstitutional.

To the dismay of the challengers, however, after deciding for us on the Constitution, the chief justice provided the fifth vote to uphold Obamacare, over the vehement joint dissent of Justices Kennedy, Scalia, Thomas, and Alito. Although we had saved the enumerated powers scheme of the Constitution for the country when these four justices and the chief justice accepted *all* our constitutional arguments, somehow we had lost our fight to save the country from Obamacare. *How was this possible?*

At its core, this book is about the answer to this question.

How We Lost: Judicial Restraint

On June 28, the last day of the Supreme Court's term, another full courtroom greeted the justices as they assumed the bench at 10 a.m. This time I wasn't there. I had committed myself to interviews and writing some instant reaction pieces, so I monitored the proceedings on my computer from my office at Georgetown Law, not far from the Supreme Court. As it happened it was a good thing I did.

When Chief Justice Roberts read the first part of his opinion, which I summarized above, most everyone in the courtroom assumed that the challengers had defeated Obamacare. Indeed, both CNN and Fox News issued news flashes that the challenge had succeeded, and my thrilled mother texted me congratulations. But sitting in my office reading the report of the written opinions on *SCOTUSBlog*, I knew better.

To explain how we lost, I need to return to the immediate aftermath of the oral argument in March. The tenor of the oral argument shocked supporters of the law and law professors, and their shock soon turned to anger. The Supreme Court normally votes in its cases in conference on Friday of the week of argument.

On the Monday following the argument—and presumably after the justices had voted on our challenge—President Barack Obama made the following statement from the Rose Garden:

> Ultimately, I'm confident that the Supreme Court will not take what would be an unprecedented, extraordinary step of overturning a law that was passed by a strong majority of a democratically elected Congress.
>
> And I'd just remind conservative commentators that for years what we've heard is the biggest problem on the bench was judicial activism or a lack of judicial restraint, that an unelected group of people would somehow overturn a duly constituted and passed law. Well, this is a good example. And I'm pretty confident that this—this court will recognize that and not take that step.[13]

Fed by the president's statement and those of others, defenders of Obamacare's constitutionality launched an angry public campaign against the conservative justices.[14] They derided as political and partisan any decision that would hold Congress to its limited powers. And some trained their fire specifically on Chief Justice Roberts.

In a *New Republic* column, Jeffrey Rosen praised "the commitment of more traditional conservatives . . . to judicial restraint," and challenged the chief justice to remain true to his judicial conservatism: "This, then, is John Roberts's moment of truth: In addition to deciding what kind of chief justice he wants to be, he has to decide what kind of legal conservatism he wants to embrace." By voting to strike down Obamacare, Rosen said, the chief justice would "be abandoning the association of legal conservatism with restraint—and resurrecting the pre–New Deal era of economic judicial activism with a vengeance."[15]

Rosen's theme was taken up by Senator Patrick Leahy, who

was then the chair of the Senate Judiciary Committee. Leahy admonished the chief justice to "do the right thing." In a Senate floor speech, the senator claimed to "trust that he will be a chief justice for all of us and that he has a strong institutional sense of the proper role of the judicial branch." He then observed that "[t]he conservative activism of recent years has not been good for the court. Given the ideological challenge to the Affordable Care Act and the extensive, supportive precedent, it would be extraordinary for the Supreme Court not to defer to Congress in this matter that so clearly affects interstate commerce."[16]

We will never know if these and many other sometimes vituperative attacks on the more conservative justices had an effect on the outcome of the case. But it was reliably reported that the chief justice had voted in conference to hold that the individual insurance mandate was unconstitutional, and that sometime after these attacks commenced, he switched his vote.[17] But instead of upholding the constitutionality of the individual insurance mandate as the four progressive justices would have, he *changed the statute so it was no longer an unconstitutional mandate.* By so doing, he could uphold the rest of the law. And he did this in the name of judicial restraint that requires deference to Congress.

Although the chief justice admitted that the law was most naturally read as a mandate to buy insurance—it was, after all, called a "requirement" that was enforced by a "penalty"—he then proceeded to adopt what he called a "saving construction" that rewrote the law in the name of judicial "deference" to Congress. "The Government asks us to interpret the mandate as imposing a tax, if it would otherwise violate the Constitution," he wrote. "Granting the Act *the full measure of deference* owed to federal statutes, it can be so read."[18]

To accomplish this, he needed to eliminate the mandate that he agreed was beyond the power of Congress to enact. Gone was what the statute called a "requirement" enforced by a "penalty."

In its place, he said the statute could be read to provide an option either to buy insurance or to pay a small and "noncoercive" tax if one did not.[19] By finding this noncoercive tax, rather than a purchase requirement, to be constitutional, he was able to uphold the rest of the Affordable Care Act.

In this way, the chief justice followed the advice of President Obama. Although the chief justice insisted that "there can be no question that it is the responsibility of this Court to enforce the limits on federal power by striking down acts of Congress that transgress those limits," by twisting the meaning of the law, he could defer to Congress.[20] As he put it, "[i]t is not our job to protect the people from the consequences of their political choices."[21] By this circuitous route, Obamacare was saved.

As President Obama had accurately observed, for years "conservative commentators" had claimed that "the biggest problem on the bench was judicial activism or a lack of judicial restraint." Chief Justice Roberts was selected by President George W. Bush precisely because of his professed commitment to judicial restraint, which during his confirmation hearings he called "judicial minimalism."

The chickens of the conservative commitment to judicial restraint had thus come home to roost. Ironically, conservatives had inherited their commitment to judicial restraint from the progressive supporters of the New Deal, who had opposed the Supreme Court holding Congress to its enumerated powers. Just as judicial restraint was invoked by progressive justices to expand the scope of the federal government by Roosevelt appointees, now a conservative chief justice invoked judicial restraint to uphold a federal takeover of the health care system.

The tragedy of the Obamacare challenge teaches that it is not enough to debate *what the Constitution means*, which is the subject of my previous book, *Restoring the Lost Constitution*. As we have seen, that only takes us half the way. As Chief Justice Roberts's ruling shows, we also need to debate *the proper role of judges* in enforcing that meaning.

In this book, I explain why judicial deference to what President Obama called the will of a "majority of a democratically elected Congress" is in fact misguided and inconsistent with the most basic premises of the Constitution.

To understand why this is wrong, we must return to the very first concept upon which the Constitution is based: "We the People."

Two Visions of "We the People"

Americans today are divided politically, ideologically, and culturally. Some of us live in blue states and watch CNN; others live in red states and watch Fox News. Some Americans want more government, others less. We engage in passionate debate over myriad issues: gun control, health care, same-sex marriage, immigration, the war on terrorism—the list of issues that divide Americans goes on and on. Our divisions are reflected in print, on the airways, and increasingly online. Battles are fought in city councils, state legislatures, and in the halls of Congress.

Of course, as we saw with Obamacare, the Supreme Court, too, is divided. This is because Americans are not just divided about politics, culture, and ideology. Americans are also divided about the Constitution itself. Every open seat on the Supreme Court is an occasion for intense partisan conflict. Confirmation hearings for Supreme Court justices become Kabuki theater in which our deep political conflicts are transformed into competing visions of the Constitution.

In this book, I call these divergent visions the "Democratic Constitution" and the "Republican Constitution," but I don't intend these labels to be partisan. There are political conservatives who hew to some aspects of the Democratic Constitution and some progressives who adopt aspects of the Republican one. Many people flit between conceptions depending on which happens to conform to the results they like. I chose the terms *democratic* and *republican* constitutions because both terms have deep roots in our constitutional history, and neither is pejorative. I dislike arguments by labels and both these labels today have a positive connotation.

At its core, this debate is about the meaning of the first three words of the Constitution: "We the People." Those who favor the Democratic Constitution view We the People as a group, as a body, as a collective entity. Those who favor the Republican Constitution view We the People as individuals. This choice of visions has enormous real-world consequences.

Each vision of We the People yields a different conception of what is called "popular sovereignty." Those who adhere to the Democratic Constitution hold a different conception of popular sovereignty than those who adhere to the Republican Constitution. So let me begin by explaining the role that popular sovereignty plays in our thinking about the Constitution.

The concept of popular sovereignty was first developed in the United States at the time of our founding. Back then it was a first principle of political theory that sovereignty—or the right to rule—must reside somewhere in any polity. While the ultimate sovereign was thought to be God, who ruled the world, on earth, monarchs claimed to be the sovereign rulers of their own people, ruling by delegation from God, or what was called divine right.

When the Americans had their revolution and rejected the rule of the English king, political theory required them to say who was sovereign in their new polity. The answer they gave was that "the people themselves" were the ultimate sovereign. But this raised at least as many questions as it solved. If "sovereignty" was an answer to the question of who has the right to rule, in what sense do the people rule? This seems like a contradiction. We need government to rule the people, and yet the people themselves are supposed to be the ultimate ruler. What sense does this make?

THE DEMOCRATIC CONSTITUTION

What I am calling the Democratic Constitution is one way to address the problem of how the sovereign people can be said to rule. If sovereignty is conceived as residing in the people collectively, then popular sovereignty means rule by the people *as a body*. And rule by the people as a body then means rule according to the "will of the people."

Of course, it makes perfect sense to talk about the will or desires of a sovereign monarch. But in what sense does a body of individual persons have a collective will or desire? No one who makes claims about the will of the people claims that there must be, or ever is, a unanimous consensus of everyone to some particular desire. In practice, the collective "will of the people" must rest on the desires of a majority or supermajority of the people. It does not—because it cannot—rest on the desires of everyone.

Therefore, in operation, a conception of popular sovereignty based on rule according to the will of the people means rule according to the will of a majority of the people. So the Democratic Constitution:

• starts with a *collective* vision of We the People;
• which leads to a conception of popular sovereignty based on the "will of the people" *as a group*;
• which, in practice, can only be the *will of the majority*.

For this side of our constitutional divide, then, a legitimate constitution is a Democratic Constitution. It sets up institutional mechanisms by which the desires of a majority of the people can be expressed.

If a well-constructed Democratic Constitution, based on a collective conception of popular sovereignty, is one that allows the will of the majority to prevail, then a number of important implications follow.

First and foremost, any principle or practice that gets in the way of the will of the majority or majority rule is presumptively illegitimate and requires special justification.

Under a Democratic Constitution, the only individual rights that are legally enforceable are a product of majoritarian will—whether the will of majorities in the legislature who create ordinary legal rights, or the will of majorities who ratified the Constitution and its amendments and created constitutional rights.

So, under a Democratic Constitution, *first comes government and then come rights*. First one needs to establish a polity with a legislature to represent the will of the people. And then this legislature will decide which rights, if any, get legal protection and which do not.

A Democratic Constitution is a "living constitution" whose meaning evolves to align with contemporary popular desires, so that today's majority is not bound by what is called "the dead hand of the past." The will of yesterday's majority cannot override the will of the majority today.

Under a Democratic Constitution, unelected judges who are not accountable to the majority present what Alexander Bickel called the "counter-majoritarian difficulty."[22] Judges are not selected to represent the desires of anyone. They are appointed, not elected, and in the federal system they serve for life. To the extent they invalidate popularly enacted laws, these unelected and unaccountable judges are thwarting the will of the people as expressed by their elected representatives.

Because of all this, under a Democratic Constitution, judges are told they should exercise their power of judicial review with "restraint." They should "defer" to the will of the popularly elected branches by adopting a "presumption of constitutionality" that simply presumes—perhaps irrebuttably—that properly elected legislatures have acted properly when they restrict the liberties of the people. For the people are only restricting themselves, we are told, and how they are to govern themselves is for their democratically selected representatives to decide.

Ultimately, this is *how* the Obamacare case was decided as it was: a majority of the Supreme Court could assert they were deferring to Congress, the popularly elected and most democratically accountable branch. Who was the unelected Supreme Court to obstruct the will of We the People as manifested by a majority of representatives in Congress? In short, five justices hewed to the vision of a Democratic Constitution.

Today, belief in the correctness of a Democratic Constitution is so pervasive among both progressives and conservatives—and among Democrats *and* Republicans—that you might be sitting there wondering what other view of the Constitution there could be. Perhaps the most important purpose of this book is simply to identify and describe this other view—what I am calling a Republican Constitution—so that you can recognize it as a distinct vision of the Constitution.

THE REPUBLICAN CONSTITUTION

What separates a Republican Constitution from a Democratic Constitution is its conception of "popular sovereignty." Where a Democratic Constitution views sovereignty as residing in the people collectively or as a group, a Republican Constitution views sovereignty as residing in the people *as individuals*.

If one views We the People as a collection of individuals, a completely different constitutional picture emerges. Because those in government are merely a small subset of the people who serve as their servants or agents, the "just powers" of these servants must be limited to the purpose for which they are delegated. That purpose is not to reflect the people's will or desire—which in practice means the will or desires of the majority—but to secure the pre-existing rights of We the People, each and every one of us.

Under a Republican Constitution, then, the first duty of government is to equally protect these personal and individual rights from being violated by both domestic and foreign transgressors. The agents of the people must not themselves use their delegated powers to violate the very rights they were empowered to protect. But how may these delegated powers be effectively limited to their proper exercise?

A Republican Constitution views the natural and inalienable rights of these joint and equal sovereign individuals as preceding the formation of governments, so *first come rights and then comes government*. Indeed, the Declaration of Independence tells us, it is "to secure these rights" that "Governments are instituted among Men." What are the implications of adopting an individual rather than a collective conception of popular sovereignty?

Under a Republican Constitution, because We the People consists of each and every person, We the People as a whole never govern. Instead, the power to govern must be delegated to some subset of the people. The small subset of individuals who are empowered to govern the rest of us are not to be confused with the people themselves, but are considered to be the servants of the people. The people are the principals or masters and those in government merely their agents. As agents they are to govern on behalf of the people and subject to their ultimate control.

Under a Republican Constitution, to ensure that these servants remain within their just powers, this lawmaking power must itself be limited by law. The Republican Constitution, then, provides *the law that governs those who govern us* and it is put in writing so it can be enforced against the servants of the people, each of whom must swear a solemn oath to obey "this Constitution." Those servants or agents who swear the oath to "this Constitution"—the written one—can no more change the "law that governs them" than we can change the speed limits that are imposed on us.

In short, under a Republican Constitution, *the meaning of the written Constitution must remain the same until it is properly changed*—which is another way of saying that the written Constitution must be interpreted according to its original meaning until it is properly amended.

Under a Republican Constitution, a completely different picture of judges emerges. Like legislators, judges too are servants of the people, and their primary duty is to adhere to the law of the Constitution above any statute enacted by Congress or by the states. Judges are given lifetime tenure precisely so they may hold democratic legislatures within the proper scope of their just powers and by so doing protect the individual "rights . . . retained by the people"—and "the privileges or immunities of citizens"—from being denied, disparaged, or abridged by their servants in the legislature.

But what are these individual rights that are retained by the people? The idea of individual popular sovereignty helps us to better understand just what rights and powers, privileges and immunities are retained by the sovereign people as individuals. Indeed, under a Republican Constitution, the rights and powers retained by the people closely resemble those enjoyed by sovereign monarchs.

- Just as sovereign monarchs claim jurisdiction over their territories and possessions, sovereign individual citizens have jurisdiction over their private property.
- Just as one monarch may not interfere within the territorial jurisdiction of other monarchs, no citizen may interfere with the person and property of any other.

- Just as monarchs may use force to defend their people and territory from the aggression of other monarchs, so too may individual citizens use force in defense of themselves and their possessions.
- Just as monarchs may consensually alter their legal relations with other monarchs by entering into treaties, so too may individual citizens freely alter their legal relations with their "fellow citizens and joint sovereigns" by entering into contracts with each other.

Of course, a Republican Constitution is established, in part, so that these liberties of the individual may be regulated by law. But the proper purpose of such regulation must be limited to the equal protection of the rights of each and every person. Any law that does not have this as its purpose is beyond the just powers of a republican legislature to impose on the citizenry. In short, when the liberty of a fellow citizen and joint sovereign is restricted, judges as agents of these citizens have a judicial duty to critically assess whether the legislature has improperly exceeded its just powers to infringe upon the sovereignty of We the People.

It is important to recognize that the Democratic and Republican views of popular sovereignty and We the People are ultimately incompatible. Adopting one of these worldviews will have implications that will differ in all these ways from adopting the other. However, because both worldviews are deeply rooted in our constitutional history and traditions, holders of each have tried to incorporate the most appealing features of the other.

Those who hold a democratic or collective vision of popular sovereignty based on majoritarian rule have strained to justify the protection of some personal or individual rights—but not so many as to thwart unduly the will of the majority. And those who hold a republican or individualist vision of popular sovereignty will acknowledge that popular elections provide a vital constraint on the exercise of power by the agents or servants of the people.

So, in practice, a constitution that hews to one of these visions may still accommodate some significant element of the other, albeit in a subordinate way. To identify the nature of a particular constitution, then, the key is to distinguish the features that are the exceptions from those that reflect the more fundamental worldview that animates that constitution. Which worldview underlies and animates the Constitution of the United States? In this book, I explain how our Constitution is a Republican Constitution.

RECLAIMING THE LABEL "REPUBLICAN"

In 2008, Sanford Levinson published his provocative book, *Our Undemocratic Constitution: Where the Constitution Goes Wrong.*[23] In reviewing it, I freely admitted that our Constitution was undemocratic in the way he suggests, but went on to say that these features are what made the Constitution exceptional and good. True, they were "undemocratic," but that was because they were "republican."[24] Thinking about Levinson's book provoked me to write this one and to title it *Our Republican Constitution*.

Were the founders really against democracy? You bet. They blamed the problems in the states under the Articles of Confederation on an excess of democracy. For example, Edmund Randolph, the first attorney general of the United States, under George Washington, observed that "the general object was to provide a cure for the evils under which the U.S. laboured."[25] And that "in tracing these evils to their origin every man had found it in *the turbulence and follies of democracy*."[26] Others said the same thing.

Elbridge Gerry from Massachusetts stated: "The evils we experience flow from the *excess of democracy*." Roger Sherman, of

Connecticut, contended that the people "immediately should have as little to do as may be about the Government."[27] Gouverneur Morris, delegate from Pennsylvania, noted that "[e]very man of observation had seen in the democratic branches of the State Legislatures, precipitation—in Congress changeableness, in every department excesses against personal liberty private property & personal safety."[28] Even those who remained more amenable to democracy, like George Mason of Virginia, admitted that *"we had been too democratic"* in forming state governments.[29]

And yet, having deliberately devised what Professor Levinson calls "our undemocratic constitution," these framers all insisted that it was still a *republican* constitution. As historian Richard Beeman reminds us, the "vast majority of the Founding Fathers were republicans, not democrats."[30] Nearly all "harbored keen misgivings about the desirability of democracy as a guiding principle for the new government."[31] Yet, at the close of the Philadelphia convention, when Benjamin Franklin was asked what form of government the convention had devised, he famously replied, "A republic, if you can keep it." So, if the founders rejected an excess of democracy in favor of a new, undemocratic form of government they called "republican," then I believe it is fair for me to call our undemocratic Constitution "republican."

The fact that our Republican Constitution has democratic elements does not make it what I am calling a Democratic Constitution. The bare fact that a particular form of government has elected legislators or an elected president does not by itself tell us whether it is a democracy or a republic. Representative government is consistent with *both* conceptions of popular sovereignty. Representative government can be favored as a practical way to "re-present" the will of the sovereign people, when direct democracy is infeasible. Alternatively, such a form of government can be viewed as a popular "check" on the servants of the people who are tasked with governing on their behalf.

Therefore, to decide whether a particular form of government is democratic or republican, we need to look to other features to see whether "first come rights and then comes government," or whether the rights of the people are considered to be the result of democratic deliberation. To the extent that the individual rights retained by the people are recognized and effectively protected from the will of majorities, that polity is a true republic.

I do not claim that everyone who used the term *republican* at the founding or thereafter necessarily meant the Republican Constitution as I am defining it. The more democratic governments of the states under the Articles of Confederation were called "republican," too. But when that system failed, the founders opted for a new approach. For this reason, the meaning of *republican* necessarily changed in 1787, when this new "undemocratic" form of government went public.

Ultimately what matters, however, is not the labels we use to describe these differing views of popular sovereignty, or what they were called in the past. Nor does it really matter which exact view was held by those who wrote the Constitution. What matters is the type of constitution they wrote and whether we today believe it to be a good enough constitution to follow.

In this book, I will examine the text of the Constitution to show that it was republican in nature, and I will then argue that our Republican Constitution is a good constitution, the meaning of which should remain the same until it is properly changed by amendment. But it is not enough to get that meaning right. Judges must then protect our Republican Constitution by enforcing the limitations on power that it imposes on the other branches, and on state legislatures.

PART I

CREATING
OUR REPUBLICAN
CONSTITUTION

CHAPTER I

"TO SECURE THESE RIGHTS"

The Political Theory of the Declaration of Independence

ON APRIL 19, 1775, seventy-seven armed Minutemen formed up on the village green of Lexington, Massachusetts, to confront seven hundred British regulars under the command of Lieutenant General Thomas Gage. Shots were fired and several of the Massachusetts men were killed in the exchange. When the British force moved on to Concord, they were routed at the North Bridge by a contingent of five hundred armed Minutemen. In their retreat to Boston, the British suffered many casualties as they were attacked by thousands of militiamen along the road. The battles of Lexington and Concord marked the start of the American rebellion, but it was not until a year later that the United States was born.

Our country—indeed our people—has a discrete starting point, a singular moment in time when its founding was expressly defended in abstract and theoretical terms. That moment was July 4, 1776, when the Continental Congress formally adopted the Declaration of Independence. To appreciate the republican nature of our Constitution, we must begin at the beginning, some thirteen years before the Constitution was enacted in 1789, when the principles upon which the new nation was formed were authoritatively declared.

THE DRAFTING OF THE DECLARATION OF INDEPENDENCE

On June 11, 1776, the Continental Congress appointed a committee to draft a declaration to effectuate Richard Henry Lee's motion "[t]hat these United Colonies are, and of right ought to be, free and independent states; that they are absolved from all allegiance to the British Crown: and that all political connexion between them and the state of Great Britain is, and ought to be, totally dissolved."[1] As John Hancock later put it, such a declaration would provide "the Ground & Foundation of a future Government."[2]

The Committee of Five consisted of the senior Pennsylvanian Benjamin Franklin, Roger Sherman of Connecticut, New York's Robert Livingston, the Massachusetts stalwart champion of independence John Adams, and a rather quiet thirty-three-year-old Virginian named Thomas Jefferson. After a series of meetings to decide on the outline of the Declaration, the committee assigned Jefferson to write the first draft.[3]

Jefferson did not have much time. With no executive, the war was run entirely by congressional committees, and the business of waging war pressed heavily on its members. Over a six-month period, Jefferson served on some thirty-four different committees, which kept him very busy. On June 17, for example, the committee overseeing the Canadian campaign submitted two reports to Congress, both in Jefferson's own hand. Two members of the Virginia delegation had left Philadelphia, increasing the pressure on Jefferson to attend the sessions of Congress.

So with the press of other matters, Jefferson did not have three leisurely weeks to write. He had merely a few days. Needing to work fast, Jefferson had to borrow, and he had two sources in front of him from which to crib. The first was a list of grievances in his draft preamble for the Virginia constitution—a list that was strikingly similar to the first group of charges against the king that ended up in the Declaration. The second was a preliminary version of the Virginia Declaration of Rights that had been drafted by George Mason in his room at the Raleigh Tavern in Williamsburg, where the provincial convention was being held.

Unlike today, when such cribbing might detract from Jefferson's accomplishment, achievement in the eighteenth century "lay instead in the creative adoption of preexisting models to different circumstances, and the highest praise of all went to imitations whose excellence exceeded that of the examples that inspired them." For this reason, younger men "were taught to copy and often memorize compelling passages from their readings for future use since you could never tell when, say, a citation from Cicero might come in handy."[4]

Mason's May 27 draft proved handy indeed in composing the Declaration's famous preamble. Its first two articles present two fundamental ideas that lie at the core of a Republican Constitution.

The first idea is that *first come rights and then comes government.* Here is how Mason expressed it:

THAT all men are born equally free and independent, and have certain inherent natural rights, of which they cannot, by any compact, deprive or divest their posterity; among which are, the enjoyment of life and liberty, with the means of acquiring and possessing property, and pursuing and obtaining happiness and safety.[5]

So, in Mason's draft, not only do all persons have "certain . . . natural rights" of life, liberty, and property, but these rights cannot be taken away "by any compact." These inherent individual natural rights, of which the people cannot divest their posterity, are therefore retained by them. Mason's words would become even more canonical than Jefferson's more succinct version in the Declaration of Independence, as variations were incorporated into several state

constitutions, and they would be echoed in the Ninth Amendment, and much later in the Privileges or Immunities Clause of the
Fourteenth Amendment.

Article 2 of Mason's draft then identified the persons who
make up a government as the *servants* of the sovereign people,
rather than their master: "That all power is vested in, and consequently derived from, the people; that magistrates are their trustees *and servants*, and at all times amenable to them."[6] As trustees
and servants, those people who serve as governing magistrates are
to respect the inherent natural rights retained by the people.

All this was compressed by Jefferson into fifty-five compelling
words:

> We hold these truths to be self-evident, that all men are
> created equal, that they are endowed by their Creator with
> certain unalienable Rights, that among these are Life, Lib-
> erty and the pursuit of Happiness. That to secure these
> rights, Governments are instituted among Men, deriving
> their just powers from the consent of the governed.

John Adams later recalled that Jefferson took only a day or
two to write the first draft, which was then turned over to the
committee for its feedback before it was submitted to Congress.
Although this draft was then heavily edited and shortened by
Congress sitting as a Committee of the Whole, its Preamble was
left pretty much as Jefferson had submitted it.

I turn now to that Preamble, for these two paragraphs identify
the theory of what I am calling our Republican Constitution.

WHAT THE DECLARATION OF INDEPENDENCE CLAIMED

Today, while most Americans have heard of the Declaration of Independence, all too few have read more than its second sentence.

Yet the Declaration shows the natural rights foundation of the American Revolution and provides important information about what the founders believed makes a constitution or government legitimate.[7] It also raises the question of how these fundamental rights are reconciled with the idea of "the consent of the governed," another idea for which the Declaration is famous.

When reading the Declaration, it is worth keeping in mind two very important facts. The Declaration constituted high treason against the Crown. Every person who signed it would be executed as a traitor should he be caught by the British. Second, the Declaration was considered to be a legal document by which the revolutionaries justified their actions and explained why they were not truly traitors. It represented, as it were, a literal indictment of the Crown and Parliament, in the very same way that criminals are now publicly indicted for their alleged crimes by grand juries representing "the people."

But to justify a revolution, it was not thought to be enough that officials of the government of England, the Parliament, or even the king himself had violated the rights of the people. No government is perfect; all governments violate rights. This was well known.

So the Americans had to allege more than mere violations of rights. They had to allege nothing short of a criminal conspiracy to violate their rights systematically. Hence the Declaration's famous reference to "a long train of abuses and usurpations" and the list that followed. In some cases, these specific complaints account for provisions eventually included in the Constitution and Bill of Rights.

But before this list of particular grievances came two paragraphs succinctly describing the political theory on which the new polity was founded. To appreciate all that is packed into these two paragraphs, it is useful to break down the Declaration into some of its key claims.

When in the Course of human events, it becomes necessary for one people to dissolve the political bands which have connected them with another, and to assume among the powers of the earth, the separate and equal station to which the Laws of Nature and of Nature's God entitle them, a decent respect to the opinions of mankind requires that they should declare the causes which impel them to the separation.

This first sentence is often forgotten. It asserts that Americans as a whole, rather than as members of their respective colonies, are a distinct "people." And this "one people" is not a collective entity, but an aggregate of particular individuals. So "they" not *it* should "declare the causes which impel *them* to the separation."

To "dissolve the political bands" revokes the "social compact" that existed between the Americans and the rest of the people of the British commonwealth, reinstates the "state of nature" between Americans and the government of Great Britain, and makes "the Laws of Nature" the standard by which this dissolution and whatever government is to follow are judged. As Committee of Five delegate Roger Sherman observed in 1774, after hostilities broke out with the British, "We are Now in a State of Nature."[8]

But what are these "Laws of Nature"? To answer this, we can turn to a sermon delivered by the Reverend Elizur Goodrich at the Congregational Church in Durham, Connecticut, on the eve of the Philadelphia Constitutional Convention. At the time of the founding, it was a common practice for ministers to be invited to give an "election sermon" before newly elected government officials, in this case the delegates to the Constitutional Convention, to encourage them to govern according to God's ways.

In his sermon, Goodrich explained that "the principles of society are the laws, which Almighty God has established in the moral world, and made necessary to be observed by mankind; in order to promote their true happiness, in their transactions and intercourse."[9] These laws, Goodrich observed, "may be considered as principles, in respect of their fixedness and operation," and by knowing them, "we discover the rules of conduct, which direct mankind to the highest perfection, and supreme happiness of their nature."[10] These rules of conduct "are as fixed and unchangeable as the laws which operate in the natural world. Human art in order to produce certain effects, must conform to the principles and laws, which the Almighty Creator has established in the natural world."[11]

In this sense, natural laws govern every human endeavor, not just politics. They undergird what may be called "normative disciplines," by which I mean those bodies of knowledge that guide human conduct—bodies of knowledge that tell us how we *ought* to act if we wish to achieve our goals. To illustrate this, Goodrich offered examples from agriculture, engineering, and architecture:

> He who neglects the cultivation of his field, and the proper time of sowing, may not expect a harvest. He, who would assist mankind in raising weights, and overcoming obstacles, depends on certain rules, derived from the knowledge of mechanical principles applied to the construction of machines, in order to give the most useful effect to the smallest force: And every builder should well understand the best position of firmness and strength, when he is about to erect an edifice.[12]

To ignore these principles is nothing short of denying reality, like jumping off a roof imagining that one can fly. "For he, who attempts these things, on other principles, than those of nature, *attempts to make a new world*; and his aim will prove absurd and his labour lost."[13] By making "a new world," Goodrich meant denying the nature of the world in which we live. He concluded:

"No more can mankind be conducted to happiness; or civil societies united, and enjoy peace and prosperity, without observing the moral principles and connections, which the Almighty Creator has established for the government of the moral world."[14]

The fact that Goodrich was a relatively obscure public figure—though his son would become a Federalist congressman from Connecticut—shows the commonplace understanding of natural law. And Goodrich's task was to remind the Connecticut delegates of the proper understanding of what the Declaration referred to as "the Laws of Nature and of Nature's God."

> We hold these truths to be self-evident, that all men are created equal, that they are endowed by their Creator with certain unalienable Rights, that among these are Life, Liberty and the pursuit of Happiness.

The most famous line of the Declaration, and for some the only line they know. The Committee of Five's draft referred to these as "inalienable" rights, but for reasons unknown the word was changed to "unalienable" sometime in the process of printing it for the public. *Inalienable* was the more common term.

What does it mean for a right to be "inalienable"? It means that it is a right you cannot give up *even if you want to* and even if you consent to do so, unlike other rights that you can agree to transfer or waive.[15] In Mason's words, it is a right that cannot be deprived or divested by any compact. Why the claim that these rights are inalienable? The founders wanted to counter England's claim that, by accepting colonial governance, the colonists had waived or alienated their rights. With inalienable rights, however, you always retain the ability to take back any right that has been given up. Unlike an alienable right—like a right to a car that can be sold and then belongs to the buyer—with an inalienable right, you can always change your mind.

The standard trilogy throughout this period was "life, liberty, and property." For example, in 1774, the Declaration and Resolves of the First Continental Congress had asserted that "the inhabitants of the English colonies in North America, by the immutable laws of nature, the principles of the English constitution, and the several charters or compacts,"[16] have the following rights: "That they are entitled to life, liberty *and property*: and they have never ceded to any foreign power whatever, a right to dispose of either without their consent."[17] Or, as the influential British political theorist John Locke wrote, "no one ought to harm another in his life, health, liberty, *or possessions.*"[18]

George Mason's oft-repeated formulation combines the right of property with the pursuit of happiness: "the enjoyment of life and liberty, with the means of acquiring and possessing property, and pursuing and obtaining happiness and safety." Interestingly, Mason's draft was slightly altered by the Virginia Convention in Williamsburg on June 11, 1776. After an extensive debate, the adopted version read:

> That all men *are by nature* equally free and independent, and have certain *inherent rights*, of which, *when they enter into a state of society*, they cannot, by any compact, deprive or divest their posterity; namely, the enjoyment of life and liberty, with the means of acquiring and possessing property, and pursuing and obtaining happiness and safety.[19]

The Virginia Convention balked at Mason's specific wording because "it was not compatible with a slaveholding society."[20] It changed "are born equally free" to "are by nature equally free," and "inherent natural rights" to "inherent rights." Then by adding "when they enter into a state of society," defenders of slavery could contend that slaves were not covered because they "had never entered Virginia's society, which was confined to whites."[21]

Yet it was the language of Mason's radical draft—rather than either Virginia's final wording or Jefferson's more succinct formulation—that became the canonical statement of first principles. Massachusetts, Pennsylvania, and Vermont adopted Mason's original references to "born equally free" and to "natural rights" into their declarations of rights while omitting the phrase "when they enter into a state of society." Indeed, it is remarkable that these states would have had Mason's draft language, rather than the version actually adopted by Virginia, from which to copy.

Virginia slaveholders' concerns were warranted. Mason's formulation proved to be judicially enforceable when, in 1783, the Massachusetts Supreme Judicial Court relied upon it to invalidate slavery in that state. And its influence continued. In 1823, it was incorporated into an important opinion by Justice Bushrod Washington defining the "privileges and immunities" of citizens in the several states as "protection by the Government, *the enjoyment of life and liberty, with the right to acquire and possess property of every kind, and to pursue and obtain happiness and safety.*"[22]

Justice Washington's opinion, with Mason's language at its core, was then repeatedly quoted by Republicans in the Thirty-Ninth Congress when they explained the meaning of the Privileges or Immunities Clause of the Fourteenth Amendment, which reads: "No state shall make or enforce any law which shall abridge the privileges or immunities of citizens of the United States." It was this constitutional language that Republicans aimed at the discriminatory Black Codes by which Southerners were seeking to perpetuate the subordination of blacks, even after slavery had been abolished.

Although Jefferson's version in the Declaration would later become an embarrassment to a people who allowed the continuation of chattel slavery, making a public claim like this has consequences. That is why people make them publicly—to be held to account. Eventually, the Declaration became a linchpin of the moral and constitutional arguments of the nineteenth-century abolitionists. It had to be explained away by the Supreme Court in *Dred Scott*.[23] It was much relied upon by Abraham Lincoln. And ultimately it needed to be repudiated by defenders of slavery in the South because of its inconsistency with that institution. But all this lay in the future.

> That to secure these rights, Governments are instituted among Men . . .

Another overlooked line, but for our purposes, possibly the most important. Here, even more clearly than in Mason's draft, the Declaration stipulates that the ultimate end or purpose of republican governments is "to *secure* these" preexisting natural rights that the previous sentence affirmed were the measure against which all government—whether of Great Britain or the United States—will be judged. This language identifies what is perhaps the central underlying "republican" assumption of the Constitution: that governments are instituted to secure the preexisting natural rights that are retained by the people. In short, that *first come rights and then comes government.*

> . . . deriving their just powers from the consent of the governed.

For reasons I will explain in this book, there is a tendency today to focus entirely on the second half of this sentence, referencing "the consent of the governed," to the exclusion of the first part, which refers to securing our natural rights. Then, by reading "the consent of the governed" as equivalent to "the will of the people," the second part of the sentence seems to support majoritarian rule by the people's "representatives." In this way, "consent of the governed" is read to mean "consent to majoritarian rule."

Put another way, the people can consent to anything, including rule by a majority in the legislature who will then decide the scope of their rights as individuals.

But read carefully, one sees that in this passage the Declaration speaks of "just powers," suggesting that only *some* powers are "justly" held by government, while others are beyond its proper authority. And notice also that "the consent of *the governed*" assumes that the people do not *themselves* rule or govern, but are "governed" by those individual persons who make up the "governments" that "are instituted among men."

The Declaration stipulates that those who govern the people are supposed "to secure" their preexisting rights, not impose the will of a majority of the people on the minority. And, as the Virginia Declaration of Rights made explicit, these inalienable rights cannot be surrendered "by any compact." Therefore, the "consent of the governed," to which the second half of this sentence refers, cannot be used to override the inalienable rights of the sovereign people that are reaffirmed by the first half.

In modern political discourse, people tend to favor one of these concepts over the other—either preexistent natural rights or popular consent—which leads them to stress one part of this sentence in the Declaration over the other. The fact that rights can be uncertain and disputed leads some to emphasize the consent part of this sentence and the legitimacy of popularly enacted legislation. But the fact that there is never unanimous consent to any particular law, or even to the government itself, leads others to emphasize the rights part of this sentence and the legitimacy of judges protecting the "fundamental" or "human" rights of individuals and minorities.

If we take *both* parts of this sentence seriously, however, I believe this apparent tension can be reconciled by distinguishing between (a) the ultimate end or purpose of legitimate governance and (b) how any particular government gains jurisdiction to rule.

So, while the protection of natural rights or justice is the ultimate end of governance, particular governments only gain jurisdiction to achieve this end by the consent of those who are governed. In other words, the "consent of the governed" tells us *which* government gets to undertake the mission of "securing" the natural rights that are retained by the people. After all, justifying the independence of Americans from the British government was the whole purpose of the Declaration of Independence.

In Chapter 3, I will explain how the tension between the concepts of "natural rights" of the people and "the consent of the governed" was also resolved by the idea of *presumed consent.* The people as a whole can only be presumed to have consented to what was actually expressed in the written Constitution and, absent a clear statement to the contrary, they cannot be presumed to have consented to surrender any of their natural rights.

Later in our history, the uncertainty of ascertaining natural rights will be addressed by shifting the question from specifying particular rights to critically examining whether any particular restriction of liberty can be shown to be within a "just power" of government—that is, a power to which any rational person would have consented, such as the equal protection of their fundamental rights, including their health and safety.

> That whenever any Form of Government becomes destructive of these ends, it is the Right of the People to alter or to abolish it, and to institute new Government, laying its foundation on such principles and organizing its powers in such form, as to them shall seem most likely to affect their Safety and Happiness.

This passage restates the *end* of government—human "safety and happiness" (again echoing Mason)—and identifies the "form of government" as simply a *means* to this end. Therefore, the people have a right "to alter or to abolish" any form of government when it "becomes destructive of these ends," as the Americans declared the British colonial government to be in the list that followed.

Jefferson adopted this passage from Article 3 of George Mason's draft Declaration of Rights, which affirmed "that whenever any government shall be found inadequate or contrary to these purposes, a majority of the community hath an indubitable, unalienable, indefeasible right, to reform, alter, or abolish it, in such manner as shall be judged most conductive to the publick Weal."[24]

∽

The political theory announced in the Declaration of Independence can be summed up by the proposition I mentioned above: *First come rights and then comes government.* According to this view:

- The rights of individuals do not originate with any government, but preexist its formation.
- The equal protection of these rights is both the purpose and first duty of government.
- Even after government is formed, these rights provide a standard by which its performance is measured, and in extreme cases, its systemic failure to protect rights—or its systematic violation of rights—can justify its alteration or abolition.
- At least some of these rights are so fundamental that they are "inalienable," meaning they are so intimately connected to one's nature as a human being that they cannot be transferred to another even if one consents to do so.

WHY THE DECLARATION WAS RIGHT

This is powerful stuff. At the founding, these ideas were considered to be "self-evident." Today, however, the idea of natural rights is obscure and controversial. Oftentimes, when the idea comes up, it is deemed to be archaic. Moreover, the Declaration's claim that such rights "are endowed by their Creator" leads many to characterize natural rights as religiously based rather than secular. This is a misunderstanding of the concept of natural rights.

So let me now turn from what the founders said and believed to why they were correct to do so. To turn from what they wrote in the Declaration of Independence and the Constitution to why what they wrote still makes sense—if properly translated into ideas that are commonly held today. In short, I want to explain why we the living *ought* to follow the text of our Republican Constitution.

As the explanation by Rev. Goodrich shows, these laws of nature are based on the regularities of nature, *and then* "the Almighty Creator" is identified as the source of this order. In the Declaration, this same relationship is reflected in the distinction between "the Laws of Nature" and "Nature's God." So natural law operates to guide human conduct even if the natural order was not divinely established. Even if there is no deity, crops will fail and buildings will fall if these laws are ignored.

So too will societies fail to provide the conditions under which human beings can pursue happiness while living in proximity to each other if the natural rights of the people are not respected and protected. As the renowned Dutch natural rights theorist Hugo Grotius famously (and bravely) affirmed: "What we have been saying [about the existence of a natural law of justice] would have a degree of validity even if we were to concede what cannot be conceded without the utmost wickedness, that there is no God, or that the affairs of men are of no concern to Him."[25]

But was the founding generation right to believe in natural rights? How do we identify these rights? In what sense can we say that they precede government? I have presented a fuller explanation and defense of natural rights in my previous book, *The Structure of Liberty: Justice and the Rule of Law*, which I will merely summarize here. I do not claim that this normative defense of natural rights was held by all the founders. My object now is not historical but is instead to provide a reason why we today should share the founders' belief in natural rights.

Let's start by distinguishing between "natural law" and "natural rights." The idea of natural law is mysterious to us today. We are accustomed to thinking of law as a command of the legislature, or perhaps the command of a government official or judge, that is enforced by a government. A natural law, whatever that might be, that was not incorporated into a command enforceable by government seems hardly worth the paper it isn't written on. How can there be a law in any meaningful sense in the absence of government recognition and enforcement?

But when we think of the disciplines of engineering or architecture, the idea of a natural law is not so mysterious. For example, engineers reason that, *given* the force that gravity exerts on the structure of a building, *if* we want a building that will enable persons to live or work inside it, *then* we need to provide a structural foundation, walls, and roof of a certain strength. The principles of engineering, though formulated by human beings, are not a product of their will.

I am not claiming that these natural laws are like the "laws" of the physical sciences. The physical sciences are purely *descriptive* and explanatory disciplines. They say nothing about what human beings should or should not do. In contrast, the disciplines of engineering and architecture are *normative* in that they instruct us on how we *ought* to act—given the nature of the human beings, the world in which they live, and the purpose at hand.

Nor need one be an engineer or an architect to formulate similar "natural law" normative principles. For example, the existence of gravity and the nature of the human body lead to the following natural law injunction for human action: *given* that gravity will cause us to fall rapidly and that our bodies will not withstand the impact, *if* we want to live and be happy, *then* we had better not jump off tall buildings.

The "principles of society" to which Goodrich referred are natural "laws" of this type. So *given* the nature of human beings and the world in which we live, *if* we want persons to be able to pursue happiness while living in society with each other, *then* they had best adopt and respect a social structure that reflects these principles.

True, any such natural law principles may be more difficult to discern and consequently more controversial than the principles of engineering or architecture. Partly this is because human beings are so amazingly complex and, unlike the materials from which buildings are constructed, are self-directed in pursuit of their own purposes.

But the mere existence of controversy does not render such principles nonexistent, nor does the fact that we cannot see, hear, taste, or touch them. After all, we cannot see, hear, taste, or touch the principles of engineering or architecture, either. Both sets of principles, or "laws," are humanly constructed concepts used to explain, predict, and guide our conduct in the world in which we live.

The idea that the world, including worldly governments, is governed by laws or principles that dictate how society *ought* to be structured, in the very same way that such natural laws dictate how buildings *ought* to be built or how crops *ought* to be planted, was well accepted by Americans at the founding of the United States. Indeed the assumption that *first come rights and then comes government* was considered so obviously true as to be, in the words of the Declaration, "self-evident." As Justice Samuel Chase famously wrote in the 1798 case of *Calder v. Bull,*

[t]here are certain vital principles in our free republican governments, which will determine and overrule an apparent and flagrant abuse of legislative power. . . . An act of the legislature (for I cannot call it a law), contrary to the *great*

first principles of the social compact, cannot be considered a rightful exercise of legislative authority.[26]

When one mentions "natural law" some ask, "Where are these natural laws? Are they 'out there' somewhere? Show them to me!" Yet we do not demand that the humanly developed principles of engineering or agriculture be found somewhere in the dirt, or brick, or steel. We don't demand of engineers and architects, "Show us where these principles are!" Nevertheless, everyone accepts that these principles must be respected if bridges are to stand and crops to grow. The "principles of society" Goodrich spoke of have the same status. If they are valid, they *must* be respected if people are to pursue happiness while living in society with one another.

This natural law account of the "principles of society" assumes, of course, that "happiness . . . peace and prosperity" are appropriate ends. Yet, once again, the normative disciplines of agriculture, engineering, and architecture are also based on the assumption that human existence and happiness are worthwhile. If you want to create human misery by building buildings and bridges that collapse, then feel free to ignore these natural laws.

Let me now introduce one final but important distinction that most contemporary popular discussions of natural law overlook: the distinction between natural law *ethics* and natural *rights*. As I have sketched it here, natural law describes a *method of reasoning* of the following type: "*Given* that the nature of human beings and the world in which they live is X, *if* we want to achieve Y, *then* we ought to do Z." The subject of any particular natural law analysis fills in the "if." When the subject is agriculture, the "if" might be "if we want to raise crops so that human beings may eat." When the subject is engineering, the "if" might be "if we want to build a bridge so that human beings may cross a river."

By the same token, the study of *ethics* may be conceived as an inquiry into the question, "How should individuals live their lives?" So "given the nature of human beings and the world in which they live (*X*), *if a person wants to live a good life* (*Y*), then he or she ought to do *Z*." Whether we attempt to feed ourselves, build bridges, or live a good life is a matter of choice. Having made this choice, how we go about making our attempts—and whether they succeed or fail—will be constrained by natural laws at play in the real world.

Thus, applying a natural law method of reasoning to the ethical question of how people ought to live their lives would begin with an inquiry into the nature of a "good life," resting this judgment, at least in part, on human nature. What a good life is for a human is not the same as what is good for a dog or a tree. Then, given a conception of the good life, a "natural law ethics" could potentially address nearly every choice a person confronts. Should I go to school? Which one? What should I study? Should I use drugs? With whom should I have sex? Each one of these questions can potentially be addressed by the natural law method of "given-if-then" analysis.

But the subject of a natural *rights* analysis is different. Or perhaps it is more accurate to say that "natural rights" are the conclusion of a natural law analysis of a different problem. Rather than asking, "How should one live one's life?" one can ask a different question, "How should society be structured so that individuals can pursue happiness while living in proximity to others?"

Given the various problems that arise when humans live and act in society with others, the answer to this question that was universally accepted at the time of the founding was that each person needs a "space" over which he or she has sole jurisdiction or *liberty* to act and within which no one else may rightfully interfere. The concepts defining this "liberty" or moral space came to be known as *natural rights*.

Thus it is a mistake, and an all-too-common one, to equate

natural law with natural rights. *Natural law* is a broader term referring to the "given-if-then" method of evaluating choices based on the "given" of human nature and the nature of the world. A natural law approach to *ethics* uses a "given-if-then" analysis to evaluate the propriety of any human action to ascertain how individuals ought to live their lives.

In contrast, a natural *rights* analysis seeks to determine the appropriate social structure within which people ought to be free to pursue their own happiness. It uses a natural law, "given-if-then" methodology to identify the *liberty* or space within which persons ought to be free to make their own choices. Whereas natural law ethics provides guidance for our actions, natural rights define a moral space or liberty in which we may act free from the interference of other persons.

Although principles of natural law ethics can be used to guide individual conduct, they should not be coercively enforced by human law if doing so would violate the moral space or liberty defined by natural rights.

In short, *natural law ethics instructs us on how to exercise the liberty that is defined and protected by natural rights.*

Again, I do not claim that everyone at the founding accepted this particular account of natural law and natural rights, although Elizur Goodrich's election sermon strongly suggests that at least some did. I offer it here in defense of the Declaration's assertion that it is "to secure these [natural] rights" that governments are instituted among men.

The belief that "first come rights and then comes government" and that these rights provide the criteria of the "just powers" of legitimate governance is the keystone of a Republican government. When properly translated into modern terms, the founding generation's belief in natural rights no longer seems so mysterious. In fact, it is true! And this same belief animated those later Americans who founded an antislavery Republican Party and who amended our Republican Constitution to make it even more protective of these inalienable rights.

Yet, while the Declaration of Independence stated the legal basis for separation from Great Britain and the underlying political theory that justified forceful resistance to the king and Parliament, it did not provide the governing structure of the United States. Indeed, thirteen years separate the Declaration of Independence from the adoption of the Constitution of the United States, during which time the United States was governed by the much different Articles of Confederation.

Did the Constitution that was later adopted recognize the underlying political theory of the Declaration, with its roots in the natural and inalienable rights of individuals? How did it differ from government under the Articles? To answer these questions, we now turn to the framing of the Constitution, why the prevailing "democratic" theory of republicanism was rejected, and how the founders' conception of "republicanism" was modified.

CHAPTER 2

REVISING "REPUBLICANISM"

Solving the Problem of Too Much Democracy

JAMES MADISON HAD a problem. After living for ten years under the Articles of Confederation, he had worked tirelessly behind the scenes to bring about a convention to devise a new constitution. In September 1786, he participated in a preliminary convention in Annapolis, Maryland. By 1787 he had secured enough support of key players like George Washington and Benjamin Franklin to convene a constitutional convention in Philadelphia.

Now, with his friend and mentor Thomas Jefferson in Paris serving as the ambassador to France, the pressure was on the thirty-six-year-old Madison. Before journeying to Philadelphia, he crammed for the gathering like a student for his exams. Jefferson had sent along a chest of books on political theory and history from his private library, which Madison assiduously studied. For the cerebral Madison had a truly fundamental problem to solve.

Like many others, he had concluded that the American regime governed by the Articles of Confederation was grossly inadequate and contrary to what the Virginia Declaration of Rights referred to as "the common benefit, protection, and security of the people." Even most of the "anti-federalists" who ended up opposing the new Constitution conceded as much. But why was this happening? Why had the "republicanism" of the founding generation failed them so?

Madison needed to figure this out.

Identifying the Majoritarian Difficulty

In the thirteen years between the Declaration of Independence in 1776 and the adoption of the Constitution in 1789, the United States was governed primarily by thirteen separate entities. Although the form of each government differed, most tended to elevate the legislature above the executive and judiciary, and made the legislature as responsive to majoritarian sentiments as possible.

State governments under the Articles were thought to be "republican." The founders had thrown off the rule by an aristocratic few in favor of rule by the democratic many. If, under aristocracy, the many are screwed by the few, the democratic or republican alternative was premised on the belief that "the people won't screw themselves." But under the Articles of Confederation, this "republican" theory had unexpectedly proved to be false.

State legislatures began enacting debtor relief laws that both undermined the rights of creditors and impaired economic prosperity, which requires a credit market that can safely rely on the obligation of private contracts to collect from debtors. States also erected a debilitating assortment of trade barriers to protect their own businesses from competing firms in neighboring states. The result was a nationwide economic downturn that was blamed on these ruinous policies.

So, "republican" government as it was then conceived was clearly not working for "the common benefit, protection, and security, of the people," but *why not*? To answer this question, in April 1787, largely for his own benefit, Madison composed an essay on "The Vices of the Political System of the United States."

Historian Jack Rakove has described this memorandum or working paper as "a truly remarkable as well as historic document."[1] For one thing, "it marks one of those rare moments in the history of political thought where one can actually glimpse a creative thinker at work, not by reading the final published version of his ideas, but by catching him at an earlier point, exploring a problem in the privacy of his study." For another, "it matters that this was not a merely academic exercise. The drafting of this memorandum was essential to Madison's self-assigned task of formulating a working agenda that would allow the coming convention to hit the ground running."[2]

Reviewing Madison's memorandum helps us see how he identified the constitutional problem now facing the country, and how he believed that the prevailing majoritarian or democratic conception of "republicanism" needed to be fundamentally revised.

In "Vices," Madison complained about the "Injustice of the laws of States." The causes of "this evil," he contended, could be traced to the "the Representative bodies" in the states and, ultimately, to "the people themselves."[3] This then called "into question the fundamental principle of republican Government, that the majority who rule in such Governments, are the safest Guardians both of public Good and of private rights."[4]

Madison concluded that we must be far more realistic about popular majorities. All civilized societies, he explained, "are divided into different interests and factions, as they happen to be creditors or debtors—Rich or poor—husbandmen, merchants or manufacturers—members of different religious sects—followers of different political leaders—inhabitants of different districts—owners of different kinds of property," etc.[5]

In a democracy, the debtors outnumber the creditors and the poor outnumber the rich. The larger group can simply outvote the smaller. The "majority however composed, ultimately give the law. Whenever therefore an apparent interest or common passion unites a majority what is to restrain them from unjust violations of the rights and interests of the minority, or of individuals?"[6]

To illustrate the problem, Madison posed the following thought experiment: "Place three individuals in a situation wherein the interest of each depends on the voice of the others, and give to two of them an interest opposed to the rights of the third? Will the latter be secure? The prudence of every man would shun the danger."[7] Likewise, will "two thousand in a like situation be less likely to encroach on the rights of one thousand? The contrary is witnessed by the notorious factions & oppressions which take place in corporate towns limited as the opportunities are, and in little republics when uncontrouled by apprehensions of external danger."[8]

The idea of democracy and democratic rule can be traced back to the ancient Greeks, where the term *demagogue* also arose. Although democracy or rule by the many had been posited as the alternative to aristocracy, or rule by the few, the problem Madison identified with "republican Government" as it had been implemented was that it was simply too democratic or majoritarian.

Three states—Pennsylvania, Georgia, and Connecticut—had unicameral or one-chamber legislatures, elected annually. Another three states—Massachusetts, New Jersey, and North Carolina— had bicameral legislatures with an upper and lower house, and representatives to both chambers were elected annually. Rhode Island elected members to both chambers every six months. In New Hampshire the members of the upper chamber or council were selected annually by members of the annually elected house. Only five states—Delaware, Maryland, New York, South Carolina, and Virginia—had upper chambers whose members sat for longer terms than did those in the lower house.[9]

Equally important was the dependence of the executive and judiciary on the will of the legislature. In ten states, the executive was chosen by one or both houses of the legislature. Only in Massachusetts, New York, and Rhode Island was the governor elected by the voters. Only in Delaware, Massachusetts, Maryland, Virginia, New York, and North Carolina were judges clearly appointed to serve "on good behavior," meaning for life unless impeached. The rest either served for a period of years or were apparently removable by a simple vote of the legislature.

Later, when defending the proposed Constitution in the tenth of a series of newspaper essays called *The Federalist*, Madison (writing pseudonymously as Publius) publicly presented the critique he had developed in his "Vices" essay: "Complaints are everywhere heard from our most considerate and virtuous citizens, equally the friends of public and private faith, and of public and personal liberty, that our governments are too unstable, that the public good is disregarded in the conflicts of rival parties."[10] Why? Because legal "measures are too often decided, *not according to the rules of justice and the rights of the minor party*, but by the superior force of an interested and overbearing majority."[11]

According to Madison, this majoritarian difficulty had led to the "prevailing and increasing distrust of public engagements, and alarm for private rights, which are echoed from one end of the continent to the other."[12] As he had in "Vices," Madison identified the source of these violations of private rights as the problem of faction. "By a faction," he wrote in *Federalist* 10, "I understand a number of citizens, whether amounting to *a majority* or a minority of the whole, who are united and actuated by some common impulse of passion, or of interest, *adverse to the rights of other citizens*, or to the permanent and aggregate interests of the community."[13]

The problem of faction was an inevitable product of democratic republicanism itself. "If a faction consists of *less than a majority*," he explained, "relief is supplied by the republican principle, which enables the majority to defeat its sinister views by regular vote."[14] However, when "*a majority* is included in a faction, the form of popular government . . . enables it to sacrifice to its ruling passion or interest both the public good and the rights of other citizens."[15]

In short, under democratic republicanism, there is nothing stopping a majority of the polity from engaging in self-dealing at

the expense of the minority. What Madison and his allies in Philadelphia decided was needed was a new republican form of government that would address the weakness of the too-democratic
state constitutions, while preserving the notion of popular sovereignty. Madison believed that "to secure the public good and
private rights against the danger of such a faction, and at the same
time to preserve the spirit and the form of popular government, is
then the great object to which our inquiries are directed."[16]

As we've already seen, Madison was not alone in identifying
"democracy" as the source of the nation's ills. These comments
bear repeating. At the Constitutional Convention, Elbridge
Gerry from Massachusetts stated: "The evils we experience flow
from the excess of democracy." After listing a number of abuses,
he admitted that he "had been too republican heretofore." He
"was still however republican, but had been taught by experience
the danger of the levelling spirit." Experience, he claimed, had
shown "that the State legislatures drawn immediately from the
people did not always possess their confidence."[17]

Roger Sherman, of Connecticut, contended that the people
"immediately should have as little to do as may be about the
Government."[18] Virginian Edmund Randolph observed that
"the general object was to provide a cure for the evils under
which the U.S. laboured,"[19] and that "in tracing these evils to
their origin every man had found it in the turbulence and follies
of democracy."[20]

Gouverneur Morris, a delegate from Pennsylvania who is
credited with helping select the actual wording of the Constitution,[21] noted that "[e]very man of observation had seen in the
democratic branches of the State Legislatures, precipitation—in
Congress changeableness, in every department excesses against
personal liberty private property & personal safety."[22] Even those
who remained more amenable to democracy, like George Mason
of Virginia, "admitted that we had been too democratic" in

forming state governments though he "was afraid that we should incautiously run into the opposite extreme."²³

So, at the convention, pretty much everyone agreed on the problem. What divided them was the appropriate solution. With the problem of majoritarian democracy in the forefront throughout the summer of 1787, the delegates wrestled with how to devise a new "republican form of government" in which the people's "personal liberty private property & personal safety" would be better secured from a majority of the people themselves.

Although Madison's initial proposals were not accepted, neither were anyone else's. Instead, gradually and painfully, piece by piece, element by element, the convention delegates devised a more perfect Republican Constitution: the Constitution of the United States.

Republicanism Revised

Madison defended the new Constitution as "republican" by expressly distinguishing between a democracy and a republic. "The two great points of difference *between a democracy and a republic* are: first, the delegation of the government, in the latter, to a small number of citizens elected by the rest; secondly, the greater number of citizens, and greater sphere of country, over which the latter may be extended."²⁴ He then now-famously claimed that the larger the territory governed by such a government, the more difficult it would be for factions to form a majority that can then oppress the rights of the minority. The bigger the republic, "the greater obstacles opposed to the concert and accomplishment of the secret wishes of an unjust and interested majority."²⁵

Then, in *Federalist* 51, Madison contended there needed to be a separation of powers that would constrain the power of the legislature because in "republican government, the legislative authority necessarily predominates."²⁶ The remedy for this "inconveniency is to divide the legislature into different branches; and to render them, by different modes of election and different principles of action, as little connected with each other as the nature of their common functions and their common dependence on the society will admit."[27] In addition, as "the weight of the legislative authority requires that it should be thus divided, the weakness of the executive may require, on the other hand, that it should be fortified."[28]

But, in addition to the separation of powers, the powers of the federal government were limited by the Constitution. "The powers delegated by the proposed Constitution to the federal government, are few and defined. Those which are to remain in the State governments are numerous and indefinite," Madison wrote in *Federalist* 45.[29] The national government's powers "will be exercised principally on external objects, as war, peace, negotiation, and foreign commerce; with which last the power of taxation will, for the most part, be connected."[30] In contrast, "the powers reserved to the several States will extend to all the objects which, in the ordinary course of affairs, concern the lives, liberties, and properties of the people, and the internal order, improvement, and prosperity of the State."[31]

This scheme of limited federal power was important for fighting the problem of faction: where there are fewer legislative powers, there are fewer opportunities for factions to capture the legislature to feed their interests at the expense of others. Conversely, the more government does, the more incentive exists for factions to form and fight over the spoils.

The responsibility of enforcing these limits on federal power ultimately fell to an impartial judiciary. In *Federalist* 78, Alexander Hamilton explained that "the courts were designed to be an intermediate body between the people and the legislature, in order, among other things, to keep the latter within the limits assigned to their authority."[32] So, if "the courts of justice are to be

considered as the bulwarks of a limited Constitution against legislative encroachments," this argues strongly "for the permanent
tenure of judicial offices, since nothing will contribute so much as
this to that independent spirit in the judges which must be essential to the faithful performance of so arduous a *duty*."[33]

It is worth noting that nowhere in *Federalist* 78 did Hamilton
speak of a "*power* of judicial review." Instead he referred to "courts
of justice, whose *duty* it must be to declare all acts contrary to the
manifest tenor of the Constitution void."[34] Indeed he used the
term *duty* five times. Hamilton admitted that "it would require an
uncommon portion of fortitude in the judges to do their *duty* as
faithful guardians of the Constitution, where legislative invasions
of it had been instigated by the major voice of the community."[35]
But it was their duty nonetheless.[36]

Later, in *Marbury v. Madison*, when Chief Justice John Marshall employed Hamilton's argument from *Federalist* 78 in favor
of the judicial nullification of unconstitutional laws, he too never
referred to a power of judicial review. Instead, like Hamilton, he
used the term *duty*: "It is emphatically the province and *duty* of
the judicial department to say what the law is."[37]

The constitutions of thirteen states, which had been designed
to implement the will of the majority, were found to be defective
because they neglected safeguards for the individual rights of the
minority. These more democratic forms of government were then
quite self-consciously repudiated by a new Republican Constitution in which federalism, the separation of powers, and independent courts of justice would protect the rights of the sovereign
individual from the will of the democratic majority at the federal
level. One by one, each state soon replaced its more democratic
constitution with a variation on the new republican one.

Yet the Constitution was still defective in major ways. As
we will soon see, it fell to a new political party—aptly named
the Republican Party—and another generation of framers to

improve our Republican Constitution. But first I want to explain how the difference between a more democratic and the new-and-improved republican view of the proper form of government presupposes two distinct and ultimately incompatible conceptions of We the People.

CHAPTER 3

"WE THE PEOPLE" AS INDIVIDUALS

*Popular Sovereignty in the Constitution
and Supreme Court*

———

AT THE CONCLUSION of the Constitutional Convention in Philadelphia in 1787, anxious citizens gathered outside Independence Hall to learn what had been produced behind closed doors. As I mentioned earlier, it is said that, as Benjamin Franklin left the building, a woman in the crowd asked him, "Well, Doctor, what have we got, a republic or a monarchy?" Franklin is reported to have responded, "A republic, if you can keep it."

We have seen that, though the new form of government devised in Philadelphia was not a monarchy, neither was it democratic. Nevertheless, Franklin still called it "a republic." This was because the meaning of that term had just been altered by the men in the building Franklin was leaving. A Republican Constitution was no longer a democratic one (if it ever truly was).

In this chapter, I explain how the text of the original Constitution that was drafted by the framers in Philadelphia acknowledges the individual sovereignty of the people. We will then see how the Supreme Court recognized this in its first great constitutional case. Then, in Chapter 4, we'll examine how the text of the Constitution was amended by a new Republican Party to complete our Republican Constitution.

INDIVIDUAL SOVEREIGNTY IN THE CONSTITUTION

The text of the Constitution expressly acknowledges the underlying political theory of the Declaration, namely, its roots in the natural and inalienable rights of individuals—that is, that first come rights and then comes government. This is why whole passages of its text must be ignored or interpreted out of existence to transform it from a Republican Constitution into a democratic one.

To be clear, the question of whether the *meaning* of the Constitution specifically references individual natural rights is separate from the question of whether the courts are empowered to *enforce* that meaning against Congress or state legislatures. One can accept that the answer to the first question is yes, while still maintaining that the answer to the second question is no.

Later on, I will suggest that courts have a duty to protect the natural rights of the people, but that they can accomplish this by enforcing the structural features of our Republican Constitution and by holding federal and state governments to what the Declaration called their "just powers." At this point, however, I am concerned only with how the original meaning of the text of the Constitution is republican.

Masters and Servants, Principals and Agents

To begin with, the Constitution nowhere speaks of the "rights" of either states or of the federal government. Instead, it speaks of "powers," which are what masters delegate to their servants. A master or "principal" delegates powers to her servant or "agent." And according to long-standing principles of agency law, an agent must exercise these powers *on behalf of* and *subject to the control of* the principal.[1] This is because the principal is the ultimate sovereign power in the relationship of principal and agent.

The Constitution is fastidious in this regard. Consider the Tenth Amendment, which reads: "The powers not *delegated* to the United States by the Constitution, nor prohibited by it to the states, are *reserved* to the states respectively, or to the people." This is pure agency talk. The Constitution delegates powers to the national government. That which is not delegated is reserved *either* to state governments, *or* to the ultimate sovereign, the people themselves.

In some ways, the Tenth Amendment is merely restating the first sentence of Article I, which defines the "legislative power" of Congress. "All legislative power *herein granted* shall be vested in a Congress of the United States, which shall consist of a Senate and House of Representatives." Neither the executive nor judicial powers are qualified by "herein granted."

For this language to serve any purpose, "herein granted" must refer to a limited set of legislative powers. Otherwise the sentence would mean the same as if it said "all legislative power shall be vested in a Congress of the United States." But that is not what it says.

Further, "herein granted" is an express reference to the written Constitution. Therefore, the only powers that may be justly or properly exercised by Congress are those found somewhere within the Constitution's text.

The "Rights . . . Retained by the People"

Although the underlying assumption that "first come rights and then comes government" pervades the document, it is expressly recognized in the Ninth Amendment, which reads: "The enumeration in the Constitution of certain rights shall not be construed to deny or disparage others retained by the people."[2]

Notice the use of the term *retained*, which means these rights preceded the adoption of any enumeration or listing of rights, whether in the original Constitution or in any of its later amendments. We know that the rights that were "enumerat[ed] in the Constitution," such as the freedoms of speech, press, assembly, and the free exercise of religion, are clearly individual rights. This strongly implies that "other" unenumerated rights belong to individuals, too.

Furthermore, "the people" to whom the Ninth and Tenth Amendments refer are expressly distinct from the governments of both the United States and the states, including their respective legislatures. Because all "powers not delegated" by the people are reserved to them, this means that the *only* powers the federal government has are those "delegated . . . by the Constitution." In other words, the government of the United States has no inherent power, but only those that are "herein granted" as a matter of written positive law.

In sum, the "retained" rights to which the Ninth Amendment refers belong to the people as individuals rather than as a group. So too do the reserved powers not delegated by "the people" to either the state or federal governments. Thus, when read together, the text of the Ninth and Tenth Amendments strongly implies that sovereignty resides jointly in the people as individuals, each and every one.

The Rights Retained by the People Are Natural Rights

That "rights . . . retained by the people" is a reference to natural rights is supported by the weight of the available evidence of original meaning, which I have surveyed in detail elsewhere.[3] I won't rehearse all that evidence here, but consider a proposal that circulated among members of the House select committee that, in 1791, was charged with drafting amendments in response to the demands of several state ratification conventions.

This proposal was found in the 1980s among the papers of

James Madison, who served on that House select committee and was determined to be in the handwriting of fellow committee member Roger Sherman, a representative from Connecticut who had previously been a delegate to the Constitutional Convention in Philadelphia. Before that Sherman served with Jefferson on the Committee of Five, which composed the Declaration of Independence.

The second amendment in Sherman's draft begins as follows: "*The people* have certain *natural rights* which are *retained* by them when they enter into Society."[4] In this passage, Sherman uses all the terminology eventually employed in the Ninth Amendment— "the people," "rights," and "retained." Then the "rights . . . retained" by "the people" are explicitly characterized as "natural rights." Sherman's proposal ends with the following injunction: "Of these rights therefore they Shall not be deprived by the Government of the united States."[5] This indicates what is meant by "deny or disparage" in the Ninth Amendment.

But what was meant by the term *natural rights*? The middle of Sherman's draft provides some examples: "Such are the rights of Conscience in matters of religion; of acquiring property, and of pursuing happiness & Safety; of Speaking, writing and publishing their Sentiments with decency and freedom; of peaceably assembling to consult their common good, and of applying to Government by petition or remonstrance for redress of grievances."[6] While some of these natural rights were enumerated in the First Amendment, the rights "of acquiring property, and of pursuing happiness & safety" were not. These individual rights remained unenumerated rights retained by the people. And "such are" signals that the rights listed by Sherman were not the only ones that were retained by the people.

Sherman's rendition of natural rights was entirely commonplace. You will recognize that language from the Declaration of Rights in the Virginia Constitution of 1776, which had been drafted by

George Mason. By 1791, Mason's language had become the canonical statement of natural rights. In addition to Virginia, four more states included a variation in their constitutions, while a fifth employed Jefferson's compressed version from the Declaration:

- Massachusetts: "All men are born free and equal, and have certain natural, essential and unalienable rights; among which may be reckoned the right of enjoying and defending their lives and liberties; that of acquiring, possessing, and protecting property; in fine, that of seeking and obtaining their safety and happiness."[7]
- New Hampshire: "All men have certain natural, essential, and inherent rights; among which are—the enjoying and defending life and liberty—acquiring, possessing and protecting property—and in a word, of seeking and obtaining happiness."[8]
- New York: "We hold these Truths to be self-evident, that all Men are created equal; that they are endowed by their Creator with certain unalienable Rights; that among these are Life, Liberty, and the Pursuit of Happiness."[9]
- Pennsylvania: "That all men are born equally free and independent, and have certain natural, inherent and unalienable rights, amongst which are, the enjoying and defending of life and liberty, acquiring, possessing and protecting property, and pursuing and obtaining happiness and safety."[10]
- Vermont: "That all Men are born equally free and independent, and have certain natural, inherent and unalienable Rights, amongst which are the enjoying and defending Life and Liberty; acquiring, possessing and protecting Property, and pursuing and obtaining Happiness and Safety."[11]

It is perhaps no coincidence that, other than Mason's and Jefferson's Virginia, all these were northern states that had or would abolish slavery.

Similar provisions were proposed by state ratification conventions. Given its Declaration of Rights, it is unsurprising that Virginia offered the following as its first proposed amendment: "That there are certain natural rights, of which men, when they form a social compact, cannot deprive or divest their posterity; among which are the enjoyment of life and liberty, with the means of acquiring, possessing, and protecting property, and pursuing and obtaining happiness and safety."[12] From New York came the following proposal: "That the enjoyment of Life, Liberty, and the pursuit of Happiness are *essential rights* which every Government ought to respect and preserve."

Though Sherman's wording was not adopted by the House, very similar wording was again proposed in the Senate: "That there are certain natural rights, of which men, when they form a social compact, cannot deprive or divest their posterity, among which are the enjoyment of life and liberty, with the means of acquiring, possessing, and protecting property, and pursuing and obtaining happiness and safety."[13]

We can only speculate about why Congress declined to propose this language be added to the federal Constitution. Perhaps this was due to the fact that, in 1783, this language had been used by the Massachusetts Supreme Judicial Court to find that slavery was unconstitutional under its constitution. Still, this well-known legal development in Massachusetts did not stop Virginia from recommending its addition.

All these provisions affirm that the natural, inherent, and inalienable rights retained by the people include the rights to acquire, possess, and protect property and the right to pursue happiness and safety. Today we would characterize the right to acquire, use, and possess property as an "economic" liberty, and the right to pursue happiness as a "personal" liberty, but this distinction is anachronistic when applied to the founding, when these unenumerated natural rights were considered inextricably intertwined.

Indeed, the right to acquire, possess, and use property is a vital means to the pursuit of happiness, as the Massachusetts and Vermont constitutions both say.

But the last sentence of Sherman's draft is also evidence that what has come to be known as the Bill of Rights as a whole, and the Ninth Amendment in particular, was a limitation on federal as opposed to state power. "Of these rights therefore they Shall not be deprived *by the Government of the united States.*" What of the states?

While Article I, Section 10 bars states from making any "law impairing the obligation of contracts," in *Barron v. Baltimore*[14] the Supreme Court denied that the Takings Clause of the Fifth Amendment could be enforced against a state in federal court, and this came to be the prevailing doctrine.

For better or worse, the original Constitution included very few protections of the rights retained by the people against their own state governments. As a result, from the perspective of the federal Constitution, state governments were deemed to be powerful enough to authorize the enslavement of some of their people by a subset of their citizenries.

This grave and nearly fatal flaw of the original Constitution almost destroyed the United States. But it was corrected by a different group of framers and ratifiers who improved our Republican Constitution by providing greater protections of the rights retained by the sovereign people.

INDIVIDUAL POPULAR SOVEREIGNTY IN THE SUPREME COURT

During the Revolutionary War, the state of Georgia contracted with South Carolina merchant Robert Farquhar to supply some goods on credit for the war effort. Georgia later refused to pay for the goods, because Farquhar was a British loyalist. In 1792, after

Farquhar died, the executor of his estate, Alexander Chisholm, who also hailed from South Carolina, brought an action on the still-uncollected account in the Supreme Court of the United States.[15]

Article III, Section 2 of the Constitution says, "The judicial power of the United States shall extend to . . . controversies, *between a state and citizens of another State*." So the text of the Constitution seemed quite clearly to allow "a state"—here the state of Georgia—to be sued in federal court by a citizen "of another State," here a citizen of South Carolina.

Despite this, not only did Georgia contest the jurisdiction of the federal courts, it refused even to show up in the Supreme Court to make its argument, so an attorney needed to be appointed to argue its side. Georgia asserted that, as a "sovereign" state, it could only be sued if it consented to such a lawsuit.[16] Then and now this was known as the doctrine of "sovereign immunity."

Arguing on behalf of the estate was Edmund Randolph, who at the time was also the first attorney general of the United States.[17] Before that, Randolph had served on the Committee of Detail, which was charged by the Philadelphia convention to create the first written draft of the Constitution.

Decided in 1793, just four years after the enactment of the Constitution, *Chisholm v. Georgia* was the Supreme Court's first great constitutional case. In its decision, the Court, by a vote of four to one, rejected Georgia's assertion of sovereign immunity. Although the justices might have rested their opinions on the plain text of Article III, two of them went further to explain why the text comports with the underlying republican theory of the Constitution. They concluded that members of the public could sue state governments because "sovereignty" rests with the people rather than with state governments. In short, they affirmed that, in America, the states are not kings, and their legislatures are not the supreme successors to the Crown.

In *Chisholm*, because each justice delivered his own opinion "seriatim," there was no joint opinion of the Court. The practice of adopting an "opinion of the court" was later adopted by John Marshall, the third chief justice. Ever since, issuing opinions of the court has served to elevate the text of the Court's opinion to the status of written law to be studied and followed as "precedents," rather than being mere "opinions" in which each justice explains his individual vote.

Justice James Wilson had been a highly influential member of both the Continental Congress and the Constitutional Convention in Philadelphia. At the convention he had served with Randolph on the Committee of Detail. In his opinion, Wilson began by stressing that the Constitution nowhere uses the term *sovereignty*. "To the Constitution of the United States the term Sovereign, is totally unknown," he wrote.[18] There was only one place in the Constitution "where it could have been used with propriety," referring to the Preamble.[19] "But, even in that place it would not, perhaps, have comported with the delicacy of those, who ordained and established that Constitution. They might have announced themselves 'Sovereign' people of the United States: But serenely conscious of the fact, they avoided the ostentatious declaration."[20]

Wilson contended that, if the term *sovereign* is to be used at all, it should refer to the individual person. Laws "derived from the pure source of equality and justice must be founded on the CONSENT of those whose obedience they require. The sovereign, when traced to this source, must be found in *the man*."[21] In other words, obedience to law must rest on the consent of the individual person who is asked to obey the law. Wilson believed that the only reason "a free man is bound by human laws, is, that he binds himself."[22]

For Wilson, states were nothing more than an aggregate of free individuals. "If *one free man*, an original sovereign," may bind himself to the jurisdiction of the court, "why may not an aggregate of free men, *a collection of original sovereigns*, do this likewise? If the dignity of each singly is undiminished; the dignity of all jointly must be unimpaired."[23] In this sentiment, Wilson was not alone.

Our first chief justice, John Jay—who, with James Madison and Alexander Hamilton, had authored some of the early *Federalist Papers*—offered his own opinion in which he referred tellingly to "the joint and equal sovereigns of this country."[24] Jay then affirmed the "great and glorious principle, that the people are the sovereign of this country, and consequently that *fellow citizens and joint sovereigns* cannot be degraded by appearing with each other in their own Courts to have their controversies determined."[25] Notice that both "citizens" and "sovereigns" are plural, not singular. And in this discussion Jay expressly said he was talking about "that *popular sovereignty* in which every citizen partakes."[26]

Neither Wilson's nor Jay's individualist conception of popular sovereignty conforms to the modern notion of popular sovereignty as a purely "collective" concept. Their opinions in *Chisholm* present the radical yet fundamental idea that if anyone is sovereign, it is We the People as individuals, in contrast with the modern view that locates popular sovereignty in Congress or state legislatures, which supposedly represent the "will of the people," or in a majority of the citizenry, rather than residing in each and every citizen who constitutes the citizenry as a whole.

In *Chisholm*, only Justice James Iredell, of North Carolina, appeared to favor the concept of legislative supremacy. In his opinion—which was based mainly on his analysis of Article III and the Judiciary Act, which empowered the federal courts—he contended that legislatures have all the powers formerly held by the king unless expressly constrained by a written constitution or by a constitutional act of Congress. "A State is altogether exempt from the jurisdiction of the Courts of the United States, or from any other exterior authority," he stated, "unless in the special instances where the general Government has power derived from the Constitution itself."[27]

Later, in his 1798 opinion in *Calder v. Bull*, Iredell made this even clearer. In contrast to the opinion of Justice Chase, Iredell maintained that, if a constitution "imposed no limits on the legislative power, the consequence would inevitably be that whatever the legislative power chose to enact would be lawfully enacted, and the judicial power could never interpose to pronounce it void."[28] In other words, only the will of a democratic majority in adopting constitutional limits on legislative power can be enforced by the judiciary.

Iredell was here anticipating the theory of the Democratic Constitution, which would soon arise in the nineteenth and twentieth centuries. With the triumph of the Democratic Constitution, Iredell's opinions in *Chisholm* and *Calder* would later come to be hailed, and those of Jay, Wilson, and Chase dismissed.

RECONCILING INDIVIDUAL SOVEREIGNTY WITH "THE CONSENT OF THE GOVERNED"

The Declaration of Independence famously declared: "We hold these truths to be self-evident, that all men are created equal, that they are endowed by their Creator with certain unalienable Rights, that among these are Life, Liberty and the pursuit of Happiness." It then affirmed "[t]hat to secure these rights, Governments are instituted among Men, deriving their just powers from the consent of the governed." This last sentence has proven to be problematic.

If the "consent of the governed" is taken to mean the consent of *a majority* of the people, then the "consent of the governed" can be used to violate the unalienable rights for which "governments are instituted among Men." The situation is still worse if the consent of a majority of a small body of men and women called "legislators" and "representatives" is taken to be the same as the consent of the people themselves. The problem with the "collective" conception of popular sovereignty based on "the will of the people" is that it invites this majoritarian interpretation of the "consent of the governed." For it would seem that the "will" of We the People could not be identified in any other way. After all, the citizenry will never be unanimous about anything.

Suppose, however, that the flaw in this reasoning is to insist that popular sovereignty entails rule by the people themselves. Rather, rule is by "governments . . . instituted among Men," who are not to be confused with people themselves. What the people must consent to is the scheme of governance, not to the individual laws that may be imposed upon them. And yet, each "joint sovereign" individual is never asked for his or her explicit consent. The Constitution itself was only ratified by a majority of elected delegates to state ratification conventions.

How do we reconcile the individual conception of popular sovereignty based on the consent of each and every person with the fact that such unanimous consent to governance is never expressly solicited, and would be impossible to obtain? If the only reason "a free man is bound by human laws, is, that he binds himself," as Justice Wilson insisted, in what sense can an individual who is never asked for his or her consent be said to have consented to be governed?

As it happens, there was an answer to this question that can also be found at the time of the founding and long before. If we start with the republican proposition that it is the people as individuals who are sovereign, and that they retain their preexisting rights while delegating powers to their agents, then, in the absence of such express consent, we must ask what each person could be *presumed* to have consented to.

In his 1845 book, *The Unconstitutionality of Slavery*, radical abolitionist Lysander Spooner contended that, since the consent of the governed "exists only in theory," the people cannot be presumed to have given up their preexisting rights.[29] "Justice," he said, "is evidently the only principle that everybody *can be presumed* to agree to, in the formation of government."[30] Although this is where I first noticed the concept, Spooner was far from the first to make this argument, which crops up in some interesting places.

In his *Second Treatise of Government*, John Locke observed that "men, when they enter into society, give up the equality, liberty, and executive power they had in the state of nature, into the hands of the society, to be so far disposed of by the legislative, as the good of the society shall require." He then considered the scope of the legislative or police power that is given up, employing an analysis based on "supposed" consent very similar to Spooner's reference to "theoretical" consent:

> [Y]et it being only with an intention in every one the better to preserve himself, his liberty and property; (for no rational creature *can be supposed* to change his condition with an intention to be worse) the power of the society, or legislative constituted by them, *can never be supposed* to extend farther, than the common good; but is obliged to secure every one's property, by providing against those three defects . . . that made the state of nature so unsafe and uneasy.[31]

In the absence of any explicit consent from the individual, like Spooner, Locke asked what a "rational creature can be supposed" to have consented to when leaving the state of nature. And the individual can only be "supposed" to have consented to the common good, which consists of the protection of each person's life, liberty, and property.

This idea of "supposed" or presumed consent appears again in an official opinion of our first attorney general of the United States, Edmund Randolph—the attorney who represented Alexander Chisholm in the Supreme Court. President George Washington had queried each member of his cabinet as to whether the Constitution gave Congress the power to incorporate a national bank.[32]

In his opinion, Randolph observed that a legislature governed by a written constitution without an express "demarcation of powers, may perhaps, *be presumed* to be left at large, as to all authority which is communicable by the people," provided that such authority "does not affect any of those paramount rights, which a free people *cannot be supposed* to confide even to their representatives."[33] Once again, given the sovereignty of the people as individuals, the people cannot be "presumed" or "supposed" to have confided in their legislature any power to violate their fundamental rights.

But perhaps the most striking use of this notion of the presumed or supposed consent of the governed appears in the 1798 Supreme Court case *Calder v. Bull. Calder* has become known for its clash between Justice Samuel Chase, who invoked "the great first principles of the social compact," which he said restrict the "rightful exercise of legislative authority,"[34] and Justice James Iredell, who seemed to assert a far more unlimited conception of legislative power. Generally overlooked, however, is the fact that, like Locke, Randolph, and Spooner, Chase too employed the notion of supposed or presumed consent.

Justice Chase began by providing examples of legislative acts that violate these "great first principles," such as a law "that punished a citizen for an innocent action," or "a law that destroys, or impairs, the lawful private contracts of citizens," or "a law that makes a man a Judge in his own cause; or a law that takes property from A. and gives it to B."[35] Such an "act of the legislature (*for I cannot call it a law*)" was beyond the legislative power, he said, because "[i]t is against all reason and justice, for a people to entrust a Legislature with SUCH powers; and, therefore, *it cannot be presumed* that they have done it."[36]

In other words, just because a legislature enacts a statute does not automatically make the statute *a law*. And a court may need to pass on the question of whether or not a statute is a product of a "rightful exercise of legislative power." If not, then such a statute would deprive a person of life, liberty, or property without what the Fifth and Fourteenth Amendments call the "due process *of law*." Even if it is enacted according to the established legislative procedures or "process," a statute that exceeds the just powers of the legislature to enact cannot properly be considered a "law." And no person can be presumed to have consented to being deprived of his or her life, liberty, or property except by a proper law.

When discussing presumed or supposed consent, the issue is the relevant default rule when the legislature is exercising implied powers rather than those that were expressly delegated. For Chase in *Calder*, the legislature has only those powers that are expressly delegated, together with those implied powers that are not fundamentally unjust, such as punishing a person for acts that were legal when performed. Like Locke, Chase asked whether, in the absence of a clear statement in a written constitution, a free and rational person could have consented to *that*.

Just seven years after *Calder*, in the case of *United States v. Fisher*, Chief Justice John Marshall adopted a similar "clear statement rule" with respect to presumed legislative intent: "Where rights are infringed, where fundamental principles are overthrown, where the general system of the laws is departed from, the legislative intention must be expressed with irresistible clearness to induce a court of justice *to suppose* a design to effect such objects." To come full circle, in his book, *The Unconstitutionality of Slavery*, Lysander Spooner relied heavily on Marshall's rule of construction in *Fisher*.

To be sure, natural justice or natural rights lurk in the

background of all these considerations of "presumed consent." But these rights are not identified and then directly protected as such. Instead, the prior existence of such rights justifies skepticism about the claim of implied legislative power in the absence of an *express* consent.

When combined with the concept of individual popular sovereignty, all these invocations of "presumed," "supposed," or "theoretical" consent cast the issue of popular sovereignty and the "consent of the governed" in a new light and support the approach to constitutional legitimacy I presented in *Restoring the Lost Constitution*.[37]

The argument has the following steps:

- First, ultimate sovereignty rests not in the government, but in the people themselves, considered *as individuals.*
- Second, to be legitimate, the government must receive the consent of *all* these sovereign individuals.
- Third, in the absence of an express consent by each person, the only implied consent that can be attributed *to everyone* is a consent only to such powers that do not violate their retained fundamental rights.
- Fourth, the *equal protection* of these rights retained by the people is what assures them that the government is actually conforming to the consent that it claims to be the source of its just powers.
- Finally, only if such protection is *effective* will the commands of a legislature bind in conscience on the individual.

Did the Eleventh Amendment Repudiate Individual Popular Sovereignty?

Some believe that the Supreme Court's decision in *Chisholm* was swiftly repudiated by the passage of the Eleventh Amendment, which reads, "The judicial power of the United States shall not be construed to extend to any suit in law or equity, commenced or prosecuted against one of the United States by citizens of another state, or by citizens or subjects of any foreign state."[38] For example, according to Bruce Ackerman, however inspiring may be the opinions of Jay and Wilson, "Americans of the Founding era emphatically disagreed. It took them only one year to mobilize in Congress and the states to enact the Eleventh Amendment which repudiated *Chisholm* and propelled the Constitution in a different direction."[39]

While the Eleventh Amendment certainly stops citizens like Chisholm from suing states like Georgia in federal court for breach of contract, did it repudiate the conception of individual popular sovereignty expressed by James Wilson and John Jay? I think not.

Ackerman is claiming that the highly technical language of the Eleventh Amendment construing Article III's state citizen diversity should be read as a repudiation of the idea expressed in *Chisholm* that the people as individuals are sovereign. He offers no evidence whatsoever that the amendment was so read at the time, and this reading of the text itself is so implausible as to border on absurdity.

Nor does the original meaning of the Eleventh Amendment "repudiate" the principle of individual popular sovereignty announced in *Chisholm* in favor of a general unwritten principle of state sovereignty or, perhaps more narrowly, state sovereign immunity. Instead, it merely does what it says and nothing more: insulate a state from suits in federal court by citizens of other states and of foreign nations.

It was not until 1890 that the Supreme Court first alleged that the underlying principle of *Chisholm* had been repudiated by the Eleventh Amendment. In *Hans v. Louisiana*, decided nearly one hundred years after *Chisholm* but just six years before *Plessy v. Ferguson*,[40] Justice Joseph Bradley claimed that the views of state sovereignty articulated by Justice Iredell in his solo dissent "were clearly right, as the people of the United States in their sovereign capacity subsequently decided"[41] when they enacted the Eleventh Amendment.

As it happens, however, Chief Justice John Marshall did not agree. In a little-noted passage of his opinion in *Fletcher v. Peck*,[42] some twenty years after the Eleventh Amendment was adopted, Marshall observed: "The Constitution, *as passed*, gave the courts of the United States jurisdiction in suits brought against individual States. A State, *then*, which violated its own contract was suable in the courts of the United States for that violation."[43] Marshall then concluded that, although "*this feature is no longer found in the Constitution*," it nevertheless still "aids in the construction of those clauses with which it was originally associated."[44]

In other words, according to John Marshall, *Chisholm* was a faithful interpretation of the original meaning of the Constitution at the time it was decided. And it remained a correct reading of the general principles of our political institutions even after the text was amended to carve out a limited immunity for states.

The text of the Eleventh Amendment, which reversed the outcome of *Chisholm*, said nothing to repudiate the underlying principle of individual popular sovereignty articulated by Jay and Wilson—the principle that was reiterated by Justice Chase in *Calder*. It merely changed the text of Article III to deny federal courts the jurisdiction to hear such cases. This far narrower proposition has been endorsed by a broad swath of ideologically and methodologically diverse Eleventh Amendment scholars.[45]

To repudiate the republican principle that sovereignty resides in the people as individuals, the Eleventh Amendment would have to have said and done a lot more than it did.

∽

Although the text of the original Constitution established a new republican form of government to supersede the more democratic governments of the states, the new federal system was still incompletely republican. Some states continued to allow the enslavement of blacks; free blacks in the North were often treated as second-class citizens; and women, though citizens, lacked some of the privileges of citizenship enjoyed by men. The rise of a new Democratic Party in the 1820s, committed both to slavery and to majoritarian rule within the states, exacerbated these problems and led to the establishment of a new antislavery Republican Party in the 1850s.

In Part II, I explain how these political developments eventually led to the adoption of amendments that greatly improved our Republican Constitution. I then tell the story of how the rise of progressivism in *both* political parties led to an assault on our Republican Constitution that has greatly undermined its republican features to this day. The progressives gave us the concepts of "judicial restraint" and "deference" to the majoritarian branches, along with the concept of "a living constitution."

All of these tropes were devised to evade the constraints on their progressive legislative agenda imposed by our Republican Constitution. So our Republican Constitution had to go. This story will make clear how the tragedy of the Supreme Court's decision in the Obamacare case was made possible by modern-day "judicial conservatives" accepting as valid the progressive attack on our Republican Constitution, and why it is entirely legitimate for judges to preserve its republican structural features.

PART II

IMPROVING
OUR REPUBLICAN
CONSTITUTION

CHAPTER 4

HOW SLAVERY LED TO A MORE REPUBLICAN CONSTITUTION

The New Republican Party and Its Amendments

THE FIRST REPUBLICAN PARTY

The original Republican Party was organized by Thomas Jefferson and James Madison to oppose the Federalists, who dominated the early Congress.¹ At the time, Jefferson was the secretary of state in the administration of George Washington, and Madison was a member of Congress from Virginia. Behind the scenes, the Federalists who dominated Congress were led by Secretary of the Treasury Alexander Hamilton. Hamilton, who served under Washington during the war, had the president's ear.

In the summer of 1791, under the ruse of taking a botanical study trip, Madison and Jefferson traveled throughout New England and New York to rally support for their anti-Hamilton cause. Their effort resulted in the formation of the first Republican Party. Jefferson recruited Philip Freneau, a journalist from New York, to publish the official party newspaper, called the *National Gazette*, giving him a position in the State Department as a translator.

Hamilton's nationalist sentiments were well known. At the Philadelphia convention, as a delegate from New York, he had proposed his own nationalist scheme for the new constitution that was reportedly received by the other delegates with a stony silence. Had the *Federalist Papers*, to which he contributed importantly, not been published pseudonymously under the name of Publius, his essays on behalf of limited national power would have been dismissed by many as disingenuous.

As Treasury secretary, Hamilton proposed the formation of the first National Bank of the United States. Hamilton succeeded in getting President Washington to support the bank over the constitutional objections of Madison in the House and Secretary of State Jefferson and Attorney General Edmund Randolph in the cabinet.

Hamilton, a highly skilled lawyer, penned a lengthy defense of the constitutionality of the bank that relied on an expansive reading of Congress's power under the Necessary and Proper Clause, which authorizes Congress "to make all laws which shall be necessary and proper for carrying into execution" the enumerated powers of Congress.[2] Some thirty years later, Chief Justice John Marshall would crib from Hamilton's analysis of the Necessary and Proper Clause when upholding the constitutionality of a national bank in the 1819 case of *McCulloch v. Maryland.*

So, in its early days, the Republican opposition to the Federalists was in defense of the constitutional limitations of national power that characterizes what I am calling our Republican Constitution. Republicans opposed the egregious Alien and Sedition Acts by attempting to rally state opposition in the form of the Virginia resolution, written by Madison, and the Kentucky resolution, penned by Jefferson. In his report of 1800, Madison condemned the acts as outside the enumerated powers of Congress to enact and, secondarily, as a violation of the freedom of speech protected by the First Amendment.

Republican Thomas Jefferson's election to the presidency was so momentous a repudiation of the Federalists, it was known as the "Revolution of 1800." The Alien and Sedition Acts were repealed by the newly elected Republican Congress. Jefferson pardoned those who had been convicted for violating it, and his

Republican allies even made private compensation to those who had been imprisoned.

As president, Jefferson adopted a far more constrained view of federal powers than had the Washington and Adams administrations before him. So too did his successor as president, James Madison, who had served as Jefferson's secretary of state.

In those days, political "parties" were considered evil. Just as the term *democracy* had the same valence that the term *demagogue* has today, the term *party* had the valence of *partisan*. A party was viewed as a faction motivated by passion or interest adverse or indifferent to the common good of all. So "Federalist" and "Republican" were convenient labels for loosely associated groups of individuals—like we use the terms "conservative" or "liberal"—rather than names for the sort of political organizations we associate with political parties today. The modern party organizations with which we are so familiar originated later. First came the Democrats, and then came the Republicans.

THE ORIGINS OF THE DEMOCRATIC AND REPUBLICAN PARTIES

The story of the rise of modern political parties is complex.[3] Suffice it to say that, after the War of 1812, the Federalist Party fell apart and was replaced by the Whigs. And the Republican Party of Jefferson and Madison was succeeded during the presidencies of Andrew Jackson (1829–37) and Martin Van Buren (1837–41) by a new organization that came to be known as the Democratic Party.

In its early years, the Democratic Party often called itself "the Democracy" because it presumed to speak for the people as a whole. The central idea was that "there existed a body called 'the democracy' and that the Constitution made the democracy sovereign."[4] The Democratic Party was "the institutional device by which the democracy might exercise its sovereignty in practice."[5]

Speaking for the ascendant Democratic Party, Martin Van Buren "articulated a radically democratic theory of the Constitution in which the will of the people as expressed through the party became the authoritative word on both policy and constitutional meaning."[6]

The concept of the will of the people was central to Van Buren's "true democracy." He believed that the "great principle first formally avowed by Rousseau 'that the right to exercise sovereignty belongs inalienably to the people,' sprung up spontaneously in the hearts of the colonists, and silently influenced all their acts from the beginning." In one respect, "Van Buren's concept of democracy was close to Rousseau's." He "seems to have conceived of the democracy almost as a unified body with a single true will."[7] To say the least, this was an anachronistic view of the founding generation's political views.

By this time, the nation was increasingly torn over the issue of slavery. At the founding, there was a national consensus that slavery was unjust and in conflict with the principles of the Declaration. Though dissenters surely existed, even slaveholders—especially Virginians like Washington, Jefferson, and Madison—agreed. They could rationalize a gradualist approach to ending the institution by telling themselves that slavery was an economically inefficient institution that would eventually die out on its own. For one thing, producing cotton on plantations was a highly labor-intensive activity that required the separation by hand of the fibers from the sticky seeds.

With the invention of the cotton gin in 1794, however, that work could be automated, and growing cotton on slave plantations became enormously profitable. This increased economic efficiency of plantation farming with slaves was soon to be further enhanced by the development of steamboats that could bring cotton upriver on the Mississippi to the North, greatly reducing the cost to market slave-produced cotton.

As these two technological developments made slavery vastly more lucrative, for the first time in American history there developed an ardently proslavery ideology to defend its continuation and even its expansion into the territories. Slaveholders began to justify their practice as both humane and superior to the wage labor system. Some even defended slavery as a form of "socialism," in which the slaves would be cared for from cradle to grave, unlike the capitalist free labor system, which cast out workers when they became too old or enfeebled to be productive.

"Slaves in all ages and countries have had their physical wants well supplied," wrote George Fitzhugh in the essay "Centralization and Socialism."[8] Taking the offensive against the capitalist "free labor" system in the North, he asserted that "man emancipated from human masters, and remitted to the unfeeling despotism of capital, has, so far, lost by the exchange, both physically and morally."[9]

Above all, the new Democratic Party was founded on the idea of states' rights in defense of slavery. "The only principle as important as the party's right to dictate to the officeholders—functionally overriding all the structural checks designed by the Framers—was the principle of states' rights." By the 1820s, "the Democrats' radical states' rights positions were dominant, and Van Buren and the Democrats hoped that a firm states' rights position would help them solve the problem of slavery." The Democracy was organized "nationally on the basis that each state's domestic arrangements were off limits to the national government."[10]

With the rise of this fervid proslavery ideology, and a new political party to advance it, came a corresponding and increasingly radical movement for its complete abolition. Most were somewhere in the middle of this battle between abolitionists and the Slave Power, but as time passed and the ferocity of the conflict continued to grow, Americans were increasingly forced to choose sides.

The wing of the radical abolitionists led by William Lloyd Garrison—a Massachusetts newspaperman—contended that, because the Constitution sanctioned slavery, it constituted a "covenant with death, and an agreement with hell."[11] To avoid being bound to adhere to the so-called Fugitive Slave Clause of Article IV, these Garrisonian radicals advocated for the northern states to secede from the Union so that fugitives from the border states could find safe harbor in the North. The Garrisonians believed that, when border states were turned into free states by this flight to the North, this would lead to the draining of slaves from the deeper South. Many Garrisonians also turned against political action and advocated withdrawal from the political process.[12]

Another antislavery group advocated political action within the existing constitutional order. In their view, the Constitution was not proslavery but instead was antislavery at the national level, while only tolerating its existence at the local or state level. They argued that, because slavery was contrary to natural rights, it could only receive protection as a matter of positive law. So the question was, what exactly did the Constitution say about slavery?

The Constitution itself did not expressly recognize property in human beings, they insisted. Instead, it recognized only a condition of servitude—"persons held to service." For this reason, it gave no express warrant to chattel slavery and was fundamentally antislavery.

This group freely conceded that the federal government had no power under the Constitution to interfere with slavery within the original states that still recognized it. But they contended that, nevertheless, it had power to abolish slavery in the District of Columbia, in the territories, and in federal installations. Their constitutional slogan was "freedom national, slavery local."[13]

In this way did the Democrats' proslavery states' rights stance beget the assertion of states' rights *against* slavery and the federal Fugitive Slave Acts. And with it, the formation of a new antislavery Republican Party to oppose the proslavery Democrats.

SALMON CHASE AND THE REPUBLICAN CONSTITUTION

The person most responsible for developing this constitutional approach was a young Ohio antislavery lawyer named Salmon P. Chase. Chase first developed these arguments in tandem with abolitionist newspaper publisher and lawyer James Birney in 1837, when they defended a runaway slave named Matilda. Like many in Ohio, Birney and Chase were transplants.

Birney had been a practicing attorney in Kentucky and a plantation slave owner in Alabama. Eventually he turned sharply antislavery and moved to the free state of Ohio, where he could more freely advocate for its abolition. There he founded the antislavery newspaper the *Philanthropist*.

Chase was born in New Hampshire. After his father died, his mother sent the twelve-year-old boy to live with his uncle in Ohio. Chase returned East to attend college at Dartmouth and study law with Attorney General William Wirt in Washington, D.C. Upon passing the bar, Chase returned to Ohio to practice law, eventually landing the Bank of the United States as his principal client.

Chase was active in local politics, in part as a way of generating legal business. But he was not involved in the antislavery movement until a mob attacked the printing press of the *Philanthropist* and went searching for Birney. When Chase heard that the mob was heading to the Franklin House to tar and feather the publisher, he raced to the hotel to warn him.

As the mob surged forward, Chase braced his arms against the door frame, blocking the hotel's entrance with his body. Six feet two, with broad shoulders, a massive chest, and a determined set to his jaw, Chase gave the rioters pause. The crowd demanded to know who he was. "Salmon P. Chase," the young lawyer replied. "You will pay for your actions," a frustrated member of the mob told him. "I [can] be found at any time," Chase said.[14] In fact, it was members of the mob who were made to pay damages when Birney retained Chase to bring a successful tort action against them for the property damage they had caused.

Matilda had accompanied her owner and father to the northern states, passing as his white daughter. When her father reached Cincinnati on his way back to the South, Matilda pleaded with him to leave her behind. When he refused her entreaties, she fled to the enclave of free blacks in Cincinnati. Eventually she was employed by Birney in his household. After a time, she was captured by slave catchers who had been sent to Ohio by her father.

Given their history, it was only natural for Birney to engage Chase as counsel to seek a writ of habeas corpus to prevent Matilda's return. Together the two lawyers hastily developed a constitutional challenge to the federal Fugitive Slave Act of 1793, under which authority she had been seized.[15]

Chase's principal constitutional argument was based on the fact that Congress had only those legislative powers "herein granted" by the Constitution. He contended that the Fugitive Slave Act was unconstitutional because Congress lacked any enumerated power to enforce the Fugitive Slave Clause of Article IV, which reads:

> No Person held to Service or Labour in one State, under the Laws thereof, escaping into another, shall, in Consequence of any Law or Regulation therein, be discharged from such Service or Labour, but shall be delivered up on Claim of the Party to whom such Service or Labour may be due.[16]

Later on, some abolitionists like Lysander Spooner would claim that, because it did not specifically reference "slavery" or property in man, the public meaning of this clause was confined to the capture of runaway indentured servants. Chase, however, conceded that it was indeed about slavery.[17] Instead, he based his defense of Matilda on the limited nature of Congress's enumerated powers.

Chase contended that the provisions of Article IV were merely "articles of compact" among the several states, to be enforced by them like treaties are enforced by sovereign nations. Congress had no enumerated power to enforce the provisions of Article IV unless, as in the Full Faith and Credit Clause, such power was specified in Article IV itself. And he denied that the Necessary and Proper Clause can be stretched to empower Congress to enforce a part of the Constitution that did not itself identify a power.[18]

Sadly, Chase lost the case and Matilda was sent "down the river," never to be heard from again. But his argument in the *Matilda* case was published and distributed widely throughout the country. The pamphlet provided the legal basis for other challenges to the constitutionality of the Fugitive Slave Act and sparked a movement among antislavery advocates that has been called "constitutional abolitionism."[19] The pamphlet also greatly raised Chase's political visibility.

Now fully engaged in the antislavery cause, Chase continued to develop his constitutional arguments, eventually presenting them to the Supreme Court in the 1846 case of *Jones v. Van Zandt*. At the end of his lengthy brief to the Court (which ran 107 pages when printed as a pamphlet), Chase included an invocation of *Calder v. Bull*.

Chase identified "certain great principles of natural right and justice," which while they were included in the "written law" of the Constitution, also "exist independently of all such sanction."[20] These great principles are:

No Legislature is omnipotent. No Legislature can make right wrong; or wrong, right. No Legislature can make light, darkness; or darkness, light. No Legislature can make men, things; or things, men. Nor is any Legislature at liberty to disregard the fundamental principles of rectitude or justice. Whether restrained or not by constitutional provision, there are acts beyond any legitimate or binding legislative authority.[21]

A legislature:

cannot authorize injustice by law; cannot nullify private contracts; cannot abrogate the seeurities [*sic*] of life, liberty and property, which, it is the very object of society, as well as of our constitution of government, to provide; cannot make a man a judge in his own case; cannot repeal the laws of nature; cannot create any obligation to do wrong, or neglect duty. No court is bound to enforce unjust law; but, on the contrary, every court is bound, by prior and superior obligations, to abstain from enforcing such law.[22]

Chase then allowed that it "must be a clear case, doubtless, which will warrant a court in pronouncing a law so unjust that it ought not to be enforced; but, in a clear case, the path of duty is plain."[23]

Chase was fighting an uphill battle in the Supreme Court, which had previously upheld the constitutionality of the Fugitive Slave Act in the 1842 case of *Prigg v. Pennsylvania*. In *Prigg*, Justice Joseph Story adopted the view of judicial restraint and deference, as well as a capacious reading of the Necessary and Proper Clause. In these respects, *Prigg* was really quite modern. Despite Chase's plea that the justices reconsider their previous decision, the Court summarily denied Chase's claims in *Van Zandt* without even allowing an oral argument in the case.

Prigg is perhaps the earliest example of the Supreme Court undermining the system of federalism with an expansive reading of the Necessary and Proper Clause. In this case, federalism was protecting the liberty of the free blacks from being wrongfully kidnapped and removed from a free state. In the name of federal power, the Supreme Court invalidated the "personal liberty laws" enacted by northern states to provide for due process before their removal.

After Congress passed the new and harsher Fugitive Slave Act of 1850, Wisconsin attorney Byron Paine successfully used Chase's constitutional arguments to free a newspaper editor named Sherman Booth, who had been charged under the new law with assisting the escape of a captured slave.[24] But the ruling of the lower court was reversed by the Supreme Court in the 1859 case of *Ableman v. Booth* in an opinion written by Chief Justice Roger Taney, the author of the infamous proslavery opinion of *Dred Scott v. Sandford*.[25]

By this time, Chase had long since shifted his attention from the courts to politics.[26] Unlike such abolitionists as William Lloyd Garrison and Wendell Phillips, Chase and his cohorts decided to attack slavery within the electoral process. First, he and Birney helped create the expressly antislavery Liberty Party. The party's strategy was to vet Whig and Democratic candidates for office and throw support to the one who was more antislavery. But both Whigs and Democrats paid scant attention to the Liberty men, and most voters cared more about the economic and other issues dividing Whigs from Democrats than they did the slavery question.

Chase then participated in another, more successful, though less radical, swing party called the Free Soil Party. The Free Soil Party was organized around the principle of "nonextension" of slavery into any new territories. Its slogan, coined by Chase, was "Free Soil, Free Labor, Free Men." (When the Republicans ran John Frémont as their first presidential candidate in 1856, they recycled the slogan as "Free Soil, Free Men, and Frémont!")

The Missouri Compromise of 1820 prohibited slavery in the former Louisiana Territory above the northern parallel of 36˚30' except within the boundaries of the proposed slave state of Missouri. In 1854, when it came time to consider the statehood of the Kansas and Nebraska territories, which were both located north of that line, Democrats in Congress scuttled the Missouri Compromise. Instead they proposed the Kansas-Nebraska Act, which would allow the admission of both territories as slave states if the white male settlers in those territories voted to approve a pro-slavery constitution.

This policy was famously promoted by Illinois Democrat Stephen A. Douglas as an exercise of "popular sovereignty," a usage that had been coined by Senator Lewis Cass, a leading Democrat from Michigan and the Democratic presidential nominee in 1848.[27] Under this theory, because the people of a community were rightfully entitled to decide such issues for themselves, the people of a territory, not Congress, should decide whether to permit or exclude slavery.

Here is how Douglas later summarized his "great principle of popular sovereignty":

> Now, my friends, if we will only act conscientiously and rigidly upon this great principle of popular sovereignty, which guaranties to each State and Territory the right to do as it pleases on all things, local and domestic, instead of Congress interfering, we will continue at peace one with another. . . . And why can we not adhere to the great principle of self-government, upon which our institutions were originally based?[28]

Under this Democratic conception of popular sovereignty, a majority of the people gets to speak for everyone. And the majority, if it wishes, can even authorize the enslavement of the minority! Of course, here the proposal was for just a majority of white males to vote, but the principle of majoritarian or collective popular sovereignty would operate the same if suffrage were extended to free blacks or even slaves. Under the collective notion of popular sovereignty, a majority—or what James Madison characterized as a "faction . . . amounting to a majority . . . of the whole"—gets to speak for We the People.

The repudiation of the Missouri Compromise was viewed by Free Soilers and many abolitionist northerners as an aggressive, expansionist maneuver by the slave-owning South. It showed that there was no quenching the ambitions of the Slave Power. Douglas's democratic conception of popular sovereignty was widely condemned.

In 1854, as a Free Soil U.S. senator from Ohio, Salmon Chase put it this way in a speech to the Senate:

> Sir, the Senator from Illinois tells us that he proposes a final settlement of all territorial questions in respect to slavery, by the application of popular sovereignty. What kind of popular sovereignty is that which allows one portion of the people to enslave another portion? Is that the doctrine of equal rights? Is that exact justice? Is that the teaching of enlightened, liberal, progressive Democracy? No, sir; no! There can be no real Democracy which does not fully maintain the rights of man, as man.[29]

Although employing the rhetoric of "liberal, progressive Democracy," Chase was actually challenging the majoritarian conception of democracy itself by appealing to the bedrock principle of the Republican Constitution: that governments are instituted among men to secure their natural rights.

After the Kansas-Nebraska Act passed Congress over bitter opposition, "popular sovereignty" led to gruesome violence that engulfed the Kansas Territory, as warring factions vied to control the content of its new constitution. Just as the War of 1812 led to the demise of the Federalists, now in the wake of the debate that resulted in "Bleeding Kansas," the Whig party collapsed. In its place rose a new party committed to a different conception of the Constitution than that of the Democrats. It was called the Republican Party and its constitutional platform was imported from the platform of the Free Soil Party, which had been written by Salmon Chase.[30]

In 1860, Chase was a leading candidate for the Republican presidential nomination, but he was beaten by Abraham Lincoln of Illinois. After his election, Lincoln chose his political rival to be his secretary of the Treasury. Inside the Lincoln cabinet, Chase was viewed as the champion of the more radical Republicans in Congress, who were distrustful of the president.

A NEW REPUBLICAN PARTY

Though the Republican platform conceded the constitutional power of states to preserve slavery ("slavery local"), it advocated a national antislavery program in which slavery would be abolished in the District of Columbia, in the territories, and in federal enclaves ("freedom national"). So threatening was this program to the Slave Power that the southern states seceded even before the Republicans could take power to implement it. In the face of this antislavery platform, the South left while the leaving was still good.

When they captured the presidency and the southern states seceded, Republicans found themselves in complete control of Congress as well. While continuing to insist that they had no authority under the Constitution to abolish slavery within an existing state, they moved swiftly to abolish slavery in the District of Columbia. The admission of new states, such as West Virginia, was conditioned on their abolishing slavery within. As authorized by Congress, the Union army began "confiscating" slaves as contraband of war under the doctrine of military necessity. In 1862, Congress barred the U.S. military from enforcing the Fugitive Slave Clause. As historian James Oakes describes the Republicans' actions after taking power, "it's hard to imagine how emancipation could have begun any sooner."[31]

Congress authorized the president to emancipate any slave upon the president's determination that it was necessary to advance the military objectives of the Union army. This culminated in the Emancipation Proclamation, which declared that any slave held in disloyal territory was hereafter and forever free. Moreover, the Proclamation also authorized enlistment of blacks into the Union Army from border slave states in the Union, which had the effect of emancipating them, too.

The Militia Act of 1862 had already "explicitly freed any slave who enlisted in the Union army and at the same time freed 'his mother and his wife and his children.'"[32] Because only American citizens were eligible to serve in the army, however, the Lincoln administration had to determine whether free blacks could be citizens of the United States,[33] a conclusion that had been denied by Chief Justice Taney in his infamous 1857 opinion in *Dred Scott*.[34]

In response to a request from Treasury secretary Chase, in November 1862 Attorney General Edward Bates issued a lengthy written opinion that free blacks were indeed citizens of the United States and, as such, were entitled to all of the "privileges and immunities" of citizens of the United States, protected by the Privileges and Immunities Clause of Article IV. "In my opinion," he wrote, "the Constitution uses the word citizen only to express the political quality of the individual in his relations to the nation; to declare that he is a member of the body politic, and bound to it by the reciprocal obligation of allegiance on the one side and

protection on the other."[35] This was the standard abolitionist constitutional theory that maintained the duty of protection recip-
rocally followed from the demand for allegiance and obedience.

"Every citizen of the United States is a component member of
the nation," Bates continued, "with rights and duties, under the
Constitution and laws of the United States, which cannot be destroyed or abridged by the laws of any particular State."[36] If they
conflict with the laws of the nation, the laws of a state are of no
force. Over and above any special rights, privileges or immunities
he may hold as a citizen of a state, a citizen of the United States
has those rights that "legally and naturally belong to him in his
quality of citizen of the United States."[37]

Blacks were U.S. citizens because they were born in the United
States and "the Constitution says not one word, and furnishes
not one hint, in relation to the color or to the ancestral race of
the 'natural born citizen.'"[38] Obliquely referring to the Supreme
Court's denial of this proposition in *Dred Scott*, Bates wrote that
regardless of what

> may have been said, in the opinions of judges and lawyers,
> and in State statutes, about negroes, mulattoes, and persons
> of color, the Constitution is wholly silent upon that subject.
> The Constitution itself does not make the citizens, (it is, in
> fact, made by them.) It only intends and recognizes such of
> them as are natural—home-born—and provides for the nat-
> uralization of such of them as were alien—foreign-born—
> making the latter, as far as nature will allow, like the former.[39]

In this way, the Republican reading of the Constitution enabled blacks to be citizens, and consequently eligible for service in the Union army. And this then emancipated them and
their families, even if they resided in a slave state that was not
then in rebellion and not subject to the other provisions of the

Emancipation Proclamation. Thus, when combined with the Militia Act of 1862 and Attorney General Bates's opinion on black citizenship, the Emancipation Proclamation's legal effect on January 1, 1863, extended well beyond the slaves who were behind Confederate lines.

INVOLUNTARY SERVITUDE AND THE PROTECTION OF ECONOMIC LIBERTY

Under the Republican antislavery reading of the Constitution, emancipating slaves in all these ways did not end the institution of slavery in states where slavery continued to be maintained locally. In those states, while slaves freed by military necessity were forever free, slavery could be reinstituted, for example by importing slaves from the border states that had not yet abolished slavery. And the risk that when southern states returned to Congress federal policy would change to allow them to reenslave their blacks could not be dismissed lightly.

Therefore, under the Republican reading of the Constitution, even after thousands of slaves had been freed, the end of slavery as a legal institution required a constitutional amendment. With great effort, the Republicans in Congress drafted and eventually approved the Thirteenth Amendment, which, as dictated by Republican constitutional theory, included an express "power to enforce this article by appropriate legislation."[40] In 1865 the amendment was ratified.

Contrary to the long-held assumption of abolitionists, the institution of slavery turned out not to be tottering and weak. Even after a punishing war, its legal abolition did not end the subordination of free blacks. Southern states responded with "Black Codes" making the freedmen second-class citizens, and local authorities looked the other way as the freedmen were brutalized and intimidated.

In response to the continued legal and extralegal persecution of the free blacks and white Republicans in the South, the Republicans in Congress enacted the Civil Rights Act of 1866. After adopting Attorney General Bates's definition of U.S. citizens as "all persons born in the United States and not subject to any foreign power," the act then mandated that

> such citizens, of every race and color, without regard to any previous condition of slavery or involuntary servitude . . . shall have the same right . . . to make and enforce contracts, to sue, be parties, and give evidence, to inherit, purchase, lease, sell, hold, and convey real and personal property, and to full and equal benefit of all laws and proceedings for the security of person and property, as is enjoyed by white citizens . . . any law, statute, ordinance, regulation, or custom, to the contrary notwithstanding.[41]

Notice how Congress identified the civil rights of all persons, whether white or black, as the rights "to make and enforce contracts . . . to inherit, purchase, lease, sell, hold, and convey real and personal property." In other words, at the very core of civil rights were the economic rights of contract and property, though, I repeat, characterizing these rights as "economic" is anachronistic.

So now we must ask, what did the Republicans in Congress think empowered them to enact the Civil Rights Act, protecting the economic rights of contract and property against infringements by the states? For many, the answer may be surprising. It is the Thirteenth Amendment, the first section of which reads: "Neither slavery nor involuntary servitude, except as a punishment for crime whereof the party shall have been duly convicted, shall exist within the United States, or any place subject to their jurisdiction." Today, the claim that the Thirteenth Amendment empowered Congress to protect the rights of contract and property from infringement seems strained, but this is largely because we take the injustice of slavery for granted in ways critics of slavery did not.

The abolitionist critique of slavery was multifaceted, but at its core was the idea of natural rights, in particular the right of property that each person has in him or herself—called self-ownership—as well as the liberty of each person to exchange his or her labor for wages and other mutually agreeable terms—called "free labor." The fundamental divide between the Slave Power and abolitionists concerned the rights of property and contract. Could a person be owned as property and be denied the right to refrain from laboring except on terms contractually agreed upon, so long as a legislature said so? Or did every person own him or herself, with the inherent right to enter into contracts by which they would acquire property in return that no legislature could properly restrict?

That today we think of these rights as "economic" should not be surprising. After all, slavery was, first and foremost, an economic system designed to deprive slaves of their economic rights. The key to slavery was labor. Restrictions imposed on what we would consider "personal liberties"—such as the freedom of slaves to speak or to read—were often instrumental to enabling the Slave Power to keep blacks working in bondage, and to reinforce the claim that blacks were inferior beings whose labor could be exploited without their consent.

The Slave Power considered the arguments of abolitionists to be so insidious that southern states made it a crime for anyone— whether white or black, free or slave—to publish or speak them. The legal punishment for communicating the ideas of self-ownership and free labor was whipping or even death. And mobs meted out their own punishments, including tarring and feathering. While today we consider the freedoms of speech, press, and assembly to be personal, back then these rights were denied specifically when it came to advocating that enslaved blacks had the right to their own labor, along with their right to own property and freely enter into contracts.

Therefore, by abolishing slavery, the Thirteenth Amendment was thought to have ipso facto empowered Congress to protect the economic liberties that slavery had for so long denied, in particular the "right . . . to make and enforce contracts, . . . to inherit, purchase, lease, sell, hold, and convey real and personal property, and to full and equal benefit of all laws and proceedings for the security of person and property."

This defense of the constitutionality of the Civil Rights Act under the Thirteenth Amendment can be simplified as follows: The Thirteenth Amendment prohibited slavery and *the opposite of Slavery is Liberty*. Any unwarranted restrictions on liberty that were imposed on emancipated slaves were simply partial "incidents" of their previous conditions of servitude. And Section 2 of the Thirteenth Amendment empowered Congress to protect any citizen from such unjust restrictions on their liberty.

The Privileges or Immunities of Citizens of the United States

To the dismay of the Republicans in Congress, President Andrew Johnson vetoed the Civil Rights Act. Johnson, a "War Democrat" from Tennessee, was Lincoln's vice president and became president upon Lincoln's assassination. In his lengthy veto message, Johnson objected to the measure because it attempted to impose by federal law "a perfect equality of the white and black races in every State of the Union."[42] Objecting to its conferral of citizenship on the freedmen, Johnson echoed Chief Justice Taney's opinion in *Dred Scott* by asking: "Can it be reasonably supposed that they possess the requisite qualifications to entitle them to all the privileges and immunities of citizens of the United States?" With respect to the civil rights enumerated in the bill, Johnson offered the following reply:

> Hitherto every subject embraced in the enumeration of rights contained in this bill has been considered as exclusively belonging to the States. They all relate to the internal police and economy of the respective States. They are matters which in each State concern the domestic condition of its people, varying in each according to its own peculiar circumstances and the safety and well-being of its own citizens.[43]

Johnson denied that the power to protect these rights was properly "incident" to the power of Congress to enforce the Thirteenth Amendment. "Slavery has been abolished," he wrote, "and at present nowhere exists within the jurisdiction of the United States; nor has there been, nor is it likely there will be, any attempt to revive it by the people or the States."[44]

Johnson conceded that the civil rights enumerated in the act "are, by Federal as well as State laws, secured to all domiciled aliens and foreigners, even before the completion of the process of naturalization." But he nevertheless protested that this claim of congressional power "must sap and destroy our federative system of limited powers and break down the barriers which preserve the rights of the States. It is another step, or rather stride, toward centralization and the concentration of all legislative powers in the National Government."[45] In response, Republican supermajorities in both the House and Senate overrode the president's veto.

Although it is often claimed that Congress then enacted the Fourteenth Amendment to constitutionalize the Civil Rights Act, this is an oversimplification of what happened. The initiative in Congress to protect the rights of free blacks and Republicans in the South by means of a constitutional amendment had begun even before the introduction of the Civil Rights Act and was promoted by different members.[46]

While Senator Lyman Trumbull of Illinois devised and promoted the Civil Rights Act under the auspices of the Thirteenth Amendment, Representative John Bingham of Ohio was the moving force behind the Fourteenth Amendment. Because the southern states were eventually going to resume their seats in Congress, Bingham sought to place these guarantees beyond the power of a future Congress to repeal. Bingham also sought to protect the rights of white Republicans in the South along with those of freed blacks.

To accomplish this, Bingham proposed the language that became part of Section 1 of the Fourteenth Amendment: "No state shall make or enforce any law which shall abridge the privileges or immunities of citizens of the United States." These "privileges or immunities of citizens" included the natural rights to which the Ninth Amendment refers, such as the rights that were enumerated in the Civil Rights Act of 1866. But they also included the personal guarantees that are enumerated in the original Bill of Rights.

Consider the explanation of Section 1 offered by Senator Jacob Howard of Michigan, the designated sponsor of the amendment in the Senate, in which he clearly identified two categories of "privileges or immunities." The first category was the rights to which the Privileges and Immunities Clause of Article IV referred: "The citizens of each state shall be entitled to all privileges and immunities of citizens in the several states." But what were these "privileges and immunities of citizens"?

Like many others in the House and Senate, Senator Howard quoted a lengthy passage from a circuit court opinion in an 1823 case called *Corfield v. Coryell.* The opinion was authored by Supreme Court justice Bushrod Washington—George Washington's nephew—while he was "riding circuit" as Supreme Court justices did back then. In the middle of the lengthy quote, Justice Washington offers this summary of "privileges and immunities":

> What these fundamental principles are it would, perhaps, be more tedious than difficult to enumerate. They may, however, be all comprehended under the following general heads: protection by the Government, *the enjoyment of life and liberty, with the right to acquire and possess property of every kind, and to pursue and obtain happiness and safety,* subject nevertheless to such restraints as the Government may justly prescribe for the general good of the whole.[47]

This language should be familiar. Justice Washington is here merely repeating verbatim the canonical formulation of natural rights that was penned by George Mason for the Virginia Declaration of Rights, and which was then replicated in four other state constitutions, in the Virginia ratification convention's proposed amendments to the Constitution, in Roger Sherman's list of "natural rights" "retained" by "the people," and in a proposed amendment offered in the Senate. It was the very same language upon which the Massachusetts Supreme Judicial Court had based its ruling that slavery was unconstitutional in that state.

In other words, according to Justice Washington, the "privileges and immunities of citizens in the several states," to which Article IV refers, include the very natural rights retained by the people to which the Ninth Amendment refers. And according to Senator Howard, and all those in Congress who quoted *Corfield*, these very same rights were "privileges or immunities of citizens of the United States," which no state shall abridge.

But then to these "*Corfield* rights" Senator Howard immediately added another category of privileges or immunities: "To these privileges and immunities, whatever they may be—for they are not and cannot be fully defined in their entire extent and precise nature—to these should be added the personal rights guaranteed and secured by the first eight amendments of the Constitution."[48] After specifically listing each of these personal guarantees, he summarized these two sources of rights. "Now, sir, here is a mass of privileges, immunities, and rights, some of them secured by the second section of the fourth article of the Constitution, which I have recited, some by the first eight amendments of the Constitution."[49]

Why then add the Privileges or Immunities Clause to the Constitution if these rights were already included in Article IV and in the first eight amendments? Because, Howard explained, the courts had ruled that "these immunities, privileges, rights, thus guaranteed by the Constitution or recognized by it . . . do not operate in the slightest degree as a restraint or prohibition upon State legislation."[50]

This last claim by Howard may be somewhat undercut by the enactment of the Civil Rights Act under the auspices of the Thirteenth Amendment. Perhaps Howard was among those who questioned the authority of Congress to enact the Civil Rights Act. Perhaps he thought the Thirteenth Amendment only empowered Congress to legislate against the vestiges of slavery in the Black Codes to which the Civil Rights Act was addressed, and did not authorize the protection of white Unionists and Republicans in the South, who were also under siege.

But the end result is the same. Whether by the Fourteenth Amendment alone, or in combination with the Thirteenth, states may not abridge the personal guarantees in what we now call the Bill of Rights, or the natural rights of their citizens, including the economic liberty "to make and enforce contracts" and "to inherit, purchase, lease, sell, hold, and convey real and personal property."

That Howard was affirming the primacy and now the enforceability of these fundamental natural rights is shown by his denial that the Privileges or Immunities of Citizens of the United States included the right to vote: "The right of suffrage is not, in law, one of the privileges or immunities thus secured by the Constitution. It is merely the creature of law."

In other words, the right of suffrage is a matter solely of positive law, and is not one of the rights of the people that preexist the formation of government, and which government is formed to secure. Howard made the distinction between natural and positive rights explicit when he explained that the right of suffrage "has always been regarded in this country as the result of positive local law, not regarded as one of those fundamental rights lying at the basis of all society and without which a people cannot exist except as slaves, subject to a despotism."

According to the sponsor of the Fourteenth Amendment in the Senate, then, the "privileges or immunities" of citizens of the United States that were now to be protected by the federal government against infringement by the states were the natural rights he described as "those fundamental rights lying at the basis of all society and without which a people cannot exist except as slaves, subject to a despotism." To wit: "the enjoyment of life and liberty, with the right to acquire and possess property of every kind, and to pursue and obtain happiness and safety."[51]

THE STILL INCOMPLETE REPUBLICAN CONSTITUTION

Although the Thirteenth and Fourteenth Amendments improved our Republican Constitution, in one important respect they made matters worse. Because of their concern over the injustice of slavery, women had played a pivotal role in the abolitionist movement. But women abolitionists also believed that the end of slavery in the name of equality would provide an impetus for ending the legal subordination of women as well.

For advocates of women's equality, then, the wording of Section 2 of the Fourteenth Amendment represented a significant setback. Section 2 was designed to provide an incentive for southern states to provide free blacks the right to vote without the need for an amendment to expressly mandate the right of black suffrage. A state's representation in the House would be reduced by the number of blacks who were ineligible to vote.

To accomplish this, however, the Republicans proposed a race-neutral formula that was instead pegged to sex. When "the right to vote . . . is denied to any of the *male inhabitants* of such state, being twenty-one years of age, and citizens of the United States," the amendment stipulated, "the basis of representation therein shall be reduced in the proportion which the number of such *male citizens* shall bear to the whole number of *male citizens* twenty-one years of age in such state."[52]

This was the first time that sex or gender was explicitly mentioned in the Constitution. Under the canons of abolitionist constitutional interpretation, the text of the Constitution could previously be read as completely gender neutral. Indeed, in an 1847 speech to the House, Congressman (and future Confederate general) Thomas Clingman of North Carolina displayed a close familiarity with Lysander Spooner's 1845 book, *The Unconstitutionality of Slavery*, in which Spooner employed something like what is today called an original public meaning approach to constitutional interpretation. Clingman chided Spooner for employing a methodology that might be used to prove that a woman could become the president of the United States. Spooner, he said, "proves everything he attempts without the slightest difficulty, except that a woman cannot be President of the United States."[53]

The problem was not that women were unprotected by the original meaning of the Fourteenth Amendment. Women were undeniably citizens of the United States, whose privileges or immunities no state could abridge. And women were entitled to the due process and equal protection of the law. The problem was that, as Section 2 shows, the right to vote was not considered to be a privilege of citizenship, but was instead considered to be a "political" right.

Just as there needed to be a Fifteenth Amendment to protect the rights of blacks to vote, so too did there need to be a Twentieth Amendment to protect the voting rights of women. And, just as blacks needed to organize themselves to redeem the promise of the Republicans' Thirteenth, Fourteenth, and Fifteenth Amendments in the 1950s and '60s, women would need to organize themselves in the 1910s to demand the completion of our Republican Constitution.

Are These Rights Judicially Enforceable?

When discussing the meaning of the Constitution, it is important to clearly distinguish two distinct questions: First, what does the text of the Constitution say and mean? Second, is its meaning enforceable by the courts?

On the one hand, we should not simply assume that, because the Constitution expressly refers to rights, privileges, or immunities that precede government, these rights may be adjudicated in a lawsuit against the government. On the other hand, we should not simply read our opinion about the issue of judicial enforcement into the meaning of the text itself unless the text addresses that question.

As we will see in Part III, when the text is silent, the answer one gives to the question of enforceability will depend on whether one holds a republican or democratic vision of the Constitution. In a republic, the first duty of government is the equal protection of these rights. How the judiciary contributes to their protection requires careful consideration.

In Chapters 6 and 7, I will explain how these rights, privileges, and immunities of American citizens are best protected by judicially enforcing the structural constraints on federal power, including the separation of powers and the limits on the powers of Congress provided by the enumeration in Article I, Section 8. Then, in Chapter 8, I explain why courts should keep Congress and state legislatures within the proper scope of their powers, and should ferret out when their "just powers" are being invoked as a mere pretext to exercising powers that have not been—and cannot justly be—entrusted to a republican government, where the people are the ultimate sovereigns.

CHAPTER 5

LOSING OUR
REPUBLICAN CONSTITUTION

*The Rise of Progressivism, Judicial Restraint,
and the Living Constitution*

IN 1872, COMPETING Republican and Democratic factions claimed to have won the office of judge and sheriff in Grant Parish, Louisiana. In March 1873, a group of Republican blacks, led by a local black militia leader, seized the courthouse in Colfax, the parish seat, and began arming and drilling within the city limits. The black militiamen, most members of which were armed with the rifles they had carried as Union soldiers, repulsed a party of whites.[1]

Three miles east of Colfax, a black man was killed in the presence of his wife and children, and his murder caused blacks to flee their homes and seek the protection of the more than four hundred armed militiamen entrenched around the courthouse. The pro-Democratic newspaper reported that the governor had refused to intervene and blacks were committing robbery and murder in Colfax.

On Easter Sunday, April 13, a group of 150 whites then attacked the courthouse and eventually drove out the blacks by setting fire to the building. More than one hundred blacks were shot and killed as they fled the fire. According to an official report, thirty-four blacks who had been taken prisoner were taken to the river bank two by two, executed, and hurled into the river. The report concluded that "not a single colored man was killed or wounded until after their surrender, and that then they were shot down without mercy."[2]

At the behest of a courageous U.S. attorney named James Roswell "J.R." Beckwith, ninety-seven persons were indicted by an all-Republican grand jury. Beckwith and his wife, both Republicans with antislavery backgrounds, had moved to New Orleans before the war and were stranded there until the port was captured by Union forces in 1862. Beckwith was appointed the U.S. attorney by Republican president Ulysses S. Grant in 1870, after the previous U.S. attorney was found dead in his office with his throat slit.

Beckwith was determined to arrest the men he had indicted for the massacre and requested federal troops to assist him. Grant's attorney general, George Henry Williams—a pro-Union, antislavery Democrat who became a Republican during the war—approved the request, directing Beckwith to "spare no pains or expense to cause the guilty parties to be arrested and punished, and if military aid is necessary to execute any United States process," the commanding officer "has been instructed to furnish it."[3] Later, he advised Beckwith to concentrate his effort on the ringleaders.

Beckwith initiated a prosecution against the few who were caught on the charge of murder and for violating the civil rights of two blacks who had been lynched during the affair. The defendants were charged under the Civil Rights Act of 1870, which barred conspiring to "prevent or hinder [a person's] free exercise and enjoyment of any right or privilege granted or secured to him by the constitution or laws of the United States, or because of his having exercised the same."[4] The charges included, among other things, conspiracy to interfere with the victims' rights to peaceably assemble and to keep and bear arms.

On February 23, 1874, the trial of William J. "Bill" Cruikshank, who had organized the slaughter of the captured blacks, and the other defendants began before a jury made up of nine whites and three blacks. The case relied almost exclusively on the testimony of black witnesses, as the whites refused to cooperate with the prosecution. On March 12 the case was submitted to the jury. The jury split 9–3 for acquittal of five of the men and 11–1 for acquittal of Cruikshank and two others. While the defendants were held in custody lest they flee into the woods, a public campaign was launched against retrying the men, but Beckwith persisted.

A second trial was held with Justice Joseph Bradley copresiding while he was riding circuit. In June 1874, after two weeks of proceedings, the jury, this time dominated by Republicans, convicted Cruikshank and two others of the civil rights violations, while acquitting the rest. All the men were found not guilty of murder. "The rule of law," Charles Lane observes, "had been vindicated, however minimally. James Roswell Beckwith had not exactly triumphed—but he had won."[5]

The Supreme Court Guts
the Republicans' Amendments

By the time the case reached the Supreme Court in March 1876, the Supreme Court had already begun the process of neutering the Thirteenth and Fourteenth Amendments. Three years earlier, in its 5–4 decision in *The Slaughter-House Cases*[6] and its 8–1 decision in *Bradwell v. Illinois*,[7] the majority had denied that a right to pursue a lawful occupation—such as being a butcher or a lawyer—was protected by either the Thirteenth or Fourteenth Amendment. *Slaughter-House* involved a state law granting a private company a monopoly slaughtering livestock in the city of New Orleans, so that all private butchers in the city had to use its facility. *Bradwell* involved an Illinois rule denying Myra Bradwell the right to practice law after she had passed the bar because she was female.

In both of these cases, the Thirteenth Amendment was held to be strictly limited to the prohibition of slavery and involuntary servitude. And the "privileges or immunities of citizens of the United States" was held to protect only some obscure rights of "national" citizenship, like the right to life, liberty, and property while traveling on the high seas. Having found the right to pursue a lawful occupation was not a right of national citizenship, Justice Samuel F. Miller, who wrote the opinions in both cases, could avoid examining whether the restrictions imposed on the liberty of New Orleans butchers, or of women in Illinois, were irrational or arbitrary.

The Court's decision in *Bradwell* was announced the day after *Slaughter-House*. In his opinion for the majority, Justice Miller made quick work of Myra Bradwell's claim to be protected by the Privileges or Immunities Clause of the Fourteenth Amendment. "The opinion just delivered in the *Slaughter-House Cases*," he wrote,

> renders elaborate argument in the present case unnecessary, for, unless we are wholly and radically mistaken in the principles on which those cases are decided, the right to control and regulate the granting of license to practice law in the courts of a state is one of those powers which are not transferred for its protection to the federal government, and its exercise is in no manner governed or controlled by citizenship of the United States in the party seeking such license.[8]

Notice that Justice Miller felt no need whatsoever to justify this outcome by reciting any reasonable basis for Myra Bradwell's exclusion. Under his approach, such a basis is not constitutionally required. Excluding Bradwell from the practice of law could have been entirely arbitrary, but it did not matter. No such claim of arbitrariness could even be asserted in federal court.

Both *Slaughter-House* and *Bradwell* involved the right to pursue a lawful occupation, which is not specifically enumerated in the text of the Constitution. Left open by these decisions was whether an enumerated right, such as the rights to peaceably assemble and to keep and bear arms, were privileges or immunities of national citizenship that were now protected from infringement by states. In *Cruikshank*, we learned that the Supreme Court's answer to this question was no.

The Court reversed the convictions of all the defendants, thereby taking another step in dismembering the Republicans' amendments. It found the indictment defective on a number of grounds. For example, it held that the First Amendment's protections of speech and assembly, as well as the Second Amendment's right to keep and bear arms, applied only to the federal government, not the states. In other words, though these rights were enumerated in the Constitution, they were not rights of national citizenship.

The Court also held that, because it made criminal the acts of individuals rather than regulate the conduct of states, it was outside the power of Congress to reach such acts under the enforcement clause of the Fourteenth Amendment: "The fourteenth amendment prohibits a State from depriving any person of life, liberty, or property, without due process of law; but this adds nothing to the rights of one citizen as against another."[9]

In 1883, the Court expanded upon the "state action doctrine" it announced in *Cruikshank* to invalidate the Civil Rights Act of 1875.[10] That act barred racial discrimination on common carriers, and in such public accommodations as inns and places of amusement. In a collection of lawsuits known as the *Civil Rights Cases*, a majority of eight justices held that, because the Thirteenth Amendment only reached slavery and involuntary servitude, it did not apply to the types of lesser discrimination barred by the act. And, as in *Cruikshank*, the Court then contended that the

Fourteenth Amendment barred only discriminatory actions by state governments, not acts by private parties.

The sole dissenter in the *Civil Rights Cases* was Justice John Marshall Harlan—a Kentucky Whig turned Republican who had served as an officer in the Union army and was nominated to the Court by President Rutherford B. Hayes in 1877. In his dissent, Harlan objected to the Court's cramped reading of both the Thirteenth and Fourteenth Amendments.

Slavery was a private as well as public institution, so there was no doubt that the Thirteenth Amendment reached private as well as governmental conduct. The only question was whether the particular *types* of private discriminatory conduct prohibited by the act were included in its scope, which the majority denied.

To this Harlan replied that because "there are burdens and disabilities which constitute badges of slavery and servitude," enactment of these strictures was within Congress's express enforcement power under the Thirteenth Amendment. This power "may be exerted by legislation of a direct and primary character, for the eradication, not simply of the institution [of slavery], but of its badges and incidents."[11] What was happening in the South was not merely "private" racial discrimination, but a wholesale scheme of both public and private actions—enforced as much by private as by public intimidation—by which the freedmen were to be resubordinated as slaves in all but official name.

With respect to the Fourteenth Amendment, Harlan explained how each of the categories reached by the statute was not purely private, but had a public character as well. For example, because the law gives all these businesses "special privileges," they are to be exercised on behalf of the entire citizenry, including blacks, and given that it is from the entire public that these privileges are granted, no individual member of the public may be arbitrarily denied his or her benefit.

In sum, when applying the enforcement clause of the Fourteenth

Amendment, Harlan identified a middle category between purely governmental acts on the one hand and purely private actors on the other. For example, a "mere private boarding house is not an inn, nor is its keeper subject to the responsibilities, or entitled to the privileges, of a common innkeeper."

At the extreme, we accept Harlan's public/private distinction today when we grant that the personal decisions of, say, whom to marry, admit to our homes, or have dinner with are purely private decisions and can be made for racially invidious or any other pernicious reasons. And all agree that government action may not arbitrarily discriminate against any citizen or group. At issue, then, is the existence of a middle category of "private" conduct that admits of sufficient "public" character as to be comparable to "state action" for purposes of the Fourteenth Amendment.

At any rate, were Harlan's reading of the Thirteenth Amendment to be accepted, there would be no need to invoke the Fourteenth to reach private conduct. And the Thirteenth Amendment has the singular advantage of being aimed squarely at the two-hundred-year history of chattel slavery based on race, which was then followed by a hundred years of legal apartheid in the South. On Harlan's analysis, then, the constitutionality of the Civil Rights Act of 1875 was over-determined by the Thirteenth Amendment and multiple clauses of the Fourteenth Amendment, which were now a part of our Republican Constitution.

Shifting Political Winds

The election of 1876 is commonly said to mark the end of Reconstruction. Republican president Rutherford B. Hayes was elected to the presidency after a protracted controversy caused by two southern states sending competing slates of electors to the electoral college. Although many now believe that Hayes was allowed to assume the presidency as part of a deal to withdraw federal troops from the South, he had made no secret of his intention to do so during the campaign itself.[12]

Undoubtedly, the sustained and ruthless campaign of terrorism launched by southern whites against blacks and white Republicans in the South was paying off by undercutting northern political will to fully protect the rights of the freedmen. In the wake of the economic Panic of 1873, Democrats regained control of the House of Representatives in 1874. As Pamela Brandwein writes, "[n]ow in charge of appropriation bills, Democrats could set low appropriations for rights enforcement, jamming government machinery, as inadequate as it already was."[13]

Yet, as Brandwein has shown, Republicans persisted in their efforts to expand their party into the South by protecting the civil and voting rights of blacks and white Republicans into the 1890s.[14] After "reaching a low in 1878, voting rights enforcement resurged with the 1880 election of Republican President James A. Garfield," and was "sustained throughout the Garfield and Arthur administrations (1880–85)."[15] When Grover Cleveland assumed office in 1885, the first Democratic administration in twenty-five years led to a corresponding decline in civil rights enforcement.

Although the decline of our Republican Constitution was more gradual than is commonly taught, by 1896 it reached its nadir in the case of *Plessy v. Ferguson*. While *Plessy* is roundly vilified today, it is useful to identify what exactly is wrong with its reasoning. Those who deny that *Brown v. Board of Education*—which effectively reversed *Plessy*—can be justified by the original meaning of the Fourteenth Amendment must implicitly accept that *Plessy* was rightly decided on originalist grounds. But if *Plessy* was wrong on originalist grounds, then *Brown* would likely have been right. Understanding how *Plessy* was inconsistent with our Republican Constitution, therefore, reveals how *Brown* represents its restoration.

Homer Plessy was arrested in New Orleans and charged with a criminal offense for riding in a streetcar reserved by law to whites.[16] By a vote of seven to one, the Supreme Court saw no violation of either the Thirteenth or Fourteenth Amendments.[17] Relying on both the *Slaughter-House* and *Civil Rights Cases*, it tartly dismissed any objection grounded in the Thirteenth Amendment, the scope of which it said was restricted solely to slavery and involuntary servitude.[18] "A statute which implies merely a legal distinction between the white and colored races," wrote Justice Henry Brown, "has no tendency to destroy the legal equality of the two races, or reestablish a state of involuntary servitude."[19]

And, as in *Slaughter-House*, the Court found the discriminatory ordinance to be a valid exercise of the state's police power. Its cursory and even casual analysis, contained in a single brief paragraph, was a simple restatement of the deference to the will of a majority in the legislature that is at the core of the Democratic Constitution:

> So far, then, as a conflict with the Fourteenth Amendment is concerned, the case reduces itself to the question whether the statute of Louisiana is a reasonable regulation, and, with respect to this, *there must necessarily be a large discretion on the part of the legislature.* In determining the question of reasonableness, it is at liberty to act with reference to the established usages, customs, and traditions of the people, and with a view to the promotion of their comfort and the preservation of the public peace and good order. Gauged by this standard, we cannot say that a law which authorizes or even requires the separation of the two races in public conveyances is unreasonable, or more obnoxious to the Fourteenth Amendment than the acts of Congress requiring separate schools for colored children in the District of Columbia, the constitutionality of which does not seem to have been questioned, or the corresponding acts of state legislatures.[20]

That's it. Nothing has been omitted here. That's the entire analysis of why it was "reasonable" to legally segregate on account of race by using the police power that was delegated by the people—each and every one—to legislatures. Solely because the majority of a legislature deemed racial segregation necessary to promote the comfort, and preserve the peace and good order, of the public— *and on no more than its say-so*—the Court will uphold such a law.

The Court's reasoning had four steps.

1. The issue is whether the statute was a "reasonable regulation" of the liberty of the individual citizen.
2. In assessing reasonableness, the Court will recognize "a large discretion on the part of the legislature."
3. Legislatures are "at liberty to act with reference to the established usages, customs, and traditions of the people, and with a view to the promotion of their comfort and the preservation of the public peace and good order."
4. By this standard, the Court could not "say that a law which authorizes or even requires the separation of the two races in public conveyances is unreasonable."

In this way, as Democrat Stephen Douglas had urged with respect to slavery in the territories, the Supreme Court deferred to this exercise of collective popular sovereignty in which the majority of those who are allowed to vote can restrict the liberties of the few, including, in this case, the liberty of the railway companies who themselves objected to these sorts of laws.[21] This deferential stance would soon come to be called "judicial self-restraint."

Again dissenting alone, Justice Harlan renewed the analysis he had offered in the *Civil Rights Cases* that the Thirteenth Amendment "prevents the imposition of any burdens or disabilities that constitute badges of slavery or servitude."[22] To the majority's contention that the statute did not discriminate against either race, but prescribes the same rule to white and colored citizens alike, Harlan responded that "everyone knows that the statute in question had its origin in the purpose, not so much to exclude white persons from railroad cars occupied by blacks, as to exclude colored people from coaches occupied by or assigned to white persons."[23] Its obvious purpose was to compel blacks "to keep to themselves while traveling in railroad passenger coaches. No one would be so wanting in candor as to assert the contrary."[24] To this, Harlan posited that the "fundamental objection . . . to the statute is that it interferes with the personal freedom of citizens."[25]

Compared with the Court's deferential approach, Harlan's was far more realistic about the evil of slavery and the way the southern states were restoring its incidents to the extent they could get away with. His instincts proved prescient. By overruling the constraints that the Republican Party had added to our Republican Constitution, the Supreme Court gave a green light to the subordination of the black minority for another seventy years.

Meanwhile, racist Democrats in the South and progressive Democrats in the North were already joining forces to form a coalition that served the interest of each partner in its own way. They began loudly clamoring to supplant the Republican Constitution and its constraints on majoritarian or "popular" will with a full-blown Democratic Constitution. The means to this end were creative "interpretations" of the text and invocations of judicial restraint and deference to the will of the people. And progressive Republicans would soon add their voices to the choir, one especially bombastic voice in particular.

THE PROGRESSIVE ATTACK ON THE REPUBLICAN CONSTITUTION

After the North grew tired of the occupation and left the Southerners, white and black, to their own devices, Democrats in the

South got busy reestablishing their old order of racial subordination. Meanwhile, some Democrats and Republicans in the North were pursuing what they called a "progressive" political agenda, which has been summarized sympathetically as follows:

> In state after state, progressives advocated a wide range of political, economic, and social reforms. They urged adoption of the secret ballot, direct primaries, the initiative, the referendum, and direct election of senators. They struck at the excessive power of corporate wealth by regulating railroads and utilities, restricting lobbying, limiting monopoly, and raising corporate taxes. To correct the worst features of industrialization, progressives advocated workers' compensation, child labor laws, minimum wage and maximum hours legislation (especially for women workers), and widows' pensions.[26]

While progressivism is today remembered for its advocacy of economic legislation, it also favored the use of legal coercion to achieve other types of social improvements. Most modern "moral" laws aimed at sex, intoxicants, and gambling trace, not to the founding, but to the Progressive Era. These "vice" laws— going so far as to ban masturbation—were often advocated as "public health" measures and justified by what today would be considered pseudoscience.[27] Likewise, policies of eugenics were also supposedly based on settled science. Of course, central to the northern progressive cause was the promotion of labor unions, which in those days were almost exclusively composed of whites and males. Blacks were left to form their own. And, as we shall see, progressives supported laws that benefited white male workers by "protecting" women in the labor force on the basis of their inherent weakness.

State and federal courts responded to this wave of progressive legislation by interpreting the Due Process Clause of the Four-teenth Amendment to require an assessment of the reasonableness of restrictions on the "life, liberty, and property" of individuals. In particular, they began to require some showing that a partic-ular restriction of individual liberty was not irrational or arbi-trary. They began to realistically assess whether restrictions on liberty were truly calculated to protect the health and safety of the general public, rather than being the product of "other mo-tives" beyond the just powers of a republican legislature.[28]

Thayerian Deference and the "Power" of Judicial Review

Progressive intellectuals fought back. In 1893, Harvard law pro-fessor James Bradley Thayer published his influential article, "The Origin and Scope of the American Doctrine of Constitutional Law," in the *Harvard Law Review*.[29] It was an extended defense of the deferential approach that the Court would employ just three years later in *Plessy v. Ferguson*.

Unlike Alexander Hamilton and John Marshall, who spoke of a judicial *duty* to follow the law, Thayer framed his inquiry in terms of a judicial "*power* to declare legislative Acts unconstitu-tional, and to treat them as null."[30] But even Thayer did not yet employ the modern term *judicial review*, retaining the traditional terminology of judicial nullification.[31]

Thayer denied that because the Constitution was in writing, or because judges swore to uphold "this Constitution," the judicial invalidation of popularly enacted legislation was justified. Instead he asserted that "neither the written form nor the oath of the judges necessarily involves the right of reversing, displacing, or disregarding any action of the legislature or the executive which these departments are constitutionally authorized to take, *or the determination of those departments that they are so authorized.*"[32] In other words, it was up to the other "departments" themselves, not the courts, to determine whether "they are . . . authorized" by the Constitution. According to Thayer, the servants of the sovereign people got to define the scope of the powers that had been delegated to them by their masters.

The switch from the language of "duty" to the language of "power" was useful, too. Powers can and should be exercised with discretion or "restraint," but we don't speak the same way of our duties. We don't think our duties to our children should be exercised with restraint. We don't think the duty of care we owe others should be exercised with discretion. Rather, we think these duties should be completely and fully honored. In contrast, the exercise of our powers can be characterized as a matter of discretion and moderation.

Thayer traced the historical origin of the power of judicial review to the replacement of sovereignty in the monarch by sovereignty in the people themselves. Crucially, he then adopted the collective conception of popular sovereignty by which the people themselves purport to govern by their constitution: "The sovereign himself, having written these expressions of his will, had retired into the clouds; in any regular course of events he had no organ to enforce his will, except those to whom his orders were addressed in these documents."[33]

One of the aims of this book is to reveal how this sort of shift from individual to collective popular sovereignty affects how we think about the power of the courts to protect the rights retained by the people. Thayer framed the judicial power to nullify laws in what I am calling the Democratic Constitution's concern for the will of the majority of the people, as expressed in the Constitution, rather than the Republican Constitution's vision of the Constitution as a means by which the rights retained by the sovereign people are protected from their servants. We have moved now from securing the *rights* of the people, each and every one, to honoring the *will* of the people, as expressed by a majority of a handful of "legislators"—the will of the people to which the individual must yield or be forced to comply.

Thayer then presented a highly distorted view of the early attitude toward judicial review. For example, he claimed that the power "was denied by several members of the Federal convention,"[34] but as I have shown elsewhere, no one at the convention denied a judicial duty to nullify an unconstitutional law, and many discussions of other topics presupposed its existence. Though one member expressed his distaste for the idea, even he did not deny it existed.[35]

Thayer cautioned the judiciary to reflect that "if they had been regarded by the people as the chief protection against legislative violation of the constitution, they would not have been allowed merely this incidental and postponed control."[36] Rather, they "would have been let in . . . to a revision of the laws before they began to operate."[37] But, again, I have shown that one of the main arguments against including judges in a "council of revision" with power to alter or reject laws *as a matter of policy* was that it would overlap with, and compromise, their judicial duty to nullify unconstitutional laws that came before them in due course.[38] And just because judges were not thought to be "the chief protection" against legislative usurpation of power does not mean they were not considered an important safeguard.

After questioning, though not entirely rejecting, the bona fides of the "power" to invalidate laws, Thayer then traced the history of judicial restraint, which he claimed was in conflict with current judicial practice, especially at the state level. Both from this history, and from the fact that the application of the Constitution's text to particular statutes requires more than the mere interpretation of the meaning of words, he derived the following injunction: judges "can only disregard" a statute "when those who have the right to make laws have not merely made a mistake, but have made a very clear one—*so clear that it is not open to rational question.*"[39]

In this way, the obligation of the servants of the people to explain why their restrictions on the liberty of a fellow citizen and joint sovereign are not irrational or arbitrary is transformed into a judicial duty to defer to any legislation that is not beyond all possible reason. Moreover, not only does this extreme deference apply to the rationality of any particular restriction of liberty; it applies as well to the legislature's assessment of the scope of its own power. It is the test to be applied by judges, "not merely [to] their own judgment as to constitutionality, but [to] their conclusion as to what judgment is permissible to another department which the constitution has charged with the duty of making it."[40]

This is because, "having regard to the great, complex, ever-unfolding exigencies of government, much which will seem unconstitutional to one man, or body of men, may reasonably not seem so to another; that the constitution often admits of different interpretations; that there is often a range of choice and judgment."[41] Therefore, "in such cases the constitution does not impose upon the legislature any one specific opinion, but leaves open this range of choice; and that *whatever choice is rational is constitutional*."[42]

This Thayerian presumption that a law is constitutional leads to a grave problem I call "double deference." The judiciary must defer to the legislature's judgment that a law restricting liberty is rational and therefore find it to be constitutional. Then, when you ask a legislator whether a proposed restriction on liberty is constitutional, he or she will reply, "Yes, because the courts will uphold it." While the courts are deferring to the legislature, the legislature in turn is deferring to the courts. By this ruse, any scrutiny of legislation to ensure it is within the just powers of a legislature is avoided.

It is plain that *Plessy v. Ferguson*, decided three years after Thayer's article appeared in the *Harvard Law Review*, was the embodiment of this deferential approach. As Justice Brown

wrote, "We cannot say that a law which authorizes or even requires the separation of the two races in public conveyances *is
unreasonable*."[43]

Thayer concluded his article with the following admonition:
"Under no system can the power of courts go far to save a people
from ruin; our chief protection lies elsewhere."[44] Or, as Chief Justice Roberts wrote in his opinion in the health care case, "it is
not our job to protect the people from the consequences of their
political choices."[45] Thayer might have added that, under his deferential approach, neither can the power of courts save minorities
from ruin at the hands of the majority.

The Not-So-Great Progressive Dissenter

The Supreme Court was slow to accept the theory of judicial restraint being urged upon it by progressives. On the Court, its
most notable proponent was Thayer's former colleague on the
Harvard Law School faculty, Justice Oliver Wendell Holmes Jr.,
who reiterated the Thayerian formulation of deference to majorities in his dissenting opinions.

In his famous dissent in the 1905 case of *Lochner v. New York*,
Holmes clearly connected the will of the majority with Thayerian
deference. "I think that the word liberty in the Fourteenth
Amendment is perverted when it is held to prevent the natural outcome of a dominant opinion," insisted Holmes, "unless it
can be said that a rational and fair man *necessarily* would admit
that the statute proposed would infringe fundamental principles
as they have been understood by the traditions of our people and
our law."[46]

In other words, if there exists anyone who is rational and fair
who thinks that a measure is constitutional, then it is. Rather
than requiring a realistic assessment of the rationality of a statute,
the mere existence of disagreement justifies its constitutionality.

Applying this standard to the New York statute restricting the length of working hours for bakers—though not for their proprietor owners—Holmes contended that "a reasonable man might think it a proper measure on the score of health. Men whom I certainly could not pronounce unreasonable would uphold it as a first instalment of a general regulation of the hours of work."[47]

Although some today think of Holmes as a crusty New England conservative who adopted judicial restraint solely as a matter of principle, in fact he "was an enthusiastic supporter of the *New Republic* and the men who edited it."[48] After reading its founding editor Herbert Croly's 1913 book, *The Progressive Democracy*, Holmes "wrote him a long letter filled with praise."[49]

Holmes loved hanging out in the town house in Washington where many of the magazine's progressive contributors lived and socialized. Ironically, given Holmes's public posture of moral skepticism, their town house "was nicknamed the House of Truth, and Holmes often stopped in to join the men for dinner or a game of cards on his way home from the court."[50] They, in turn, heaped their praise on him, which he relished. On Holmes's ninety-third birthday, President Franklin Roosevelt sent the retired justice a handwritten note "wishing all good things for the most splendid and wisest of all American Liberals."[51]

Teddy Roosevelt, the Bake Shop Case, and the Democratic Constitution

Holmes's majoritarian dissents were brought to wider public attention by former president Theodore Roosevelt, who had nominated Holmes to the Supreme Court. Like Holmes, Roosevelt was a graduate of Harvard College. Unlike Holmes, who graduated from Harvard Law School, Roosevelt dropped out of Columbia Law School to run for office as a New York Republican, becoming a New York State assemblyman and eventually governor. Elected vice president in the fall of 1900, Roosevelt became president six months after taking office, when Republican president William McKinley was assassinated in 1901.

During his presidency from 1901 to 1909, Roosevelt, an ardent progressive, moved the Republican Party in a progressive direction. Yet many of Roosevelt's more radical proposals were rejected by Republicans in Congress, and state and federal courts found other progressive legislation to be an unconstitutional violation of the Due Process Clause. When, in 1912, Roosevelt again sought the Republican nomination, he made the Supreme Court a major issue of his campaign, and he clearly articulated the Democratic Constitution's postulate that "the majority" have the right to rule in the name of "the will of the people."

In March of that year, Roosevelt delivered a fiery speech at Carnegie Hall in New York, titled "The Right of the People to Rule." In this address he posited himself as the progressive savior of the Republican Party:

> The great fundamental issue now before the Republican Party and before our people can be stated briefly. It is: Are the American people fit to govern themselves, to rule themselves, to control themselves? I believe they are. My opponents do not. I believe in the right of the people to rule. I believe the majority of the plain people of the United States will, day in and day out, make fewer mistakes in governing themselves than any smaller class or body of men, no matter what their training, will make in trying to govern them.[52]

In his Carnegie Hall speech, he defended a number of progressive electoral reforms at the state level, including the use of popular referenda so that "the majority may step in and legislate directly" when legislatures fail to enact progressive legislation.[53] He favored the popular recall of state court justices in states where

their terms were not already limited, direct state presidential primary elections, and a power of the voters to veto any constitutional decision made by the courts. (Today, California and other
states have referenda and initiatives, as well as judicial recall processes, that date back to this era and these progressive proposals.)
In a separate speech he also expressed support for the popular
election of senators.[54]

Roosevelt openly scoffed at concerns about the tyranny of the
majority:

> I have scant patience with this talk of the tyranny of the
> majority. Wherever there is tyranny of the majority, I
> shall protest against it with all my heart and soul. But we
> are today suffering from the tyranny of minorities. It is a
> small minority that is grabbing our coal deposits, our water
> powers, and our harbor fronts. A small minority is bat-
> tening on the sale of adulterated foods and drugs. It is a
> small minority that lies behind monopolies and trusts. It
> is a small minority that stands behind the present law of
> master and servant, the sweatshops, and the whole calendar
> of social and industrial injustice. It is a small minority that
> is today using our convention system to defeat the will of
> a majority of the people in the choice of delegates to the
> Chicago Convention.[55]

So, for Roosevelt, the "only tyrannies from which men,
women, and children are suffering in real life are the tyrannies
of minorities. . . ."[56] Roosevelt believed that "no sane man who
has been familiar with the government of this country for the last
twenty years will complain that we have had too much of the rule
of the majority."[57]

He then focused his ire on the state courts for construing "the
'due process' clause of the State constitutions as if it prohibited

the whole people of the State from adopting methods of regulating the use of property so that human life, particularly the lives of the working men, shall be safer, freer, and happier."[58] He repeatedly praised the conception of due process "pronounced by Justice Holmes": "The police power extends to all the great public needs. It may be put forth in aid of what is sanctioned by usage, or held by the prevailing morality or strong and preponderant opinion to be greatly and immediately necessary to the public welfare."[59]

Roosevelt contended that, when a "judge is ascertaining the preponderant opinion of the people (as Judge Holmes states it) . . . he has no right to let his political philosophy reverse and thwart the will of the majority."[60] He should instead follow, rather than thwart, public opinion: "In that function the judge must represent the people or he fails in the test the Supreme Court has laid down."[61] Following Holmes, Roosevelt contended that "the judgment of the people should not have been set aside unless it were irrational. . . . The courts today owe the country no greater or clearer duty than to keep their hands off such statutes when they have any reasonably permissible relation to the public good."[62]

Roosevelt took direct aim at several Supreme Court decisions, including its decision in *Lochner v. New York*, in which the Supreme Court had found that a maximum hours law for bakery employees was unconstitutional under the Due Process Clause.

> For twenty-five years here in New York State, in our efforts to get social and industrial justice, we have suffered from the tyranny of a small minority. We have been denied, now by one court, now by another, as in the Bakeshop Case, where the courts set aside the law limiting the hours of labor in bakeries.[63]

Indeed, it was the presidential campaign of Teddy Roosevelt that first made "the Bakeshop Case," as Roosevelt called it, a matter of public controversy. In 1912, the Bakeshop Case became a progressive political cause célèbre like *Citizens United* is today.

Three thousand people filled Carnegie Hall to hear the former president inveigh against his successor, Republican president William Howard Taft, and the courts. An overflow crowd awaited him at the Carnegie Lyceum when he finished his address. In its headlines, the *New York Times* highlighted Roosevelt's call for "real popular rule," and "that the people should have supervision over judicial decisions," as well as his invocation of Justice Holmes's view of the police power.[64]

When it became clear that he would be denied the Republican nomination, however, Roosevelt bolted the party to create his own "Progressive Party." In an address to its national convention in Chicago on August 6, 1912, he congratulated them on forming a new party.[65] "The time is ripe, and overripe, for a genuine Progressive movement," and the "first essential in the Progressive programme is the right of the people to rule."[66]

With respect to the judiciary, Roosevelt said, "our prime concern is that in dealing with the fundamental law of the land, in assuming finally to interpret it, and therefore finally to make it, the acts of the courts should be subject to and not above the final control of the people as a whole."[67] He then succinctly summarized the central tenet of the Democratic Constitution: "Political parties exist to secure responsible government and to execute the will of the people,"[68] which in operation Roosevelt frankly affirmed means the majority of the people, or a majority of legislative bodies.

Because Roosevelt's "Progressive Party" came to be known as the Bull Moose Party, the degree of Roosevelt's commitment to progressivism and the Democratic Constitution has been obscured. But it is widely understood that his third-party run split the Republican vote and allowed progressive Democrat Woodrow Wilson to win the presidency in 1913.[69]

Woodrow Wilson's Living Constitution

"If today we have a 'progressive' or a 'living' constitution," Christopher Caldwell writes, "Wilson can claim to be its father."[70] It was during the Wilson administration that several of Roosevelt's proposals for the states got applied to the federal government by formal constitutional amendment. Two of these formal written and ratified amendments to the Constitution have done much to change our form of government in unanticipated ways.

The Sixteenth Amendment, passed in 1913, authorized a national income tax, allowing for greatly increased federal spending and reversing a Supreme Court decision holding such a tax to be unconstitutional. Having access to this much money greatly enhanced the significance of the spending power of Congress. It has allowed the national government to buy the cooperation of the states by collecting income tax from its citizens, but only returning it to them if state governments agree to use their broader police powers to implement federal programs.

The Seventeenth Amendment, also adopted in 1913, required the direct popular election of senators, who previously were selected by state legislatures, undermining a structural constraint on federal power. Together with the effects of the enhanced spending power, state legislatures lost their ability, however indirect, to block national measures that conflicted with their individual state interests.

Wilson was not much enamored with the U.S. Constitution. From his teens he acquired a bizarre compulsion to rewrite the constitutions of whatever group or organization in which he became active. Whether the Eumeneans at Davidson College, the Princeton baseball club, or the Johns Hopkins Literary Society, he "would dig up and then rewrite its constitution, usually seizing on some neglected provision which, in an emergency, could be wielded to make the system more efficient, hierarchical, and subject to his own wishes."[71]

When it came to the U.S. Constitution, like many progressives today Wilson preferred the parliamentary system of England. At nineteen, during the centennial of the Declaration of Independence, he wrote in his diary that he wished America had "England's form of government instead of the miserable delusion of a republic. A republic too founded upon the notion of abstract liberty!"[72] Distinguishing between a republic and a majoritarian democracy, Wilson predicted that "this country will never celebrate another centennial as a republic. The English form of government is the only true one."[73] As a student, Wilson devised a plan to revise the federal government, "more along the lines of the British Cabinet system, in which executive and legislative powers would be entrusted to ministers serving at the pleasure of the majority party."[74]

As a professor at Wesleyan University, he told his students that the Constitution "was not merely a document written down on paper but is a living and organic thing, which, like all living organisms, grows and adapts itself to the circumstances of its environment."[75] Later, as president, Wilson would appoint to the Supreme Court the progressive attorney and political activist Louis Brandeis, who would help move the Court to adopt a modest version of the presumption of constitutionality that had been urged by Thayer and Holmes.

After becoming president, Wilson racially segregated federal offices for the first time in American history. Sounding much like the Supreme Court in *Plessy*, Wilson explained that "segregation was caused by friction between the colored and white clerks, and not done to injure or humiliate the colored clerks, but to avoid friction."[76] "If the colored people made a mistake in voting for me," he told the *New York Times* in 1914, "they ought to correct it."[77]

When a delegation of black professionals led by Monroe Trotter, a Phi Beta Kappa graduate of Harvard and a Boston newspaper editor, appeared at the White House to protest the new policies, Wilson treated them rudely. He declared that "segregation is not a humiliation but a benefit, and ought to be so regarded by you gentlemen."[78] When Trotter took issue with this view, Wilson replied, "[i]f this organization is ever to have another hearing before me it must have another spokesman. Your manner offends me. . . . Your tone, with its background of passion."[79] Woodrow Wilson was a peach.

To put it mildly, racial equality was not among the priorities of progressives, who did little or nothing to oppose Wilson's racist agenda. (In the midst of the public campaign on behalf of the anarchists Sacco and Vanzetti, even Holmes privately noticed that his progressive friends like Felix Frankfurter seemed to "care more for red than for black."[80]) After all, the Democratic political coalition combined southern racists, who could not be bucked, with northern progressives ardently committed to the cause of labor unions, whose membership was usually all white and all male.

A constitutional commitment to deference to majoritarian state legislatures conveniently facilitated the agenda of both these key Democratic constituencies.

Judicial Skepticism and the Protection of Minorities

Until Teddy Roosevelt made it the focal point of his attack on the Supreme Court during his progressive presidential campaign in 1912, *Lochner v. New York* was a relatively obscure and routine Due Process Clause decision. The state of New York had passed the Bakeshop Act, which regulated the health and safety of bakeries, including such minutiae as the ceiling height, the material and finishing of walls and floors, ventilation, the location of sleeping facilities and toilets for employees, and even what animals could be on the premises. (Cats only!)

With one exception, the Court easily sustained the entire Bake-shop Act as reasonable health and safety regulations. The exception was a prohibition on bakery employees, but not owners, working more than sixty hours per week that had been proposed by the bakeshop unions. For this provision, the Court could identify no health and safety rationale, and therefore suspected it had not been included for that reason. "In our judgment, it is not possible, in fact, to discover the connection between the number of hours a baker may work in the bakery and the healthful quality of the bread made by the workman," wrote Justice Rufus Peckham. "The connection, if any exists, is too shadowy and thin to build any argument for the interference of the legislature." When "tenuous assertions such as we have adverted to become necessary in order to give, if possible, a plausible foundation for the contention that the law is a 'health law,'" he continued, "it gives rise to at least a suspicion that there was some other motive dominating the legislature than the pur-pose to subserve the public health or welfare."

Of course, the other motive was obvious: helping bakeshop union members, and the larger corporate bakeries for which they worked, at the expense of the smaller, ethnic bakeries. Bakeries had to operate around the clock. The former could operate using shift workers; the latter had to rely on a single set of employees working longer hours. But because the government had failed to justify the maximum hours law as a legitimate health and safety measure, the Court did not need to speculate as to these "other motives."

In short, unlike *Bradwell v. Illinois* and *Plessy v. Ferguson*, where the Court had blindly deferred to the will of the Illinois and Louisiana state legislatures, the Court now took a realistic look at the rationale for this measure, and found it wanting. As we saw above, Justice Holmes favored simply deferring to the legislature. In place of a realistic assessment of the operation of this restriction on liberty, Holmes, like James Thayer, would have applied a formal and largely irrebuttable presumption in favor of legislative restrictions on liberty.

Although the Supreme Court at this time cannot fairly be described as generally protective of blacks, ironically it was the more "conservative" justices—the bane of the progressives—who also took a more skeptical view of seemingly neutral racist legislation in two revealing cases.

The Thirteenth Amendment makes an exception from its ban on slavery for involuntary servitude "as a punishment for crime whereof the party shall have been duly convicted." The state of Alabama took advantage of this exception by enacting a law making it a crime subject to imprisonment for a person to quit his job who had signed a labor contract and accepted an advance payment.

The scheme called for making a cash payment to blacks who signed labor contracts. Then, if they were to quit their job, the statute presumed their intent to defraud the employer when they accepted the payment. In *Bailey v. Alabama*, the jury had been instructed that "the refusal of any person who enters into such contract to perform such act or service, or refund such money, or pay for such property, without just cause, shall be prima facie evidence of the intent to injure his employer, or to defraud him."[81]

With this law in place, blacks who sought to quit their employment could then be threatened with criminal prosecution for fraud, sentenced to hard labor, and even rented out to private employers as convict laborers. In this way did Alabama seek to reimpose the incidents of slavery on black citizens.

But in 1911, the so-called *Lochner*-era Supreme Court held the statute to be unconstitutional. "If it cannot punish the servant as a criminal for the mere failure or refusal to serve without paying his debt, it is not permitted to accomplish the same result by creating a statutory presumption which, upon proof of no other fact, exposes him to conviction and punishment."

In sharp contrast with the deferential approach taken in *Brad-well* and *Plessy*, the majority in *Bailey v. Alabama* found that, viewed realistically, such enforcement of a labor contract did indeed constitute involuntary servitude in violation of the Thirteenth Amendment. "Without imputing any actual motive to oppress, we must consider the natural operation of the statute here in question, and it is apparent that it furnishes a convenient instrument for the coercion."[82]

Dissenting in this case as he had in *Lochner*, Justice Holmes favored deferring to the legislature and would have upheld the statute. He contended that "if breach of contract may be made a crime at all, it may be made a crime with all the consequences usually attached to crime."[83] With respect to the statutory presumption of fraudulent intent, he asked: "Is it not evidence that a man had a fraudulent intent if he receives an advance upon a contract overnight and leaves in the morning? I should have thought that it very plainly was."[84]

In 1917, the Court used its Due Process Clause protection of economic liberty to invalidate a racially exclusionary zoning law in Louisville, Kentucky.[85] As wealthy black businessmen and professionals began to buy houses in residential neighborhoods of Louisville, the city passed an ordinance that forbade "any colored person to move into and occupy as a residence . . . any house upon any block which a greater number of houses are occupied . . . by white people than are occupied . . . by colored people."[86] The same restriction in reverse applied to whites.

The National Association for the Advancement of Colored People (NAACP) constructed a test case to challenge the ordinance by setting up a sale by Charles Buchanan, a white home owner and real estate agent, to William Warley, a black man.[87] Buchanan then contested the ordinance that prohibited the sale because it reduced the value of his property in violation of the Due Process Clause. He also claimed that the ordinance violated the Equal Protection Clause because its purpose was to discriminate against African Americans.

The Kentucky Court of Appeals rejected the challenge, offering a typical progressive justification: "[T]he advance of civilization . . . has resulted in a gradual lessening of the dominion of the individual over private property and a corresponding strengthening of the relative power of the state in respect thereof."[88] However, the U.S. Supreme Court unanimously reversed.

Again, unlike *Bradwell* and *Plessy*, the Court realistically evaluated the state's "police power" rationales for restricting property and contract rights.[89] The state defended the law by claiming it tended "to promote the public peace by preventing racial conflicts," that it tended "to maintain racial purity," and that it prevented "the deterioration of property owned and occupied by white people," which it contended was "sure to follow the occupancy of adjacent premises by persons of color."[90] The Court was having none of this.

Justice William Rufus Day quoted from the Civil Rights Act of 1866, which "expressly provided that all citizens of the United States in any State shall have the same right to purchase property as is enjoyed by white citizens," and the Civil Rights Act of 1870, which said that "all persons within the jurisdiction of the United States shall have the same right in every State and Territory to make and enforce contracts . . . as is enjoyed by white citizens."[91]

The Court concluded that these statutes "did not deal with the social rights of men, but with those fundamental rights in property which it was intended to secure upon the same terms to citizens of every race and color."[92] It then distinguished *Plessy v. Ferguson* on the (dubious) ground that "in that case, there was no attempt to deprive persons of color of transportation in the coaches of the public carrier, and the express requirements were for equal though separate accommodations for the white and colored races."[93] The Court in *Plessy*, it said, had permitted a "classification of accommodation . . . upon the basis of equality for both races."[94]

However, the Court then rejected the police power rationale on which *Plessy* was based (and which Woodrow Wilson used to justify segregating federal offices): "It is urged that this proposed segregation will promote the public peace by preventing race conflicts. Desirable as this is, and important as is the preservation of the public peace, this aim cannot be accomplished by laws or ordinances which deny rights created or protected by the Federal Constitution."[95]

In short, the Supreme Court used its Due Process Clause doctrine—so widely vilified by progressives then and by some conservatives today—to shift away from the Democratic Constitution's majoritarian rule to the Republican Constitution's emphasis on securing the rights of the sovereign individual from the exercise of majoritarian power.

David Bernstein and Ilya Somin observe that the Court's refusal to defer to Kentucky's assertion of its police power the way it had deferred to Louisiana's in *Plessy* was remarkable for several reasons. First, in comparison to the 1890s, "the 1910s represented the worst period of post–Civil War racism in American history."[96] Second, "the Court had to go out of its way to distinguish *Plessy* and was not entirely persuasive in doing so."[97] Third, by the 1910s, "Progressive advocates of sociological jurisprudence so dominated mainstream legal thought that Charles Warren remarked that 'any court which recognizes wide and liberal bounds to the State police power is to be deemed in touch with the temper of the times.'"[98]

Fourth, the Supreme Court "had recently expressed sympathy for nonracial zoning, based on progressive precepts that could also be applied to racial zoning," and "Jim Crow racial segregation itself was part of a broader pattern of state regulation that was broadly progressive in nature."[99] Finally, even in the "*Lochner* era," by the 1910s "the Court almost always upheld state regulatory legislation as a valid exercise of the police power," and the same year had "upheld several controversial regulatory laws."[100]

For all these reasons, and given his commitment to majoritarianism and judicial restraint, it is surprising that Justice Holmes joined with the majority in invalidating the state law rather than defer to the will of the local majority. Yet we now know that he had indeed been planning to dissent. In a short opinion that was typeset, then edited by him, he avoided expressly asserting the majoritarian tenets of the Democratic Constitution. Instead, he chipped away at the NAACP challenge in a number of ways.

First, Holmes said that the Court should refuse to sustain the claim of what appeared to be a test case (which it was): "The contract sounds so very much like a wager upon the constitutionality of the ordinance that I cannot feel a doubt whether the suit should be entertained without some evidence that this is not a manufactured case."[101] He then noted that, because the plaintiff is white—which was a deliberate part of the NAACP litigation strategy—he cannot complain that the statute may discriminate against blacks. "It is possible that the ordinance unduly abridges the constitutional rights of the blacks"—possibly referring to a potential Equal Protection Clause challenge—"but that question is not before us," he wrote.[102] He concluded that "the plaintiff is a white man and cannot avail himself of this collateral mode of attack."[103]

When he drafted his dissent, Holmes believed that the plaintiff had "no interest as entitles him to complain under the Fourteenth Amendment."[104] The "only ground available to the plaintiff is in respect of his property," and the only conceivable basis for such a claim would be that the regulation might constitute a "taking" of private property for public use without just compensation.[105] This the Court had previously recognized as violation of the Due Process Clause when done by a state. But the claim was wanting, thought Holmes, because it was not a physical taking and merely affected the value of the plaintiff's property.

Rejected, *sub silentio*, in his dissenting opinion was the due process analysis of the majority, which found the restriction to be an unreasonable regulation of liberty because it was insufficiently justified as an exercise of the state's police power. Yet, in the end, Holmes, the majoritarian who so confidently affirmed in his *Lochner* dissent that "the word liberty, in the Fourteenth Amendment is perverted when it is held to prevent the natural outcome of a dominant opinion," did not deign to address this theory.[106]

Instead, for reasons unknown, the Great Dissenter meekly joined the majority's due process opinion. We can only speculate as to why. Perhaps in this case, the Democratic Constitution was just too big a pill even for Holmes to swallow, as we will see it eventually proved to be for the progressives on the Court when they finally came to hold the majority.

True, *Bailey v. Alabama* and *Buchanan v. Worley* can be considered outliers during a period in which the civil rights of blacks were being trampled. Nevertheless, they reveal that a general across-the-board realistic stance of skepticism toward restrictions of liberty can help an "out group" *before* it is politically powerful or appealing enough to demand special judicial protection. In contrast, a Thayerian-Holmesian across-the-board formal rule of deference to legislative majorities *guarantees that challenges by out groups will fail*, as did Myra Bradwell's and Homer Plessy's.

As with bread from a bakeshop, half a loaf is better than none.

The Progressive Louis Brandeis and His Briefs

Just as progressive Republican Teddy Roosevelt had appointed Oliver Wendell Holmes Jr. to the Supreme Court, progressive Democrat Woodrow Wilson nominated the progressive activist attorney Louis Brandeis. Brandeis had served as one of Wilson's key political advisors during the election of 1912, helping to craft an even "more radical approach" than was being advocated by Roosevelt, who was running as the Progressive Party nominee.[107] "Nobody embodied the principles of the New Freedom more than this essential member of candidate Wilson's first brain trust," writes Wilson biographer A. Scott Berg, and "nobody engendered more of Wilson's admiration than this profound liberal thinker, social activist, and spokesman for the voiceless."[108]

Just as racial equality was not a priority of progressives, neither was sex equality. Brandeis had made his reputation, in part, from the lengthy amicus briefs he filed to the Court on behalf of progressive statutes. Rather than citations to legal authorities, what came to be known as "Brandeis Briefs" were unconventional compilations of quotes from social science research offered to show the reasonableness of legislation.

His first such brief was submitted in the 1908 case of *Muller v. Oregon*,[109] which concerned a statute limiting the number of hours that women could work. Brandeis maintained that the statute restricting the contract rights of women was reasonable because women were physically weaker and less resilient than men. Here is how Brandeis summarized the "world's experience" with the "physical differences between men and women":

> Long hours of labor are dangerous for women primarily because of their special physical organization. In structure and function women are differentiated from men. Besides these anatomical and physiological differences, physicians are agreed that women are fundamentally weaker than men in all that makes for endurance: in muscular strength, in nervous energy, in the powers of persistent attention and application. Overwork, therefore, which strains endurance to the utmost, is more disastrous to the health of women than of men, and entails upon them more lasting injury.[110]

This summary was followed by paragraph-length excerpts from dozens of authorities. There "appears to be a general agreement," said one, "that women are more docile and amenable to discipline; that they can do light work equally well; that they are steadier in some respects." But, "on the other hand, they are often absent on account of slight indisposition, and they break down sooner under strain."[111] And so the brief went for another ninety turgid pages.

Brandeis's argument was reminiscent of Justice Bradley's infamous concurring opinion in the 1873 case of *Bradwell v. Illinois*.[112] When Myra Bradwell, the respected editor of a Chicago legal newspaper, was denied a license to practice law in Illinois, she brought suit claiming that her "privileges or immunities" as a citizen of the United States had been abridged.

The Court denied her claim in a decision announced the day after the Court had declined to protect the rights of New Orleans butchers in the *Slaughter-House Cases*. As we saw above, for Justice Miller, the *Bradwell* case was easy. If the Privileges or Immunities Clause did not protect the unenumerated right to pursue a lawful occupation, as the Court held in *Slaughter-House*, then Bradwell too could not avail herself of its protection.[113]

For Justice Bradley, however, the case was more difficult. Bradley had dissented in *Slaughter-House* on the ground that such a right was constitutionally protected. So, in *Bradwell*, he needed to show why the Illinois restriction was a reasonable exercise of the state's police power. Because he admitted the need for judicial scrutiny, unlike Justice Miller, Justice Bradley had to assess the merits of Bradwell's claim.

Like Brandeis, Bradley contended that the restriction on women's employment was reasonable because women were different. "The natural and proper timidity and delicacy which belongs to the female sex evidently unfits it for many of the occupations of civil life," he wrote.[114] "The Constitution of the family organization, which is founded in the divine ordinance, as well as in the nature of things, indicates the domestic sphere as that which properly belongs to the domain and functions of woman-hood."[115] The only thing that Brandeis offered that Bradley lacked was "scientific" authorities to back up his claims. (Much progressive economic regulation was upheld based on equally dubious "science.")

While the *Slaughter-House Case* was a 5–4 decision, *Bradwell* was decided 8–1. The sole dissenter was Chief Justice Salmon P. Chase. Too ill and weak to pen a dissent, he died on May 7, three weeks after the decisions were announced. But the official report read, somewhat unusually, and perhaps even uniquely: "The Chief Justice dissented from the judgment of the Court *and from all the opinions*"—including the sexist concurring opinion of Bradley.[116]

While the *Bradwell* case and Bradley's concurrence is rightly considered a blot on the record of the Court, *Muller v. Oregon* and Brandeis's brief is still taught as a great progressive and legal realist triumph over formalism. In *Muller*, the Supreme Court bought Brandeis's argument that the law was rational because women were the weaker sex, and upheld it as constitutional:

> That woman's physical structure and the performance of maternal functions place her at a disadvantage in the struggle for subsistence is obvious. This is especially true when the burdens of motherhood are upon her. Even when they are not, by abundant testimony of the medical fraternity continuance for a long time on her feet at work, repeating this from day to day, tends to injurious effects upon the body, and, as healthy mothers are essential to vigorous offspring, the physical well-being of woman becomes an object of public interest and care in order to preserve the strength and vigor of the race.[117]

The progressive Brandeis Brief had worked. Huzzah!

Later, in the 1923 case of *Adkins v. Children's Hospital*,[118] the Court invalidated a minimum wage law for women on the ground that the health and safety rationale of *Muller* did not extend to government-mandated disparate pay. Holmes, of course, dissented. He would have upheld the law, which, whether by design or happy coincidence, would make it harder for women to compete with male workers by making it more expensive to employ women. "The end, to remove conditions leading to ill health, immorality and the deterioration of the race," he wrote, "no one would deny to be within the scope of constitutional legislation."[119]

Applying his Thayerian standard of deference so praised by Theodore Roosevelt, Holmes concluded that "[w]hen so many intelligent persons, who have studied the matter more than any of us can, have thought that the means are effective and are worth the price, it seems to me impossible to deny that the belief reasonably may be held by reasonable men."[120] Likely because of his involvement in *Muller* and possibly also because of his daughter's job at the Minimum Wage Board (as well as the fact that his vote would not have changed the outcome), Brandeis recused himself, so the decision was five to three to invalidate the law.[121]

Across-the-board skepticism about the rationality of a restriction on liberty does not guarantee that prejudice bolstered by junk science will lose. But the need for Justice Bradley in *Bradwell* to articulate *why* the restriction on women practicing law was rational could provide a focal point for political action and set the stage for the repudiation of such restrictions. Shortly after the Court rendered its decision, Myra Bradwell received a letter from women's rights advocate Susan B. Anthony:

My dear Mrs. Bradwell:
Like the Frenchman who didn't swear on a certain
occasion—so I don't—simply because no swearing could

possibly reach the case. I am fired to White heat. Do send
me all *you* say in the [*Chicago Legal*] *News* on the decision
and do put all *your lawyer's brain* to it. Write me the best
letter you possibly can for me to read at our . . . May
meeting in New York. Don't fail—I pray you. . . . Just
don't fail to send me everything. Our convention will pour
hot shot into that old Court.

Susan[122]

(As it happened, Illinois had already modified its rule even before
the case was decided, and a nineteen-year-old woman named
Alta M. Hulett was admitted to practice law that same year.[123])

Likewise we can criticize the Brandeis Brief and the Court's
opinion in *Muller* only because the due process of law barred irrational and arbitrary restrictions on liberty, and required that such
restrictions be within the just powers of a republican legislature.
Compare this to the silence of Justice Miller in *Bradwell*, who
found that women, like the butchers in *Slaughter-House*, simply
had no right to assert.

A chance of victory is better for less politically powerful groups
than Thayerian-Holmesian "restraint," which forecloses any pos-
sibility.

Enter the Presumption of Constitutionality

As a justice, Brandeis pursued the progressive agenda of advanc-
ing the Democratic Constitution. In the 1931 case of *O'Gorman
& Young, Inc. v. Hartford Fire Ins. Co.*,[124] the Court refused to
strike down an insurance regulation, saying that "the presumption of constitutionality must prevail in the absence of some
factual foundation of record for overthrowing the statute."[125]
Writing for a 5–4 majority, Justice Brandeis described the operation of this presumption:

It does not appear upon the face of the statute, or from any facts of which the court must take judicial notice, that in New Jersey evils did not exist in the business of fire insurance for which this statutory provision was an appropriate remedy. The action of the legislature and of the highest court of the State indicates that such evils did exist. The record is barren of any allegation of fact tending to show unreasonableness.[126]

In other words, the burden was now on the person challenging the statute to establish its *un*reasonableness—perhaps by presenting his or her own Brandeis Brief *against* its rationality. In this way, the revival of a "presumption of constitutionality" that had been urged by James Bradley Thayer in his 1893 *Harvard Law Review* article had finally become accepted Supreme Court doctrine (although in somewhat more modest form than either Thayer or Holmes had urged).

Brandeis's innovation was triumphantly noted in the *Columbia Law Review* by Walton H. Hamilton. Hamilton was an economist on the faculty of Yale Law School, a New Dealer, and a sharp critic of the Supreme Court's constitutional skepticism toward social regulation:

The demand is to find an escape from the recent holdings predicated upon "freedom of contract" as "the rule," from which a departure is to be allowed only in exceptional cases. The occasion calls not for the deft use of tactics, but for a larger strategy. The device of presumptions is almost as old as law; Brandeis revives the presumption that acts of a state legislature are valid and applies it to statutes regulating business activity. The factual brief has many times been employed to make a case for social legislation; Brandeis demands of the opponents of legislative acts a recitation of fact showing that the evil did not exist or that the remedy was inappropriate. He appeals from precedents to more venerable precedents, reverses the rules of presumption and proof in cases involving the control of industry; and sets up a realistic test of constitutionality. It is all done with such legal verisimilitude that a discussion of particular cases is unnecessary; it all seems obvious—once Brandeis has shown how the trick is done. It is attended with so little fanfare of judicial trumpets that it might have passed almost unnoticed, save for the dissenters, who usurp the office of the Greek tragedy and comment upon the action. Yet the argument which degrades "freedom of contract" to a constitutional doctrine of the second magnitude is compressed into a single compelling paragraph.[127]

O'Gorman shows that the process of weakening the Due Process Clause scrutiny of the Supreme Court began well before the election of Franklin Roosevelt. After Chief Justice Taft had left the Court due to illness in 1929, President Herbert Hoover nominated Charles Evans Hughes to replace him. Progressives, who by this time were calling themselves "liberals," protested that he was too conservative.

When Hoover next selected John Parker, a southern court of appeals judge, to replace southerner Justice Edward Sanford, Felix Frankfurter took the lead in mobilizing liberals for a confirmation battle. Organized labor and the NAACP combined in opposition, though according to Walter White of the NAACP, the American Federation of Labor "was exceedingly anxious to prevent the identification of its opposition against Parker with that of Negroes."[128]

With the enthusiastic support of both Frankfurter and Brandeis, Hoover then selected Owen Roberts, who assumed Sanford's seat a week before *O'Gorman* was argued. When the

Court presumably divided 4–4, the case was set over for reargument so that Justice Roberts could participate. He and Hughes thereby determined the outcome of the case, which was decided 5–4, with Roberts and Hughes siding with Holmes and Brandeis.

When Justice Holmes retired, liberals made a full-court press for Hoover to appoint Benjamin Cardozo. Hoover was up for reelection and Frankfurter told Hoover's secretary of war, Henry Stimson, that Cardozo was "the only appointment that would be received with national enthusiasm."[129] The fact that Cardozo was yet another judge from the Northeast "would evaporate like snowflakes" in the face of the national acclaim that would greet Cardozo's appointment by the President. According to Brad Snyder, "like the liberals who had lobbied for Cardozo," Hoover "was concerned that the Court was dominated by too many conservatives."[130]

To the disappointment of the conservative justices, Hoover chose Cardozo. Justice Willis Van Devanter wrote privately that Cardozo had been chosen "because the President thought he was of a Holmes type and would follow in Holmes's footsteps."[131] To another he wrote: "I understand that some of the senators told the President they would oppose the nomination of any one whose views were not in keeping with those of the retiring justice."[132] Frankfurter was thrilled. He wrote the president that "never in the history of the Court has an appointment been made to it more fitting to the needs of the Court at the particular period than is true of your appointment of Chief Justice Cardozo."[133]

In this way was the adoption of the progressives' presumption of constitutionality led by Hoover appointees before the New Deal even began. This is less surprising when one considers that the Republican Hoover—like the Republican Theodore Roosevelt before him—was also a political progressive.[134] Progressives had been big fans of Hoover when he had served in the Wilson administration, declaring him "the best qualified man to succeed Woodrow Wilson."[135] After his service in the Harding and Coolidge administrations, however, they turned against him, as a partisan Republican. "At the same time that he was lobbying Stimson to counsel Hoover to nominate Cardozo to the Supreme Court," Frankfurter "was ramping up his campaign to replace Hoover in the White House with New York Governor Franklin D. Roosevelt."[136]

Ironically, the Brandeis Brief is still hailed today for injecting a much-needed dose of "realism" into the judicial system in place of its traditional reliance on more "formalist" methods of legal reasoning based on legal principles.[137] Yet the presumption of constitutionality merely replaced one formal presumption favoring the individual with another favoring the government. In truth, Brandeis was driven more by his progressive ends than by any principled concern for "realist" judicial decision making.

The same proved to be true about the progressives' professed commitment to "the will of the people." Having accomplished their mission of reducing the protection afforded the rights of property and contract, their commitment to the Democratic Constitution's mantra of judicial restraint did not last long. With the majority of the Court in hand, a mere seven years after *O'Gorman*, the Supreme Court began to qualify its presumption of constitutionality. The result would eventually be a partial, but still distorted, redemption of the Republican Constitution.

THE NEW DEAL COURT'S PARTIAL REVIVAL OF THE REPUBLICAN CONSTITUTION

If Brandeis's opinion in *O'Gorman* represents the triumph of the majoritarianism and judicial restraint of the Democratic Constitution, it was not quite so extreme a triumph as it may at first appear. For one thing, Brandeis never denied that the presumption of constitutionality could be rebutted by a showing—perhaps by a reverse Brandeis Brief—that a law was an unreasonable or arbitrary restriction on liberty. In this way, Brandeis's "restraint" was not as restrained as Holmes's was.

As Justice Harlan Stone would reaffirm in his 1938 opinion in *United States v. Carolene Products:*[138]

> We may assume for present purposes that no pronounce-ment of a Legislature can forestall attack upon the consti-tutionality of the prohibition which it enacts by applying opprobrious epithets to the prohibited act, and that a statute would deny due process *which precluded the disproof in ju-dicial proceedings* of all facts which would show or tend to show that a statute depriving the suitor of life, liberty, or property had a rational basis.[139]

Later in his opinion, Justice Stone reiterated that where the rationality of a law depended "upon facts beyond the sphere of judicial notice, such facts *may properly be made the subject of judicial inquiry*, and the constitutionality of a statute predicated upon the existence of a particular state of facts may be challenged *by show-ing to the court* that those facts have ceased to exist."[140] Likewise, even where a statute is constitutional on its face, it may still "be assailed by *proof of facts* tending to show that the statute as applied to a particular article is without support in reason," for example, "because the article, although within the prohibited class, is so different from others of the class as to be without the reason for the prohibition."[141]

Therefore, when we consider what the New Deal Court actu-ally *said* (as opposed to what it may have believed or intended), the presumption of constitutionality was genuinely rebuttable by those bringing a Due Process Clause challenge to a statute. It was not until 1955 that the Supreme Court moved from dispar-aging the other rights retained by the people to denying them altogether. This was the year that the Warren Court adopted the full Holmesian view that a restriction on liberty is constitutional so long as no reasonable person could think it was unreasonable or without some rational basis. This dubious honor belongs to the case of *Williamson v. Lee Optical of Oklahoma*,[142] to which I will return.

In *Carolene Products*, the Court upheld the rationality of a congressional ban on the interstate sale of "filled milk" as a means of protecting the public's health. Filled milk—like Carolene Products' Milnut drink—was made by combining skim milk with coconut oil so it tasted more like whole milk with all its original milk fat. But filled milk was less expensive than whole milk or than the competing milk substitutes like condensed or evaporated milk. As important, in the days before refrigeration was widely available, it could be shipped and stored at room temperature.[143]

Geoffrey Miller summarizes the evidence about the healthfulness of filled milk:

> The fact was that filled milk undoubtedly improved the national health. Its lower price increased consumption of skimmed milk and vegetable fats, both wholesome and nutritious foods. And to the extent that it displaced other dairy products, the result was far from undesirable. The sugar content of condensed milk (including Borden's "Eagle") was high enough to raise questions about its desirability as a baby food. Fresh whole milk was often positively dangerous. Milk was known to transmit typhoid fever, diphtheria, diarrhea, septic sore throat, and scarlet fever. It was suspected in the transmission of poliomyelitis. Most tragically, it was a leading cause of tuberculosis, a disease that carried away thousands of adults and tens of thousands of children annually. These dangers were largely absent in the case of filled milk, which was manufactured

in modern plants under hygienic conditions and sterilized at high temperature.[144]

So, although filled milk was entirely healthful—indeed more healthful than condensed milk, which consisted of 40 percent sugar—it was banned at the behest of the politically powerful dairy farm lobby, which also pushed to ban "oleomargarine," the name of the food product about which we now "can't believe it's not butter." Pressing for prohibition "were various farmer associations: breed groups; county, state, and national political organizations; dairy newspapers; agricultural colleges and universities; granges; and dairy promotional organizations. Farmers understood, correctly, that the imported coconut oil in filled milk undercut the domestic butterfat market."[145]

Despite the fact that the law was purely factional or "special interest" legislation grounded on junk science, the Court accepted the government's claim that milk fat was essential to a healthful diet, especially for children. As we will see, however, the story has a happy ending: In the 1970s the Filled Milk Act was again challenged as irrational, and was declared unconstitutional by a court that considered the presumption of constitutionality to be rebuttable by evidence! As a result, the Milnot Company, as it was now called, was allowed to sell its drink in interstate commerce.

Carolene Products is famous today, however, not for its eventually rejected view that the presumption of constitutionality was rebuttable in court. Instead, it is best known for the most famous footnote in Supreme Court history. In Footnote Four, Justice Stone identified three circumstances where "there may be narrower scope for operation of the presumption of constitutionality"[146]— that is, three circumstances when laws should *not* be presumed to be constitutional and judges should *not* be "restrained."

In short, Footnote Four describes three circumstances in which judicial restraint should be rejected and the Republican Constitution partially revived. The three exceptions are these: first, "when legislation appears on its face to be within a specific prohibition of the Constitution, such as those of the first ten Amendments, which are deemed equally specific when held to be embraced within the Fourteenth"; second, when legislation adversely affects the "political processes which can ordinarily be expected to bring about repeal of undesirable legislation"; and third, when legislation is the product of "prejudice against discrete and insular minorities."[147]

The first two of these exceptions can be rendered compatible with the Democratic Constitution's commitment to majoritarian rule, as then–Harvard law professor John Hart Ely would attempt to show many years later in his influential 1980 book, *Democracy and Distrust*.[148] The "specific prohibitions" of the Constitution can be viewed as commands of the supermajority of the people who ratified them. And the situations where an existing majority in the legislature attempts to tamper with the democratic process can be said to obstruct the ability of the people themselves to manifest their will.

But the third exception of Footnote Four is an acknowledgment of the most problematic feature of the Democratic Constitution: the abuse of the rights of a minority by those in the majority. In this regard, Footnote Four represented a retreat by the progressive justices from the full implications of the Democratic Constitution they had for so long been advocating and a partial revival of the Republican Constitution's principal tenet that the purpose of government is to secure the preexisting rights of each and every person, even against the will of the majority.

So, although the Court was now composed exclusively of justices appointed by progressive presidents, some of them started to waver in their commitment to across-the-board judicial deference to legislative majorities. Perhaps this indicates that the majoritarianism of the Democratic Constitution was seen to be problematic.

But it may also simply show that appeals to the "will of the people" and judicial restraint were merely an opportunistic means to achieve progressive ends—in particular, the regulation of the economy—by surmounting the structural barriers that our Republican Constitution placed in the way. Judicial deference would then be discarded whenever it obstructed progressive ends.

Harvard Restraint Versus Yale Activism

In a 1947 *Fortune* magazine article,[149] historian Arthur Schlesinger Jr.—an enthusiastic progressive New Deal Democrat—described the growing divide among the New Deal justices on the issue of judicial role. Indeed, it was Schlesinger who coined the term *judicial activism* to describe those justices who were not acting with what, until then, had been deemed the appropriate restraint.

In his article, Schlesinger fawningly profiled the "nine young men, each appointed by Democratic Presidents" (these "young men" were all in their fifties or sixties) who "will be on the bench in a Republican era"—referring to the Republican Congress that had been elected in 1946.[150] Naturally, he downplayed the active Ku Klux Klan involvement of former Democratic Alabama senator and now-justice Hugo Black as "but one phase in a process of self-education."[151]

Although the Court stood united on the constitutionality of New Deal legislation, Schlesinger described the emergence of "a fundamental conflict" among them "over the proper function of the judiciary in a democracy."[152] In this "great debate," he identified three groups. The first, consisting of Justices Black, Douglas, Murphy, and Rutledge, he labeled "judicial activists."[153] A second group, consisting of Justices Frankfurter, Jackson, and Burton, he called "Champions of Self Restraint."[154] And Justice Reed and Chief Justice Vinson lay somewhere in the middle.[155]

According to Schlesinger, the activist group "believes that the Supreme Court can play an affirmative role in promoting the social welfare"; these justices are "more concerned with the employment of the judicial power for their own conception of the social good."[156] For example, they are concerned with "the protection of civil liberties and of defendants in criminal cases."[157]

Schlesinger identified this group with "realist" thinkers associated with Yale Law School, who maintained that "the liberal case against the 1936 Court was based on a false and naïve issue." The true criticism was "not that the old Court engaged in judicial legislation, for this is inevitable, but that it engaged in *reactionary* judicial legislation. Judicial self-restraint . . . is at best a mirage." Because "the Court cannot escape politics . . . let it use its political power for wholesome purposes."[158] (How convenient to change the gravamen of the complaint against "political" judges allegedly enacting their "policy preferences" only after achieving control of the Court.)

In contrast, the second group, the "Champions of Self Restraint," wish to preserve the "judiciary in its established but limited place in the American system"; these justices are more concerned "with expanding the range of allowable judgment for legislatures, even if it means upholding conclusions they privately condemn."[159] If the legislatures make mistakes, "it is up to the legislature to remedy them."[160] Though Schlesinger failed to note it, perhaps it was no coincidence that Thayer, Holmes, Brandeis, and Frankfurter all hailed from Harvard, as did he.

In sum, the first "group regards the Court as an instrument to achieve desired social results; the second as an instrument to permit the other branches of government to achieve the results the people want for better or worse."[161] Schlesinger made clear that this was "not a debate between conservatives and liberals." The entire Court, except for the Republican justice Harold Burton,

Schlesinger said, "is made up of New Dealers. They disagree over the role the Court is to play in bringing about the kind of society they all want."[162]

Although generally siding with the "restraint" group, Schlesinger admitted that the "Stone doctrine" of *Carolene Products* "does indeed furnish the activists with strong logical grounds for intervention on behalf of personal rights, particularly when laws restrict political agitation."[163] But when it comes to economic legislation, he said, "Frankfurter and Jackson are surely right."[164] The "larger interests of democracy in the U.S. require that the Court contract rather than expand its power," and that "basic decisions on all questions save the fundamental rights of political agitation be entrusted as completely as possible to institutions directly responsive to popular control."[165]

A cynic would observe that this synthesis of the Yale and Harvard judicial philosophies conveniently protected the right of progressives, socialists, and communists to freely "agitate" for progressive, socialist, and communist economic legislation that would, when enacted, be immunized from constitutional challenge by individuals whose property and contract rights were being restricted. But the line Schlesinger tried to draw in the name of fidelity to the Democratic Constitution was about to be crossed in a very big way.

Brown v. Board of Education AND THE "Counter-Majoritarian Difficulty"

If *Plessy v. Ferguson* was the epitome of the Democratic Constitution's commitment to majoritarianism and judicial deference, the 1952 case of *Brown v. Board of Education* was a redemption of the Republican Constitution. I refer here not only to the result of the case, in which the Court, led by Chief Justice Earl Warren—a former Republican governor nominated by Republican president

Dwight Eisenhower—ruled that the racially segregated schools violated the Fourteenth Amendment, as a majority of Republicans in Congress had once believed.[166]

I refer also to the fact that the Supreme Court upheld the individual rights of individual schoolchildren against an invocation of the state police power by a legislative majority presumably representing the "will of the People." And I refer as well to the Court's implicit repudiation of *Plessy v. Ferguson*'s deference to the exercise of a state's police power by a majority of its legislature.

Like the cases discussed by Schlesinger, however, *Brown* too violated the central tenets of the Democratic Constitution. It raised what Alexander Bickel famously labeled "the counter-majoritarian difficulty."[167] "The root difficulty," he wrote, "is that judicial review is a counter-majoritarian force in our system."[168] After *Brown*, the task for Bickel and other academics was to reconcile the Court's use of judicial power with the precepts of the Democratic Constitution's collective vision of popular sovereignty, in which a majority of the people are supposedly entitled to govern.

Progressive academics like Bickel, Ely, and others offered a series of theories explaining the exceptions for what they took to be the general rule or baseline of judicial restraint. My objective here is not to present and critique these theories, but to draw two lessons from the felt need to defend "the power of judicial review" in this way.

First, it was the majoritarianism of the Democratic Constitution that made *counter*-majoritarianism a "difficulty." Second, the felt need to counter majoritarianism shows that the Democratic Constitution was always too noxious for Americans to fully embrace in its pure form.

In the 1780s, our Republican Constitution was devised to transcend the majoritarianism in the states by taking the regulation of interstate commerce out of their hands and barring them from impairing the obligation of contracts within their borders. In the 1850s, the Republican Party was founded to oppose majoritarian popular sovereignty in the territories.

Then, when the progressives finally got control of the Supreme Court in the 1930s, their commitment to judicial restraint lasted all of five minutes. Confronted with the majoritarian implications of the Democratic Constitution with respect to the civil and personal rights they favored—and the realization that Republicans in Congress might now enact "reactionary" legislation—progressives retreated to a watered-down form of the Republican Constitution.

The fundamental mistake of this revival is viewing the "power of judicial review" as raising a "counter-majoritarian difficulty" that must somehow be reconciled with honoring the will of the people. To the contrary, we can label the problem with democratic republicanism as the "majoritarian difficulty": as Madison observed, where the greatest power resides lies the greatest danger to the rights of the people.[169] In a republic, that power resides in a majority of the electorate. An independent judiciary with a duty to protect these rights from being unreasonably restricted by the majority is part of the answer to this majoritarian difficulty.

The majoritarian difficulty is the problematic claim that a subset of the people, whether amounting to a majority or minority of the whole, gets to rule the others. It is problematic because each and every one of the people has certain fundamental rights, and it is only "to secure these rights that governments are instituted among men."

True, the power to govern must be delegated to some subset of the people, whether a majority of a handful of elected legislators or a majority of the electorate voting in a referendum. But these persons are not themselves the sovereign, and must somehow be constrained to respect the rights of those who are.

In Part III, I turn from narrative to constitutional design—

from the story of the rise, fall, and partial revival of our Republican Constitution, to the ways the Republican Constitution is supposed to secure the sovereignty of the people, each and every one. Provided, of course, that it is actually followed and enforced. An engaged judiciary enforcing a written constitution is one way, though not the only one, to address the majoritarian difficulty. Federalism and the separation of powers are two more that I examine in the next chapter.

PART III

PRESERVING OUR REPUBLICAN CONSTITUTION

CHAPTER 6

WHY FEDERALISM MATTERS

How Structure Secures the Liberties of the People

OUR STRUCTURAL CONSTITUTION

The framers of the Constitution were like designers of a ship to transport people safely through sometimes treacherous waters. They spent countless hours devising this structure so the ship would float even in rough seas, while allowing the passengers to enjoy the voyage in better comfort and safety than any previously designed ship.

But when the time came to sell tickets, a substantial segment of the public expressed their concerns about the ship's integrity. Would it truly protect their lives, liberty, and property? And what happens if—perish the thought—the structure failed under stress and the ship sank? These consumers demanded that some additional safety equipment be installed before they would set sail.

While the designers of the ship did not all share these concerns, they appreciated that they needed to mollify potential consumers if they were going to get enough of them aboard. So, to their original structure they added lifeboats. Of course, it was not their "original intent" that these lifeboats ever be used. To the contrary, if they were needed, it would mean that their original design had been compromised. Moreover, while being in a lifeboat was better than perishing at sea, should it be necessary to use them, they were a far cry from the comfort of the ship itself.

The U.S. Constitution is primarily a structure that was

intended to protect the individual sovereignty of the people. Only secondarily, and incompletely, does it expressly protect any particular rights retained by the people. In this sense, the few rights that are enumerated in the text of the Constitution are like the lifeboats on a ship. They were never intended by the ship designers to be used, but they certainly may be when the constitutional structure proves inadequate.

The fact that today our legal system pays so much attention to the few rights that are contained in the Constitution—such as the freedoms of speech, press, assembly, and the free exercise of religion—is a bad sign. It is a sign that the structural protections of the Constitution have been breached, and we are now all in the lifeboats. While this is better than drowning, we can and should repair, restore, and even improve the structure we inherited from the framers of the Constitution and its amendments.

Protecting Retained Rights Versus Limiting Delegated Powers

As we saw in Chapter 2, the individual sovereignty of the people is recognized by the text of the Ninth and Tenth Amendments. As a reminder, the Ninth Amendment reads, "The enumeration in the Constitution, of certain *rights*, shall not be construed to deny or disparage others *retained by the people*."[1] And the Tenth Amendment says: "The *powers* not delegated to the United States by the Constitution, nor prohibited by it to the states, are *reserved* to the states respectively, or *to the people*."[2]

These provisions expressly affirm that the people are distinct from the governments of either the United States or the states. Only the sovereign people, as individuals, have rights; the sovereign people also have powers that are not delegated either to the United States or to the several states. Government, as the agent of the people, should be held to its delegated powers.

This division between rights and powers also reflects two different approaches to protecting the sovereignty of the people as individuals. The first is to establish a structure that effectively confines the servants of the people to exercising their granted powers, thereby *indirectly* protecting the individual rights of the people. The second is to empower some group of servants to identify and *directly* protect the rights retained by the people. The Constitution as amended employs both strategies as a redundant safeguard of the people's sovereignty.

Writing to George Washington while the amendments we call the Bill of Rights were being debated in the Virginia legislature, James Madison made the point that limiting powers granted and protecting retained rights were two distinct but complementary ways to accomplish the same end: "If a line can be drawn between the powers granted and the rights retained, it would seem to be the same thing, whether *the latter be secured*, by declaring that they shall not be abridged, or that the former shall not be extended."[3]

Notice here that the end or purpose of *both* strategies is that "the rights retained . . . be secured." In Madison's view, one means to accomplish this end is "by declaring they shall not be abridged." Another is "by declaring that" the "powers granted . . . shall not be extended." Although some constitutional rights constrain the "means" by which the "ends" defined by the enumerated powers are achieved—for example, the Fourth Amendment's ban on general search warrants—the idea that limiting powers and directly protecting rights are two complementary strategies to protect the natural rights of the sovereign people is still valid.

Our Republican Constitution recognizes very few specific rights retained by the people—they are the lifeboats—and largely opts for the second of these strategies for protecting popular sovereignty by establishing a structure that attempts to limit government to what the Declaration calls its "just powers." In this chapter and the next, I explain how, by hewing to this structure rather than by identifying and protecting particular rights, both the enumerated and unenumerated rights retained by the people can be protected without specifically identifying them.

Substantive Versus Structural Constraints on Power

To appreciate these two strategies, it is useful to distinguish two different types of constitutional constraints: substantive and structural. A *substantive* constraint takes the form of "thou shalt not do X," and must be enforced by the courts. A *structural* constraint is "self-enforcing" and therefore potentially more effective.

For example, despite the criticism of the Senate as radically "undemocratic" because representation is by state, and not by population, California and Delaware still only get two senators apiece, and the Congress is still divided between a Senate and a House. Bills must still be presented to and signed by the president. Presidential terms of office are still four years, and he or she is still limited to two terms in office. So structural constraints are "stickier" than substantive ones.

Precisely because they are designed to address the "majoritarian difficulty" by limiting the power of the more representative branches of government, structural constraints will very often appear to be "undemocratic."[4] This is due to the fact that these constraints on majoritarian power are part of the Republican Constitution, which is designed to protect the liberties of the sovereign people as individuals—each and every one of them—against abuse by either minorities or majorities.

Among the most important of such constraints are the divisions of powers between the federal and state governments and among the legislative, executive, and judicial branches. *Federalism* is the term used to describe the division of powers between the national and state governments. By contrast, the phrase "separation of powers" is typically used to describe the separation of legislative, executive, and judicial powers within both the federal and state governments.

In this chapter, I explain how federalism indirectly protects the rights retained by the sovereign people. In the next chapter, I will describe how federalism has waxed and waned over the years, then turn my attention to the separation of powers.

WHY FEDERALISM MATTERS

The United States began with thirteen separate colonies that became thirteen strong states tied together by what was essentially a treaty among them, called the Articles of Confederation. Our federalist system was not designed from scratch but resulted from a stronger national government with specific and limited powers being superimposed on states with general (but still not unlimited) powers.

The new national government was not formed by the states themselves through their legislatures, as some persist in claiming today. Instead it was formed by the electorate who, voting in conventions held in each state, withdrew some powers from their state governments and then delegated them to the new national one. As the Supreme Court held in *Chisholm v. Georgia*, in our federal system, the states are not the sovereigns. We the People, as individuals, are the sovereigns.

At the time the Constitution was being devised, some, like Alexander Hamilton, desired a consolidated national government, while others preferred the strong state system under the Articles. But most were unhappy with the existing situation. For example, trade barriers had been erected by individual states to favor their own businesses, which greatly reduced economic prosperity. The United States was militarily weak, which placed its independence at risk from stronger European powers. And the relative autonomy of the states meant that the United States was unable to meet its treaty commitments, which both undermined the ability to negotiate trade agreements with foreign powers and put the United States in greater jeopardy of war.

For all these reasons, even those who were skeptical about the new Constitution preferred a stronger national government than existed under the Articles. As a compromise with the nationalists, the new federal government was given limited and enumerated powers over trade with foreign nations and among the several states, the making of treaties, and the raising and deployment of the military. To these great powers were added a few more particular functions, such as establishing post offices and post roads, devising uniform rules of nationalization and bankruptcies, and granting rights for limited terms in one's writings and inventions.

This delegation of powers to the new Congress and president left the states with all other "just powers" that a free people can be presumed to have delegated to a government, though states were expressly barred from impairing the obligation of contracts, which they had been doing with debtor relief laws.

To further mollify those who remained suspicious of this new creation, eight amendments were added to expressly protect some of the rights retained by the people that had most frequently been violated in the past, as well as some procedural rights that restricted the means by which the enumerated powers could be implemented.

Then two more amendments were added to ensure that the powers of the federal government would be construed as limited. The Ninth Amendment was supposed to ensure that the eight amendments protecting rights would not be construed as exclusive. The Tenth Amendment reinforced the first sentence of Article I, which limited the powers of Congress to those that were "herein granted."

However it originated, the resulting system of federalism has yielded some enormous advantages for protecting the rights retained by the people. If the federal government has only the power to provide for the common defense as well as to protect the free flow of commerce between states, along with a few other specific tasks, most of the laws affecting the liberties of the people will be made at the state level. This would include the regulation of most economic activity as well as what are today called "social issues."

In the 1824 case of *Gibbons v. Ogden*, Chief Justice John Marshall referred to these reserved state powers as "that immense mass of legislation which embraces everything within the territory of a State not surrendered to the General Government; all which can be most advantageously exercised by the States themselves."[5] For example, "inspection laws, quarantine laws, health laws of every description, as well as laws for regulating the internal commerce of a State, and those which respect turnpike roads, ferries, &c., are component parts of this mass."[6]

Marshall then affirmed that "no direct general power over these objects is granted to Congress; and, consequently, they remain subject to State legislation. If the legislative power of the Union can reach them, it must be for national purposes."[7] But he immediately made clear that by "national purpose" he meant "it must be where the power is *expressly given* for a special purpose, or is *clearly incidental* to some power which is *expressly given*."[8]

Federalism Makes Diversity Possible

Given widespread disagreement about both economic and social policies, lodging this "immense mass of legislation" in the states enabled a diversity of approaches to develop. Sometimes states are characterized as "laboratories of experimentation," a paraphrase of a dissenting opinion by Justice Louis Brandeis in the 1932 case of *New State Ice Co. v. Liebmann*.[9] In his dissent, Brandeis described how a "state may, if its citizens choose, serve as a laboratory; and try novel social and economic experiments without risk to the rest of the country."[10]

As we have already seen, however, Brandeis was a leading progressive activist. Like the other progressives of his era, Brandeis was dissenting here in favor of state experiments in *restricting* the liberties of the people, not protecting them. In *New State Ice Co.*, Oklahoma had enacted a protectionist scheme in which no one could sell ice to customers without first obtaining a license from a local commission after showing "the necessity for the manufacture, sale or distribution of ice" to a particular community.[11] The statute gave existing ice companies a right to such a license without any such showing, but new entrants in the market needed to get permission from the commission.

Licensing schemes like this are the traditional way by which existing firms protect themselves from new competitors. The New State Ice Company sued to enjoin Liebmann's start-up from distributing ice without such a license. Liebmann challenged the constitutionality of the statute, alleging that the restriction on the start-up company was arbitrary, and the licensing regime was irrational.

Brandeis was dissenting from a 7–2 majority decision of the Court rejecting New State's claim that selling ice "is a privilege to be exercised only in virtue of a public grant, and not a common right to be exercised independently by any competent person conformably to reasonable regulations equally applicable to all who choose to engage therein."[12] Under the traditional due process standard a "reasonable" regulation was one well suited for a legitimate state purpose, such as the protection of health and safety. And a restriction was "arbitrary" if it was not equally applicable to every citizen.

Writing for the Court, Justice George Sutherland concluded that "a regulation which has the effect of denying or unreasonably curtailing the common right to engage in a lawful private business . . . cannot be upheld consistent with the Fourteenth Amendment."[13] Under the Fourteenth Amendment, "nothing is more clearly settled than that it is beyond the power of a state, under the guise of protecting the public, arbitrarily [to] interfere with private business or prohibit lawful occupations or impose unreasonable and unnecessary restrictions upon them."[14]

Responding to Brandeis's "experimentation" trope, the Court insisted that "unreasonable or arbitrary interference or restrictions cannot be saved from the condemnation of that amendment merely by calling them experimental."[15] Although states can certainly "indulge in experimental legislation," Sutherland insisted that it would be a "strange and unwarranted doctrine to hold that they may do so by enactments which transcend the limitations imposed upon them by the Federal Constitution."[16] He then reaffirmed the Republican Constitution's principle, "imbedded in our constitutional system, that there are certain essentials of liberty with which the state is not entitled to dispense in the interest of experiments."[17]

Despite this, Brandeis's "laboratory of experimentation" trope is still apt. When it comes to economic regulation, so long as they remain within the proper scope of their power to protect the rights, health, and safety of the public, fifty states can experiment with different regimes of legal regulation so the results can be witnessed and judged rather than endlessly speculated about. Confident predictions about the wonderful effects of novel regulatory schemes are commonplace. Concrete results are quite another matter.

As important, if not more so, businesses small and large can decide to relocate if they deem a particular scheme of regulation to be too onerous. In a federal system, states will be somewhat inhibited in imposing restrictions on businesses by the threat of regulatory competition. Other states will be induced to offer more receptive "business climates" to entice businesses to relocate.

Foot Voting Empowers the Sovereign Individual

Progressive critics of this competitive dynamic disparage this as a "race to the bottom" in which states are prevented from enacting beneficial regulations. When it comes to economic regulation, progressives hubristically assume they know the optimal or superior regulatory scheme from which deviations are to be condemned as "a race to the bottom." Friedrich Hayek called this "the fatal conceit" because discovering this knowledge is precisely why we need competitive experimentation.[18]

Such experimentation is impossible at the national level when adopting a one-size-fits-all regulatory scheme. Once implemented, no matter how disastrous, such "experiments" are rarely repealed, but are instead endlessly and futilely "reformed." Obamacare has proven to be a disastrous public policy, but the structural constraints that make it difficult for legislation to become federal law in the first place then work to obstruct its repeal.

Of course, it is possible that some states may enact "inferior" regulations to attract business seeking to lower their costs of production. But it is far more likely that local electorates will demand the sorts of "reasonable regulations" they witness other states successfully implementing at a reasonable cost. For some reason, those who trust Congress to produce optimal restrictions on economic activity nationwide to avoid a "race to the bottom" are skeptical of the willingness of state legislatures to protect the health and safety of their constituents.

When it comes to liberty, Ilya Somin has explained how the competition provided by federalism empowers the sovereign individual. Because one's vote in an election is swamped by the ballots of millions of others, it is simply irrational for most persons to invest too heavily the time and resources to learn what it takes to vote wisely.[19] Unless one is voting on a referendum, voters can only choose between candidates from one of two (or three) parties, each of which presents a complex package of economic and social policies that voters are not allowed to disaggregate. You must vote for one of the packages, or not vote at all.

Not only is it next to impossible to influence any particular policy by casting one's individual ballot; it is also impossible to separate that policy from others in the "package" offered by one of the contending parties. For example, for whom would the owner of Carolene Products vote to ensure he was allowed to distribute Milnut in interstate commerce? How would the one vote of the owner of Carolene Products realistically protect him from irrational or arbitrary restrictions on his business? Expecting people to protect their liberty in this way is so fantastic, one can't even tell a plausible story about how it might be done.

In sum, a system of voting does not allow the sovereign people to "rule," and it is a pernicious myth to claim that they do. For a variety of reasons, ours is generally a two-party system. The best voters can do is discipline the "in" duopoly party by shifting their electoral support to the "out" duopoly party and hope for some marginal improvement. That is the reality of majoritarian or democratic rule in which one votes for representatives in a two-party system.

By contrast, Somin explains, when voting with one's feet by moving to another city or state, one has far greater control over the results. Each person can individually control the state in which they live by selecting from among fifty choices, not just two. And they can personally experience the economic opportunities that result from different state policies. In a federal system, people are then free to move to another state for a better job, or for a cleaner and safer environment. For this reason, it is far more rational for individuals to investigate the difference between states than the difference between political candidates.

In short, what prevents a legislative "race to the bottom" in a federal system is the freedom of sovereign individuals to race to the states with a better package of results. This dynamic is much less powerful at the national level, because individuals are much more reluctant to leave their country than their state. One suspects that, at some level, progressives grasp the power of this dynamic, which is why they advocate for national legislation for every problem to defeat the individual liberty that federalism helps secure.

The Importance of Keeping Social Issues Local

When it comes to social policy, the preferences of individuals loom even larger than with economic policies. Not only is it difficult to identify the objectively "correct" social policy; it is not clear that such policies even exist. Different people subjectively prefer to live in different types of communities, not only because of differing opinions about morality, but simply as a matter of taste. Some prefer the year-round warmth and sunshine of California and Florida, while others prefer the natural rhythm of the changing seasons. Some prefer the stimulation of urban areas, while others prefer the tranquility of the countryside. Some prefer the "community" of small towns, while others find their conformity stifling. Some prefer the symmetry and homogeneity of "planned" developments, while others prefer the anarchistic heterogeneity of spontaneously evolving architecture.

A rich diversity of preferred lifestyles can only be achieved at the local level. Although many of these policies are really best decided at the municipal rather than the state level, in our federal system, states, not municipalities, are the constitutional units of government. Within each state the degree of "home rule" by towns and cities is governed by a state's constitution and statutes. Still, from the perspective of diversity, it is preferable to have the variety of options provided by fifty state governments than a one-size-fits-all national policy.

As with economic policy, subnational competition between social policies in a federal system imposes a salutary constraint on state governments by threatening an exodus of dissenting citizens to other states. On the positive side, with fifty states to choose from, it is far more likely that a person can find a state or municipality with a social environment in which he or she is more comfortable than if one social policy is imposed on the United States as a whole.

Some individuals may understandably feel aggrieved that they may have to move to find a more congenial social environment. They may ask, "Why should I have to move?" The alternative, however, is to impose their preferred social environment on all the others, who may ask, "Why do you get to change the social environment from the one that I came here to enjoy?"

By their nature, communities must have one character or another. Given that communities must be one type or another, it is best to have as many different communities as possible from which to choose to satisfy the range of individual tastes, preferences, and moral commitments. Therefore, these are the sorts of zero-sum, or all-or-nothing, decisions that are best decided as locally as is legally feasible.

As I already mentioned, the cost of exiting one state for another is far lower than exiting the United States when one disagrees with a national policy. I am speaking here not just of the price of transportation, but more important, the entire subjective cost of leaving one's home and community. For most people, leaving their state is inhibiting to be sure. But, as a comparative matter, it is far more inhibiting to leave one's country, perhaps requiring one to learn a new language.

Consequently, under a federal system citizens' enhanced power of exit not only provides a comparatively greater constraint on legislative power that is reserved to the states; it also empowers individuals to achieve their own purposes far more effectively than relying on their ability to influence national policy by their vote, or by leaving the country of their birth.

In all these ways, liberty is more robustly protected by confining lawmaking to the state and local levels in a federal system, than by moving all such decisions to the national level. This is why the southern Slave Power pushed for proslavery legislation at the national level, including increasingly onerous federal fugitive slave laws that undercut the efforts of states to protect their free blacks from being kidnapped by slave catchers. The antislavery Republicans maintained that the ultimate objective of the South was to gradually extend slavery into the northern states. This prospect further radicalized northern voters, who had been indifferent to slavery in the South, to support a new antislavery political party.

Likewise, Justice Brandeis notwithstanding, progressives have never been content to "experiment" at the local level and be judged by the results. In every way they can, they seek to push all policy decisions to the national level. There, with only the meager voting power to constrain them, they can impose their one-size-fits-all, "comprehensive" policies on everyone. They even hound those individuals and companies who seek to exit the jurisdiction of the United States for freer pastures elsewhere.

None of this is to say that states are inherently better at economic and social policy than is the federal government. Quite the contrary. Arizona Supreme Court justice Clint Bolick has referred to the policies of state governments as "grassroots tyranny."[20] My point is simply that there are structural constraints on the degree to which states can abuse their powers that are lacking at the federal level. In addition to the ones already mentioned, the Constitution also gives Congress and the courts power to ensure that states are not infringing the privileges or immunities of their citizens.

In contrast, state governments have no comparable check on federal power. Perhaps they should.

The Problem with "Cooperative" Federalism

Since the adoption of the Sixteenth Amendment, the federal government has been able to use its power to tax personal income to siphon the wealth of a state's citizens to Washington. It can then use its spending power to offer the states their own citizens' money back in return for states using their more general power to implement one-size-fits-all federal policy. If states refuse the deal, their citizens' money will be sent to the citizens of other states.

In this way, the Republican Constitution's system of *competitive* federalism has increasingly been supplanted by a scheme of "cooperative" federalism, resulting in what Michael Greve has called the "upside-down Constitution."[21] The federal government has been able to exceed the enumerated limits on its powers by bribing or coercing the states with their own citizens' money to use their more extensive powers as Congress sees fit. Indeed, under this system, states have become major supplicants and lobbyists for federal laws.

Arguably, this violates Article I, Section 8, which requires that taxes be raised only "to pay the debts and provide for the common defense and *general* welfare of the United States."[22] According to this objection, money taken from a state cannot go to a program that wholly withholds benefits from a state, because such a program would not be "general" but would be partial.

It is not the taxing that would be unconstitutional, since the Sixteenth Amendment now authorizes this. What is unconstitutional is a spending program that does not benefit every state, but rather is conditioned on such state's "cooperation." Taxes paid by citizens of a state that opts out of such a federal program would no longer be spent in support of the general welfare of each and every one of the states—including itself.[23]

Federalism Avoids a Political War of All Against All

There is another, and potentially even more powerful, way that federalism protects the individual sovereignty of the people. When any issue is moved to the national level, it creates a set of winners and a set of losers. Because the losers will have to either live under the winners' regime or leave the country, everyone will fight much harder to achieve their result or, failing that, to block the other side from achieving its goal.

Consequently, the more issues that are elevated to the national level, the more contentiousness, bitterness, and "gridlock" develops as people fight ever harder *not to lose*. The result is a political version of what Thomas Hobbes called a "war of all against all."

There was a time in Europe when religion was considered to be a national issue. Sovereign monarchs imposed one "established" religion on everyone, with members of dissenting religions legally persecuted or deprived of the equal protection of the law. If one's eternal soul depended on living according to the one true path to salvation in a community of other believers, why shouldn't one fight to the death to prevail? And why isn't it completely proper to save the souls of heretics by ensuring their conversion by any means necessary?

Nor is this a matter of ancient history. Radical Islamists take this very same position about religion today and are prepared to fight to impose their "correct" faith on others. Tens of thousands have been killed and millions more subjugated in this brutal new religious war. Whole countries have been reduced to religious despotism, and then threaten their neighbors.

The classical liberal solution to this violence, destruction, chaos, and persecution was to "decentralize" religion by delegating the choice of one's religion to the individual's own conscience, and then to "tolerate" those who make different choices than ours. In this way, sovereignty over the most important issue of all was shifted from the monarch to the individual, with each person becoming the sovereign of his own conscience, protected by an individual right to "the free exercise of religion."

Not that this was an easy transition to make. It required modifying religion itself so it did not require that everyone around you be on the same path. Individuals are allowed to vote with their feet to attend the church, synagogue, or mosque of their choice and, if they desire, to move to communities where there are more believers like them. It is precisely this "liberal" diversity approach that Islamists reject in favor of their more medieval, one-size-fits-all religious regime.

What is true of what for many is the most important social issue of all—their faith and their soul—is also true of lesser moral and economic issues. Beyond matters like prohibiting murder, rape, robbery, and the like, about which there is a universal consensus, any issue that affects the liberty of individuals is likely to be too contentious to be handled as a one-size-fits-all, love-it-or-leave-it national policy.

As with religious liberty, we avoid a political, and sometimes physical, Hobbesian war of all against all by ensuring that as many issues as possible are handled at the *personal* level of individual sovereigns, which is why individual liberty is the ultimate means to the pursuit of happiness for people living in society with others. Because of the competitive processes I have already described, reinforced by federal checks on state power, such individual liberty is far better protected at the more local level than at the national.

To repeat, it is not that the social and economic policy issues protected by a diversity of state regulations are less important than those handled at the national. To the contrary, the *more important the issue, the more likely it will engender a political war of all against all* to avoid having another's social policy imposed on you. So, the more important the issue, the less it is fit to be decided at the national level. Indeed, the First Amendment declares that "Congress shall make no law respecting an establishment of religion." And our Republican Constitution left even the supremely important policy of exactly *how* to define, prosecute, and try such offenses as murder, rape, and robbery to the diversity of state legal systems.

The United States has been a far more prosperous and contented country because of its federal system. Yet that system was not fully established at the founding. And since it was established, it has been greatly undermined. As we will see in the next chapter, there is not just one but three distinct conceptions of federalism that have developed since the founding of our republic.

CHAPTER 7

PROTECTING RIGHTS BY LIMITING FEDERAL POWER

The Rise, Fall, and Partial Revival of Federalism

———

ON AUGUST 15, 2002, deputies from the Butte County, California, Sheriff's Department and federal agents from the Drug Enforcement Administration (DEA) visited the home of Diane Monson to investigate the activities of a tenant who lived on the premises. While there, the agents spotted six marijuana plants that Diane, a forty-five-year-old wife, office manager, and bookkeeper, grew to supply the marijuana she used to relieve her severe back pain and spasms. She had turned to marijuana when various combinations of pharmaceutical medicines proved either to be ineffective or to have side effects that interfered with her ability to function normally. For her, marijuana was her only relief.

Although the deputies determined that the plants were legal under California's Compassionate Use Act, which the voters had approved by popular initiative in 1996, the DEA agents insisted that they were illegal under federal law. Marijuana is listed as a Schedule I drug under the federal Controlled Substances Act (CSA), which was part of the Comprehensive Drug Abuse Prevention and Control Act of 1970. Under the CSA, a Schedule I controlled substance must have a high potential for abuse, no currently accepted medical use in medical treatment, and a lack of accepted safety for use under medical supervision. Marijuana was placed on Schedule I in 1970 by the Congress that enacted the CSA.

At first, the deputies refused to let the DEA agents remove the plants, but the agents were insistent. For three hours Diane and her husband "talked with them, reasoned with them, and finally pleaded with them to leave the plants alone."[1] Mike Ramsey, the Butte County district attorney, went to Diane's aid by calling the U.S. attorney to ask that he instruct the agents to stand down. When, instead, the U.S. attorney approved the seizure of the plants, the deputies called their sheriff for instructions. He told them to step aside and let the plants be taken and destroyed.

Diane was in tears as she watched the DEA agents chop down her medicinal plants, and she felt the muscles in her back tighten up. After that her spasms returned and she was unable to sleep normally. She was forced to procure marijuana from other sources. Purchased marijuana was not only expensive; it was also of uncertain quality.

Thus did a clash between federal and state laws give rise to a direct conflict between federal and state law enforcement officers and prosecutors, which culminated in a three-hour standoff in the backyard of a citizen of the United States. Here state law enforcement agents attempted to protect the liberty of a sovereign individual for whom they worked. But their efforts were overridden by federal power whose political connection with Diane was far more attenuated.

In 2002, Angel Raich was a seriously ill forty-one-year-old mother of two who used marijuana grown for her by two caregivers to alleviate the life-threatening wasting syndrome from which she suffered. Two years earlier, her weight had dropped to only ninety-four pounds, which became life threatening. She also suffered from an inoperable brain tumor and several seizure disorders, the symptoms of which were alleviated by consuming marijuana in various forms. Raich was confined to a wheelchair when her doctors suggested she try marijuana, which enabled her to walk, as well as to increase her weight to a healthy level and maintain it there.[2]

In the fall of 2002, Diane and Angel brought a civil suit seeking to enjoin the federal government from enforcing the CSA against them. They claimed that the application of the law to the wholly intrastate and entirely noneconomic activities of growing and consuming marijuana exceeded the power of Congress "to regulate commerce . . . among the several states." In addition, they claimed that the enforcement unconstitutionally deprived them of their life, liberty, or property under the Due Process Clause of the Fifth Amendment. They also invoked the Ninth Amendment. But it was their Commerce Clause challenge that prevailed in the U.S. Court of Appeals for the Ninth Circuit.

Together with attorney Robert Raich, Angel's then husband, and Diane's attorney, David Michael, I represented these women in their lawsuit. I argued their case in the federal district court (where we lost), in the Ninth Circuit (where we prevailed), and eventually in the Supreme Court of the United States in the fall of 2004. Representing the federal government that day was then–acting solicitor general Paul Clement. Eight years later, Clement would be my cocounsel in challenging the constitutionality of the Affordable Care Act for exceeding the commerce power of Congress.

The day of our argument, only eight justices were present in the courtroom. Chief Justice Rehnquist was too ill from the cancer that would take his life the following year, so Justice John Paul Stevens, the next most senior justice, presided over the proceedings. In June 2005, by a vote of 6–3, the Supreme Court rejected Diane and Angel's claim.

All four of the more "progressive" justices, Justices Breyer, Ginsburg, Souter, and Stevens, ruled for the government in an opinion by Justice Stevens that was joined by Justice Kennedy.

Justice Antonin Scalia concurred in the result. Three of the five more "conservative" justices, the chief justice and Justices Clarence Thomas and Sandra Day O'Connor, dissented. The case was then remanded to the Ninth Circuit to consider our Due Process Clause challenge, which was ultimately rejected by the appellate judges.[3]

In ruling that the Controlled Substances Act trumped California's Compassionate Use Act, the four progressive justices put their principled commitment to unfettered federal power above their compassion for the sick, the suffering, and the dying. In contrast, although they upheld this exercise of federal power, both Justices Kennedy and Scalia in other cases, before and since, have affirmed that the commerce power of Congress does indeed have limits.

I tell this story because it illustrates how "federalism"—the doctrine that the federal and state governments each occupy separate spheres—can serve to protect liberty if the federal government is held by the courts to its limited and enumerated powers. Had their federalism argument been accepted by five justices instead of just three, Angel's and Diane's personal liberty would have been protected by the laws enacted by the voters of the state of California. There would have been no need for a court to acknowledge and protect their unenumerated right to preserve their lives and avoid pain and suffering under either the Ninth Amendment or the Due Process Clause of the Fifth— legal claims that ultimately failed to vindicate the most personal of their liberties.

In the last chapter, I explained how the federalism of our Republican Constitution can protect liberty without the need to directly protect individual rights. But this requires that courts hold Congress to its enumerated powers, which they failed to do in *Gonzales v. Raich*. Indeed, even without judicial enforcement, resistance to the CSA by a growing number of states like California has made marijuana for medical use available to thousands of persons under the laws of their state (though those who exercise this liberty are still criminals in the eyes of the federal government). In short, as I used to tell reporters during the pendency of the *Raich* case, "federalism is not just for conservatives."

In this chapter, I tell the story of how the federalism of our Republican Constitution has been undermined by judicial abdication.

THE RISE, FALL, AND PARTIAL REVIVAL OF FEDERALISM

In practice, federalism has waxed and waned since the founding, as it underwent three distinct phases during three different eras in our constitutional history: from the founding to the Civil War, from Reconstruction to the New Deal and Great Society, and from the Rehnquist Court to today.

Federalism 1.0: Enumerated Powers Federalism

Let's begin at the beginning. As we have seen, in 1787 the Constitution replaced the Articles of Confederation—which was essentially a treaty among sovereign states—with a new national government ratified by the voters themselves in state conventions rather than by the legislatures of existing states. Under this new system, it was important that the national government have certain powers that were lacking under the Articles and that it be able to act on the citizenry directly without going through the state governments.

But it was also very important that states hold a great deal of power over their own citizens. How much power? Well, enough power to authorize some of their people to legally own others of their people. Now *that* is a whole lot of power. This was accomplished by granting the new national government only limited and enumerated powers that would have nothing at all to do with slavery within existing states.

The scheme of limited and enumerated powers was crucial to the maintenance of this state autonomy with respect to its domestic affairs, and the original meaning of the limited powers of Congress in Article I, Section 8 reflects this imperative. If, for example, the Commerce and Necessary and Proper clauses meant at the founding what the Supreme Court has held they mean today, Congress would have had the power to prohibit the slave trade within the states, not merely with foreign nations, because slavery was an "economic" activity that "substantially affected" interstate commerce. In this way, the evil of slavery establishes beyond any doubt the greatly limited scope of the original meaning of the enumerated powers of Congress in Article I, Section 8.

This is not to say that states had unlimited power, which was then, as now, the definition of tyranny or despotism. But state legislative powers were almost exclusively limited by states' own constitutions, some of which were more "republican" than others, to say the least.

Federalism at the founding can therefore best be described as "Enumerated Powers Federalism." The national government was conceived as one of limited and enumerated powers. The powers of states were simply *everything left over* after that enumeration that the people of each state had delegated to their respective state legislatures in state constitutions.

Enumerated Powers Federalism is expressed in the first words of Article I, which created Congress: "All legislative powers *herein granted* shall be vested in a Congress of the United States."[4] This principle is then reinforced by the words of the Tenth Amendment: "The powers not delegated to the United States by the Constitution, nor prohibited by it to the states, are reserved to the states respectively, or to the people."[5]

It is useful to remember that, while versions of the Tenth

Amendment were proposed by several state ratification conventions, James Madison considered it to be superfluous and unnecessary. "Perhaps words which may define this more precisely, than the whole of the instrument now does, may be considered as superfluous," he said to the House of Representatives during his speech proposing various amendments.[6] "I admit they may be deemed unnecessary," he continued, "but there can be no harm in making such a declaration. . . ."[7]

Madison's blasé attitude about the Tenth Amendment was in stark contrast with the imperative he felt to add what eventually became the Ninth Amendment. This provision was needed, he said, to guard against "one of the most plausible arguments I have ever heard urged against the admission of a bill of rights into this system," namely, that "by enumerating particular exceptions to the grant of power, it would disparage those rights which were not placed in that enumeration."[8] And "it might follow by implication" that those rights that had not been "singled out, were intended to be assigned into the hands of the general government, and were consequently insecure."[9]

In the original Constitution, then, the "reserved" powers of states are defined solely in terms of what is left over after powers are "delegated to the United States" and then delegated to the states by their constitutions. There is no affirmative statement about the scope of state powers in the Constitution itself. Indeed, the Tenth Amendment is entirely noncommittal about which of the reserved powers are allocated to state governments and which are reserved "to the people" themselves. This allocation of "reserved" powers was to be determined by state constitutions.

States have many powers, including the power to tax and to spend, and the power to take property for public use. They also have the power to regulate and prohibit the activities of the persons within their borders. Soon after the founding, these "reserved" powers of states to regulate and prohibit activity came to be called the "police power," though that term does not appear in the Constitution and has proved notoriously difficult to define with precision. "The police power of the state," one commentator observed in 1921, "is one of the most difficult phases of our law to understand, and it is even more difficult to define it and to place it within any bounds."[10] Difficult no doubt, but not impossible.

The phrase "internal police" was used seven times by delegates to the Constitutional Convention to refer to the power of state governments; once this power was referred to as "their police." The issue of the police power of states arose when the convention was still considering making a general grant of power to the national government but wished to ensure that the national legislature not "interfere with the governments of the individual States in any matters of internal police, [in] which the general welfare of the United States is not concerned."[11] In *The Federalist*, Hamilton employs the phrase "domestic police" twice in essays denying that the national government was a threat to state power.[12]

Because at this time the scope of the "internal police" was simply whatever powers were left over after delegating enumerated powers to Congress, there was no pressing need to define it any more precisely. As we will soon see, however, the situation changed with the enactment of the Fourteenth Amendment, which empowered Congress and the federal courts to protect the privileges or immunities of citizens of the United States from being abridged by the laws of their own states. To implement this protection, it became necessary to identify the proper scope of the police power of states.

With Enumerated Powers Federalism, however, the powers of states are not protected by affirmatively defining their scope. Instead they are protected by holding Congress to its delegated powers, which means that it falls to the federal judiciary to preserve the federalist structure. Unless states violate the few constraints imposed on them by Article I, Section 10 or are interfering with one of Congress's enumerated powers, what states do with their reserved police powers is not a matter for the national government in general, or the federal courts in particular, to decide.

Early on, however, Enumerated Powers Federalism was undermined by the Supreme Court over the issue of slavery. Some today associate federalism and "states' rights" with slavery and segregation. But as we have repeatedly seen, from the very beginning, southern slave states were not content with the powers reserved to them by Enumerated Powers Federalism. Instead, they sought to enlist and expand national power in service of slavery.

Perhaps the earliest invocation of national power on behalf of slavery was the Fugitive Slave Act of 1793. But it was not until some fifty years later, in the 1842 case of *Prigg v. Pennsylvania*,[13] that the Supreme Court upheld the act by finding an implied congressional power to enforce the provision of Article IV, Section 2 that read:

> No Person held to Service or Labour in one State, under the Laws thereof, escaping into another, shall, in Consequence of any Law or Regulation therein, be discharged from such Service or Labour, but shall be delivered up on Claim of the Party to whom such Service or Labour may be due.[14]

You will recall from Chapter 4 that, in the *Matilda* case, Salmon Chase had argued that this provision, like all the provisions of Article IV, were articles of compact or treaty between the several states to be honored solely by what is called the "comity" or reciprocal respect of other state governments. Just as treaties with foreign nations do not expand the delegated powers of Congress, neither do these articles of compact or treaty among the several states.

As evidence that Congress lacked the power to enforce these articles of compact, Chase pointed to the exceptional grant of congressional power to enforce the Full Faith and Credit Clause in Article IV. Section 1 expressly states that "the Congress may by general laws prescribe the manner in which such acts, records, and proceedings shall be proved, and the effect thereof."[15] The presence of such a power here, and its absence in the clause governing persons "held to service or labor," strongly implied that such a power does *not* exist to enforce that clause.

In *Prigg*, however, the Supreme Court held that Congress did have the power to enforce this clause by enacting the Fugitive Slave Act. Moreover, this national power overrode the police power of individual states that were trying to protect free blacks within their borders from being wrongfully seized as slaves. Given that Article IV, Section 2 contained no express congressional enforcement power, how did the Court reach its conclusion?

Writing for the Court, Justice Joseph Story *implied* it by combining the injunction of Article IV with the Necessary and Proper Clause of Article I, Section 8, which gives Congress the power "to make all Laws which shall be necessary and proper for carrying into Execution the foregoing Powers, and all other Powers vested by the Constitution in the Government of the United States, or in any Department or Officer thereof."[16] With the "end being required" by Article IV, Story reasoned that "it has been deemed *a just and necessary implication*, that the means to accomplish it are given also."[17]

In this way, an unenumerated or implied federal power was deemed by the Court to override the reserved police power of states. Yet the Necessary and Proper Clause only grants Congress power to enact laws to carry into execution "all other Powers vested *by the Constitution* in the Government of the United States." And Article IV, Section 2 vested no such powers in the federal government.

Prigg is an early and egregious example of how a judicially sanctioned expansion of congressional power—often by invoking the Necessary and Proper Clause—can overwhelm Federalism 1.0 by overriding the enumerated limits on the powers of Congress that operate to reserve powers to the states and the people. For this version of federalism to work, judges must be engaged and willing to hold the line. By expanding the scope of federal power to uphold an act of Congress, Justice Story had failed to do his job as a servant of the people. Unfortunately, Story's judicial abdication was a harbinger of things to come.

Federalism 2.0: Fundamental Rights Federalism

After the Civil War, the Republicans in the Thirty-Eighth Congress enacted the Thirteenth Amendment, eliminating the power of states to enforce slavery within their borders. But southern states almost immediately used the rest of their vast police powers to enact "Black Codes" to restrict the economic and personal liberties of the freedmen. Their aim was to come as close as possible to restoring slavery in everything but name. By exerting their reserved police powers—together with their countenancing private violence—these states sought to consign free blacks to a subordinate legal class akin to slavery, and to make life treacherous in the South for white Unionists and Republicans.

In response to this, as we have seen, the Republicans in the Thirty-Ninth Congress used their enforcement power under the Thirteenth Amendment to enact the Civil Rights Act of 1866. Although they overrode the veto of President Johnson by supermajorities in both houses, some in Congress saw the need to write these protections into the Constitution lest courts question their power to enact the Civil Rights Act. And only a constitutional amendment would prevent a future Congress containing southern Democrats from repealing the Civil Rights Act, which Democrats were loudly threatening to do.

So the Republicans created the Fourteenth Amendment,

which can be viewed as a sort of "do over" of the Thirteenth. The amendment was drafted to eliminate any doubt that they were "amending" Federalism 1.0 by curtailing the power of states to violate the fundamental economic and personal liberties of their own citizens. Section 1 of the amendment defined a new Federalism 2.0 that qualified the previously hands-off approach of Federalism 1.0 by placing new federal constraints on all three branches of state governments:

- First, the new Privileges or Immunities Clause expressly prohibited states from enacting any law that infringed upon the fundamental rights of *any* or *all* of their citizens: "No state shall make or enforce *any law* which shall abridge the privileges or immunities of citizens of the United States." In other words, this clause prohibited *legislation* that either violated fundamental rights across the board, or discriminated in their recognition and protection.
- Second, the new Due Process Clause said that no state shall "deprive any person of life, liberty, or property, without due *process* of law." This authorized federal judicial scrutiny of whether a citizen of the United States was subject to death ("life"), imprisonment ("liberty"), or fine ("property") either (a) by a legislative act that was not truly a "law" because it was irrational or arbitrary, or (b) by a state *judicial process* that did not accurately apply constitutional laws to particular persons.
- Third, the new Equal Protection Clause specified that no state shall "deny to any person within its jurisdiction the equal *protection* of the laws." State *executive branch* officials were now required to enforce otherwise constitutional laws in a nondiscriminatory fashion.

In addition, while by itself Section 1 would only have authorized federal courts to police the states, the Republicans in Congress sought also to empower themselves. Section 5 of the Fourteenth Amendment gave Congress the enumerated "power to enforce, by appropriate legislation, the provisions of this article." By refusing to rely on the Supreme Court's implied powers doctrine of *Prigg v. Pennsylvania*, the Republicans reinforced Enumerated Powers Federalism by adding an additional enumerated power of Congress, as they had done with the Thirteenth Amendment.

In short, Enumerated Powers Federalism was now supplemented by new federal judicial and legislative powers to protect the fundamental rights of citizens from being violated by (a) *creating* or maintaining irrational or arbitrary statutes enacted by state legislatures, (b) inaccurately *applying* those laws to particular persons by state courts, or (c) unequally *enforcing* those laws by state executive branch officials. We can call Federalism 2.0 "Fundamental Rights Federalism" because it protected the fundamental rights of citizens of the United States from being abridged by their own state governments.

The reaction of the South to this and other measures to restrict its power over the freed blacks was a campaign of terrorism unwitnessed in this country before or since, from lynchings up to and including mass murders. Then, as we have seen, in such cases as the *Slaughter-House Cases*, *Cruikshank*, the *Civil Rights Cases*, and *Plessy*, the Supreme Court systematically neutered the Fundamental Rights Federalism of the Fourteenth Amendment.

Later, in such cases as *Lochner v. New York* and *Buchanan v. Warley*, the Supreme Court used the Due Process Clause to place some limits on the police powers of states. But its efforts were bitterly opposed by progressives who favored the rights of states to enact progressive economic legislation, and by their coalition partners, the southern Democrats, who favored the rights of states to enact the economic system of Jim Crow.

Eventually, this partial revival of Fundamental Rights Federalism using the Due Process Clause of the Fourteenth Amendment was beaten back by the Thayer-Holmes-Brandeis doctrine of judicial restraint. Then, with the New Deal Court's expansion of federal regulatory power—relying primarily, as had Justice Story in *Prigg*, on a capacious reading of the Necessary and Proper Clause[18]—came the demise of the Enumerated Powers Federalism 1.0 of the Founding Era. The Supreme Court held that Congress could regulate or prohibit any intrastate economic activity that had a substantial effect on interstate commerce, even though such activity was not itself "commerce . . . among the several states."

When these two developments were combined, Congress now had free rein to regulate or prohibit every economic activity in the country—whether interstate or intrastate—unconstrained by the Due Process Clause of the Fifth Amendment that applied to the federal government. True, under the Footnote Four approach of *Carolene Products*, individuals might still protect themselves from federal or state laws if they could assert that a statute violated an express prohibition of the Constitution or that they were members of a suspect class of persons facing discrimination. But what about the states?

If under the Necessary and Proper Clause, Congress now had the power to reach wholly intrastate economic activity that substantially affects interstate commerce, Congress also has the power to regulate the states themselves. After all, much of what state governments do is economic in nature and certainly affects interstate commerce.

So what becomes of federalism?

Federalism 3.0: State Sovereignty Federalism

Enter the Rehnquist Court. By 1992, during their three terms, Republican presidents Ronald Reagan and George H. W. Bush were able to nominate a majority of the justices, five of whom evinced great sympathy for our system of federalism. Their challenge was somehow to preserve the role of states in our constitutional system without questioning or rolling back the tremendous expansion of federal power that had been approved by the New Deal Court and further expanded by the Warren and Burger Courts.

After William Rehnquist became chief justice in 1986, the Court began developing what came to be known as the "New Federalism," but which in this story could be called "Federalism 3.0" or "State Sovereignty Federalism."

First came the Court's so-called Tenth Amendment cases of *New York v. United States*,[19] *Gregory v. Ashcroft*,[20] and *Printz v. United States*.[21] In each of these cases, the Court attempted to create a special state exemption from federal powers that would easily have reached the conduct in question if performed by a private party. Then came its so-called Eleventh Amendment cases of *Seminole Tribe of Florida v. Florida*[22] and *Alden v. Maine*,[23] immunizing states from some lawsuits in federal court.

In *Seminole Tribe*, Chief Justice Rehnquist endorsed Justice Bradley's repudiation of *Chisholm v. Georgia* in favor of state sovereignty. Under the Rehnquist Court's New Federalism, it was the sovereignty of states that justified the Court in carving out affirmative protections of state governments from the expansive post–New Deal interpretations of federal power. Its approach was reminiscent of Footnote Four, which had carved out special exceptions for discrete and insular minorities. Federalism 3.0 added states to the list of specially protected groups.

Although the New Federalism preserved some autonomy for states from the control of Congress, the more textually faithful way to protect states is to combine Enumerated Powers Federalism 1.0 with Fundamental Rights Federalism 2.0. This would involve (a) limiting Congress to its enumerated powers and letting states take up the slack except (b) where states have violated the Fourteenth Amendment or other constitutional restrictions on their power like the Contracts Clause. Very tentatively, the Rehnquist Court also began to move in this direction.

In 1995, in *United States v. Lopez*,[24] the Supreme Court invalidated a law making it a federal crime to possess a gun within one thousand feet of a school, ruling that it was beyond the commerce power of Congress. Then, in 2000, in *United States v. Morrison*,[25] the Court similarly held that the creation of a civil cause of action for gender-motivated violence was also beyond the limited and enumerated powers of Congress.

Notice that, by striking down the Gun-Free School Zone Act in *Lopez* as beyond the power of Congress to enact, the Court protected the right of the people to keep and bear arms, but did so without having to apply the specific prohibition of the Second Amendment.[26] Likewise, it also served to protect the reserved powers of states without having to appeal to any unenumerated principle underlying the Tenth or Eleventh Amendments.

Rather than returning to the scheme of limited and enumerated powers, however, the Rehnquist Court sought to preserve the New Deal vision of national economic regulation. It did this by allowing Congress to continue to reach wholly intrastate *economic* activity that had a substantial effect on interstate commerce, while drawing a line at the power to regulate *noneconomic* intrastate activity, such as possessing guns within a thousand feet of a school, or engaging in gender-motivated violence.

Rather than unwind or repudiate the so-called New Deal settlement, which accepted a vast expansion of federal power, the Rehnquist Court adopted an approach that can be summarized as (a) this far and no farther without (b) a justification that will not end the enumerated powers scheme altogether. As Chief Justice Rehnquist wrote in his opinion in *Morrison*, "*thus far* in our Nation's history our cases have upheld Commerce Clause regulation of intrastate activity only where that activity is economic in nature."[27]

In this way, the New Deal settlement was to be reconceived rather than "unsettled." First, the post–New Deal expansion of federal power to reach activity within states was taken to be a high-water mark of federal power. That power could not go any higher without special justification that would not lead to an unlimited power in Congress. Second, affirmative carve-outs from this New Deal expansion of power would be made to accommodate some continued autonomy for "sovereign states," thereby preserving some semblance of federalism.

With Obamacare, Congress pushed its regulatory power to new heights by commanding that the people buy health insurance from a private company or else pay a penalty. Further, it threatened states with the loss of all current funding for Medicaid if they did not use their police power to vastly increase their Medicaid coverage. But would the Supreme Court find that Congress had exceeded its powers, as it had in *Lopez* and *Morrison*?

After what some took to be the abandonment of the New Federalism by Justices Kennedy and Scalia in *Raich*, the death of Chief Justice Rehnquist, and the retirement of Justice O'Connor, it was reasonable to question whether there were still five votes to uphold the New Federalism of the Rehnquist Court. Most law professors thought not. But, as we have seen, the Roberts Court found both exercises of power to be unconstitutional.

Justices Kennedy and Scalia returned to the federalism fold. With their votes, a mandate to engage in economic activities was held by five justices to be beyond both the Commerce and the Necessary and Proper clause powers of Congress. Although we failed to defeat Obamacare, the principle that the federal government is one of limited and enumerated powers was vindicated.

At the same time, Chief Justice Roberts's approach of adopting a "saving construction" to uphold the rest of the statute opened the eyes of many constitutional conservatives to the problem with "judicial restraint." This highly visible refusal to enforce the

Constitution's limits on federal power may well have been a political inflection point. Now, more than at any time since the New Deal, there is a burning desire among many conservatives and libertarians for judges who will have the courage to more fully revive and redeem our Republican Constitution.

CHAPTER 8

A GOVERNMENT OF MEN AND NOT OF LAWS

The Rise of the Executive-Administrative State

———

IN JANUARY 2012, an interviewer from the Univision Spanish-language TV network asked President Barack Obama why he was continuing to deport illegal immigrants from Mexico and elsewhere. He replied that this was "because that's the law that's on the books right now. And the way our system works, the president doesn't have the authority to simply ignore Congress and say, we're not going to enforce the laws that you've passed." A few moments later, he added that the president can't "just wave away the laws the Congress has put in place. . . . And until we get comprehensive immigration reform, there's going to continue to be heartbreaking stories. That's what we're trying to change. But ultimately the way we change it, is we've got to change our politics."[1]

In giving this response, President Obama was displaying respect for the separation of powers. He was recognizing that, under Article I, "*all* legislative" or lawmaking power granted by the Constitution is vested in Congress. And, under the Take Care Clause of Article II, Section 3, the president "shall take Care that the Laws be faithfully executed."[2]

Recently, however, the president has engaged in numerous acts that seem to run afoul of this basic principle. He or his cabinet officials have waived key provisions of the Affordable Care Act that might prove to be politically unpopular. When Congress refused to enact the so-called Dream Act, legalizing whole categories of now-illegal aliens residing in the United States, the president adopted an enforcement policy that emulated the terms of the act, administratively exempting tens of thousands from deportation. Very recently he issued sweeping executive orders to do even more to implement immigration policies he formerly had conceded required congressional action. President Obama negotiated an important and highly controversial agreement with a foreign power that he refused to submit to the Senate for its advice and consent, but is implementing unilaterally.

These actions by the president constitute an end run around our Republican Constitution's separation of legislative and executive power. Although it may be fictitious to claim that Congress represents the "will of the people," the fact that Congress is elected does provide a potentially important check on the abuse of government power by the president. The electorate cannot remove a president from office until his or her term expires. But they can vote for representatives who will rein in the president's policies. Conversely, they can vote for a president who will use the veto power to block congressional action.

In this way, the liberties of the people can be protected by the structure of the government, and by the different constituencies that vote for different offices in different elections. When he defended his unilateral actions by claiming a mandate from his election by a majority of the people, President Obama was invoking the mantra of the Democratic Constitution to override the structural constraints on power provided by our Republican Constitution. In this effort, he has not been alone.

The president was encouraged by the then-Democratic majority leadership in the Senate and by the Democratic minority leadership in the House. After 2014, he was encouraged by the Democratic minority in the Senate, who would exercise their filibuster power to prevent congressional reprisals. In this way do the Democrats in Congress put their adherence to the Democratic Constitution ahead of their commitment to their institutional role in the separation of powers. Just like the progressives of old abandoned their fealty to judicial restraint when they gained control of the courts, congressional Democrats favor their current policy ends over their previous assertions that Congress represented the will of the American people.

Indeed, whenever a president seeks to exceed his powers, he is likely to be supported in his efforts by his partisan allies in Congress. The president has what Theodore Roosevelt called his "bully pulpit" to rally public support for his actions. And, if his party controls one or both houses of Congress, congressional resistance is difficult to mount.

Yet, even when Congress concurs in presidential encroachment on its legislative power, this is a problem. The powers of the national government are not separated to protect the prerogatives of Congress; they are separated to secure the sovereignty of the people. So, even when supported by members of the legislative branch, any breach of the Republican Constitution's separation of powers is dangerous.

To appreciate why, it is useful to consider the origin of this structural protection of individual liberty.

THE THREE FUNCTIONS OF GOVERNMENT

Like so much of our Republican Constitution, the idea for this feature can be traced to John Locke. According to Locke, the social compact establishes a government that addresses the inconveniences in the state of nature, primarily the inconvenience of executing or enforcing the laws of nature to protect one's natural rights. It is useful to summarize Locke's argument briefly.

Locke began by asking why, if a person in the state of nature was so free as to be the "absolute lord of his own person and possessions," would he part with this freedom to enter into a civil society with a common government?[3] For Locke, the "obvious" answer was that, though in the state of nature, a person has the natural rights to his life, liberty, and possessions, the enjoyment of such rights is "very uncertain, and constantly exposed to the invasion of others." Without a government, the enjoyment of one's property "is very unsafe, very unsecure."[4] Because the state of nature "is full of fears and continual dangers," it is reasonable for a person "to join in society with others . . . for the mutual preservation of their lives, liberties and estates."[5]

Why exactly are the natural rights of the people so unsafe and insecure without a government? Locke identified three basic problems for which a properly structured government is the solution.

The Lack of Known and Standing Law to Guide Conduct

The first problem is to ascertain what justice requires of each person. The state of nature lacks "an established, settled, known law, received and allowed by common consent to be the standard of right and wrong, and the common measure to decide all controversies between them."[6] This is due, in part, to the bias each of us has toward our own interests—and the interests of those we care about—as well as the limited time we spend thinking about these matters until we get into a dispute with someone else.

The solution to this problem is the creation of a lawmaking or *legislative power* to enact statutes that people can read in advance of acting, so they can conform their conduct to the law. And when a dispute arises, these rules can be fairly applied to determine who is in the right.

The Lack of a Known and Impartial Judge to Settle Disputes

Second, the state of nature lacks "a known and indifferent judge, with authority to determine all differences according to the established law."[7] This is a problem because, when we are both the "judge and executioner of the law of nature" in disputes with others, our judgments will naturally favor our own side. Or, as Locke put it, "being partial to themselves, passion and revenge is very apt to carry them too far, and with too much heat, in their own cases."[8]

The solution to this problem is the creation of a *judicial power* to decide cases and resolve controversies impartially. This includes private cases with fellow citizens as well as controversies with the agents or servants of the people who comprise their government.

The Inability of Individuals to Enforce Their Rights

Third, in the state of nature there is the absence of a power to enforce whatever judgments might be reached in a particular case. No one of us is strong enough to enforce our rights against everyone else, especially against a group of persons allied against us. As Locke put it, in "the state of nature there often wants power to back and support the sentence when right, and to give it due execution."[9] Resistance by criminals and other rights violators makes it dangerous to enforce our rights, and "frequently destructive, to those who attempt it."[10] The solution to this problem is the creation of an *executive power* to enforce the laws.

In this way, Locke very clearly distinguished the legislative, judicial, and executive powers.

CHECKS AND BALANCES

Although he identified the three powers or purposes for forming a government to secure the liberties of the people, Locke did not emphasize that these powers ought to be *separated* or placed in different hands to enable each to check the others as a means of securing the liberties of the people. This is understandable given that they were merged in the British political system with which he was familiar.

The idea of a separation of these powers is identified with the French political thinker Charles-Louis de Secondat, whose title was the Baron de Montesquieu, and who is best known today simply as Montesquieu. Although he did not originate the notion, in his 1748 book, *De l'Esprit des Loix*—translated in 1750 into English as *The Spirit of the Law*—Montesquieu's advocacy of a division of political power among different persons comprising an executive, a legislature, and a judiciary greatly influenced the founding generation.

Montesquieu insisted that placing any combination of these powers into the hands of a single person was extremely danger-ous. "When the legislative and executive powers are united in the same person, or in the same body of magistrates, there can be no liberty."[11] Likewise, "there is no liberty, if the judiciary power be not separated from the legislative and executive."[12] Why is this? Montesquieu explained that

> there is no liberty if the judiciary power be not separated from the legislative and executive. Were it joined with the legislative, the life and liberty of the subject would be exposed to arbitrary controul; for the judge would be then the legislator. Were it joined to the executive power, the judge might behave with violence and oppression.

Therefore, all liberty would be at an end, "were the same man, or the same body, whether of the nobles or of the people, to exercise those three powers, that of enacting laws, that of executing the public resolutions, and of trying the causes of individuals."[13]

Under the Articles of Confederation, all powers of governance resided within the states. Congress had no power to make laws binding on the people, or to establish a judiciary to adjudicate disputes or an executive to carry out the law. And, as we saw, in the states, the legislative, judicial, and executive powers of government were only imperfectly separated.

When the founders grew dissatisfied with the "democratic" constitutions of the states and created a new national government with the power to govern the people directly, they strove to further and more clearly separate each of these three functions of government. They put each of these functions into the hands of different persons comprising the legislative, or Congress (Article I); the executive, or president (Article II); and the judiciary (Article III). This separation of powers was an important innovation of their newly revised conception of "republican" government. Under our Republican Constitution, the three branches that are responsible for these three functions of government are not totally separated. The president participates in the legislative process by exercising a veto power. The Senate participates in the executive power to deal with foreign nations by requiring the president to get its advice and consent to treaties. Likewise, the Senate must consent to the appointment of executive branch officials who act on behalf of the president. So our system of checks and balances necessitates the involvement of some branches in the activities of the others.

Nevertheless, the separation of powers is a vital means to avoid the tyranny of arbitrary government in which discretionary powers are wielded by some against others. As the 1780 Massachusetts Constitution, drafted by John Adams, famously affirmed:

In the government of this Commonwealth, the legislative department shall never exercise the executive and judicial

powers, or either of them: the executive shall never exercise the legislative and judicial powers, or either of them:
the judicial shall never exercise the legislative and executive
powers, or either of them: to the end it may be *a government
of laws, and not of men*.[14]

Conversely, when the separation of powers is overridden, the
result is a government of men and not of laws.

Undermining Federal Checks and Balances

We have already seen how the progressives worked to undermine
the judicial check on legislative power provided by the Fourteenth
Amendment, which was impairing their ability to enact economic
legislation restricting liberty at the state level. They then sought
to override the system of competitive federalism by expanding
national power to supersede the "state experimentation" they had
so recently lauded. After this, they went to work undermining
the checks and balances on national power provided by a formal
separation of powers.

All this has happened in a variety of ways, involving complicated
legal doctrines that are highly technical to explain. Rather than
attempt that here, let me offer a partial summary of the ways that
the checks and balances provided by the separation of powers have
been overcome. Each of these changes to our Republican Constitution was implemented by Congress, supported by the president at
the time, and eventually sanctioned by the Supreme Court.

Just as President Obama sought—with the help of his Democratic allies in the Senate and House—to overcome the checks
on his power posed by a Republican-controlled Congress, most
of these alterations of the separation of powers were in reaction to
successful efforts to use our Republican Constitution to resist the
progressive political agenda of the day.

But, however these unchecked powers arose, they need not be employed for progressive ends. They can be made to serve other powerful interests, and can be abused whenever political conservatives are in control. What matters is that these changes to our Republican Constitution have resulted in a far more powerful federal "servant" with far fewer protections of the sovereign people who are supposed to be its "master."

Delegating the Power of Congress to the Executive-Administrative State

The separation of powers into three branches was, and to some extent remains, an impediment to the adoption of progressive legislation at the national level. Not only does such legislation have to pass two chambers of Congress, but it must be approved by the president and evaluated for constitutionality by the judiciary. This creates a number of "veto gates" that can block a measure. Sometimes these vetoes represent the sentiment of the majority, and sometimes the efforts of a concentrated minority that is particularly affected by a particular measure.

Moreover, Congress consists of a mere handful of persons: 435 representatives and 100 senators. Such a small group of individuals cannot hope to enact all that many laws. So the very smallness of Congress provides a structural limit on federal power. (Hot, muggy summers in Washington, D.C., used to limit the time that Congress could sit to enact laws, but air-conditioning has overcome this unintended structural constraint.)

In both these ways, the separation of powers built into the structure of our Republican Constitution exerted a brake on the ability of progressives to closely control the liberties of the people. What to do? Enter the administrative state, which is probably more accurately called the "executive-administrative state."

In the twentieth century, the creation of "administrative

agencies" in the executive branch enabled Congress to delegate its lawmaking power to as many people as are needed to make as many rules as are desired. In this way, the reach of the national government could be infinitely expanded. Now all the majority in control of Congress need do is to approve a goal like "clean air and water." Then the unelected staffs of the executive branch administrative agencies can do the hard work of writing the rules and regulations that would actually be applied to the people, without the need for any further action by Congress.

Once the administrative agency is up and running, Congress formally retains the ultimate power to veto any administrative rules or regulations. But here is where the veto gates of our Republican Constitution work to advance rather than inhibit the progressive agenda. Any reversal of an agency rule must pass both houses of Congress and be presented to the president for his approval. Such an action can be scuttled in a variety of ways and therefore rarely occurs. Indeed, the known difficulty in accomplishing this—like the known difficulty of amending the Constitution—deters most from even making the effort.

By establishing administrative agencies to make laws instead of Congress, the progressives were able to extend the power of the federal government to control the liberties of millions in ways that, as a practical matter, had previously been impossible. Then, once created, the checks and balances that were originally designed to protect the liberties of the people were flipped to protect the discretion of those who seek to control the people. So, not only do administrative agencies get to set the rules free of the checks and balances, but the checks and balances actually serve to insulate and shield their control of the people from being effectively checked.

Moreover, progressives in Congress can maintain control of these agencies, not by revising and repealing the rules and restrictions they impose on the people, but by controlling their funding. Congressmen with particular interests in the agenda of particular agencies serve on the committees that set funding. Here too the game is rigged in favor of progressive policies requiring more intrusive federal government.

Congressmen who favor increased expenditures for areas of their concern collude with representatives from locales with different concerns to raise the budgets of both. Members from agricultural districts and states, for example, will collude with members from districts with defense contractors to increase both agricultural and defense spending. Each threatens to cut the budget of the other as a means of extracting more for all.

By this route, the creation of the executive-administrative state results in Congress expanding both its regulatory and its spending powers to the delight of progressives.

The Supreme Court has allowed Congress to delegate legislative power so long as the legislation provides administrative agencies with an "intelligible principle" to guide their lawmaking.[15] In a recent opinion, Justice Clarence Thomas provided a detailed explanation and critique of this doctrine. "To the extent that the 'intelligible principle' test was ever an adequate means of enforcing that distinction, it has been decoupled from the historical understanding of the legislative and executive powers and thus does not keep executive 'lawmaking' within the bounds of inherent executive discretion."[16] As he concludes:

> We have too long abrogated our duty to enforce the separation of powers required by our Constitution. We have overseen and sanctioned the growth of an administrative system that concentrates the power to make laws and the power to enforce them in the hands of a vast and unaccountable administrative apparatus that finds no comfortable home in our constitutional structure. The end result may be trains that run on time (although I doubt it), but the cost is to our Constitution and the individual liberty it protects.[17]

Instead, Justice Thomas urged us to "return to the original meaning of the Constitution: The Government may create generally applicable rules of private conduct only through the proper exercise of legislative power."[18] In short, if a federal rule tells sovereign individuals what they may do and how they may do it, then it must come from the Congress, not from an agency of the executive branch.

If the courts won't enforce the separation of powers, then how about the checks on executive branch administrative power provided by the president?

Weakening the President's Power to Check Congress with Independent Agencies and Omnibus Spending Bills

Administrative agencies belong to the executive branch, so presumably they are under the control of the president, not Congress. What happens when the president is less inclined to pursue progressive policies? To counteract this, Congress has extended its lawmaking power still further by creating so-called independent agencies that are headed by officials whom the president may nominate or appoint, but not remove. This makes these agencies even more beholden to their patrons on the congressional committees that control their spending, weakening the president's check on congressional power.

Presidential power can further be checked by aggregating spending into bigger and harder-to-veto bills. There was a time when spending was authorized one program at a time, which could be vetoed by the president. But long ago, this system morphed into bigger and bigger bills to bring more and more congressmen and senators into line.

So in place of spending bills for each individual program, there was one big "agricultural spending bill" and one big "defense spending bill." No one who wanted their agriculture spending blocked would block the defense spending sought by another. So, congressmen from agriculture states could trade their support for military spending for the support of those congressmen from districts with defense contractors. The president could then be stopped from vetoing measures he opposed by tying them to programs he desired.

Even this has not satisfied the desire for logrolling and spending. After the 2010 elections, with the House of Representatives in control of Republicans, the progressives in the Senate teamed up with a progressive president to do an end run around the "regular order" of passing giant appropriation bills on particular subjects. After the 2014 elections turned the Senate over to the Republicans, the Democratic minority used the Senate's filibuster rules to block individual appropriations bills that had passed the House from being taken up in the Senate.

By refusing to pass such bills in the Senate and waiting until the last spending authorizations are about to expire, all spending can be rolled into a single "omnibus" spending bill. Senators and representatives who might oppose individual legislative measures or spending items must then vote for the bill, or else the government will "shut down," threatening the financial support that millions of Americans now rely upon. The same device can also be used against a Republican president when progressives are in control of both the Senate and the House.

This shows that progressives can use their control of the presidency and one or more houses of Congress to obviate any checks provided by the branches they do not control. Because the government now provides a flow of income to so many individuals, groups, and businesses, progressives can use any of the "veto gates" they happen to control to coerce those they may not control into compliance.

The picture just painted may seem contradictory. On the one hand, the executive-administrative state moves the lawmaking power from Congress to the executive branch. On the other hand, the creation of independent agencies helps Congress shield these agencies from presidential control. The common end of both these maneuvers, however, is the imposition on the country of a progressive legislative agenda. Congress creates administrative agencies to advance vague progressive goals, and then shields these agencies from interference by any president who might oppose them.

That this results in rule by an unelected bureaucracy at odds with the precepts of the Democratic Constitution does not faze modern-day progressives any more than did their abandonment of judicial restraint once they had control of the courts. Just as the Slave Power was committed to slavery above any principled commitment to states' rights, so too are progressives committed to their policy agenda above any principled invocation of the Democratic Constitution. When they are in control of Congress, progressives seem perfectly comfortable using this control to create an executive-administrative state that will continue to pursue their agenda, even when they can no longer claim a majority in the legislature.

But what about the independent judiciary?

Weakening the Judicial Constraint on the Other Branches by Adopting Deference and Restraint

The final check on the abuse of powers by the other two branches is the judiciary. As Gary Lawson has explained, the administrative state is in conflict with numerous constitutional limits on power.[19] So the rise of the administrative state presented many opportunities for judicial invalidation. But, as Lawson succinctly summarized, since the New Deal, the Supreme Court has largely shrunk from stopping progressives in Congress from extending the reach of national power by delegating their legislative powers to the executive-administrative state.

Justice Thomas has observed that, to the framers, "the separation of powers and checks and balances were more than just theories. They were practical and real protections for individual liberty in the new Constitution. The Judiciary—no less than the other two branches—has an obligation to guard against deviations from those principles."[20] And yet the Supreme Court has "not always been vigilant about protecting the structure of our Constitution."

Although it "has repeatedly invoked the 'separation of powers' and 'the constitutional system of checks and balances' as core principles of our constitutional design, essential to the protection of individual liberty, it has also endorsed a 'more pragmatic, flexible approach' to that design when it has seemed more convenient to permit the powers to be mixed." In his opinion, Justice Thomas explained how history shows that this "approach runs the risk of compromising our constitutional structure."[21]

Short of invalidating the delegation of congressional power to administrative agencies or their "independence" of presidential control, the courts could still check their power by critically evaluating administrative rules that restrict the liberties of the people to see if they are truly consistent with the statutory authorization of Congress. Yet, here too, the "judicial restraint" that had been urged by the progressives has largely been adopted, thereby allowing free rein to the executive-administrative state.

In 1984, the Supreme Court decided the case of *Chevron U.S.A., Inc. v. Natural Resources Defense Council, Inc.*,[22] involving a dispute over the Environmental Protection Agency's interpretation of a provision of the Clean Air Act Amendments of 1977. In *Chevron*, the Court held that a federal court must defer to interpretations of congressional statutes made by those government agencies charged with enforcing them, unless such interpretations are unreasonable.

If the statute unambiguously addresses the issue, then the

unambiguous meaning controls. But if the statute is ambiguous, then the court asks whether the agency's interpretation of the ambiguous provision is based on a permissible construction of the statute. A permissible construction is one that is not "arbitrary, capricious, or manifestly contrary to the statute." As utilized by the courts, this standard is very easy to satisfy.

The so-called *Chevron* deference doctrine is one of many arcane rules known only to those who are deeply immersed in the technicalities of what is called "administrative law." Yet it has profoundly weakened the separation of powers that is supposed to secure the sovereignty of the people from their servants in government. Here again, it provided an avenue for progressive majorities in Congress to obviate our Republican Constitution's check on their power.

All Congress need do to delegate carte blanche power to executive-administrative agencies is write an ambiguous provision that is not on its face unconstitutional, under the highly deferential stance that courts take to such delegation. The veto gates provided by separation of powers will then prevent future congresses from checking the administrative agency. And the courts will not review whether any "reasonable" implementation of this standard is actually an unreasonable restriction on the liberties of the people.

Nor will they review the reasonableness of an agency's interpretation of its own rules. As Justice Thomas has explained, just "as it is critical for judges to exercise independent judgment in applying statutes, it is critical for judges to exercise independent judgment in determining that a regulation properly covers the conduct of regulated parties."[23] And yet, under so-called *Seminole Rock* deference, judges will "accord 'controlling weight' to the agency interpretation of a regulation, subject only to the narrow exception for interpretations that are plainly erroneous or inconsistent with the regulation."[24]

In Judge Thomas's view, *Seminole Rock* deference "represents a transfer of judicial power to the executive branch,"[25] as it "precludes judges from independently determining [the] meaning" of regulations."[26] As a result, it "amounts to an erosion of the judicial obligation to serve as a 'check' on the political branches."[27] For this reason, he concludes that "the entire line of precedent beginning with *Seminole Rock* raises serious constitutional questions and should be reconsidered in an appropriate case."[28]

By delegating its lawmaking powers to the administrative agencies in the executive branch, and then insulating the law made by these agencies from the president, from the courts, and even from Congress itself, we are all today ruled by the dead progressive hand of the past. You can vote "no" on progressive legislation a thousand times. But once the combination of a legislative majority and friendly president exists for even a moment, a single "yes" vote will delegate unchecked power to administrative agencies in political perpetuity.

IT'S NOT ABOUT DEMOCRACY; IT'S ABOUT POWER

I admit that the story I have just told about the weakening of the checks and balances provided by the separation of powers seems both confusing and daunting. Perhaps you had difficulty even following it. And this is the simplified version! In part, this is because the underlying reality I am attempting to explain is deliberately tangled to obscure its evasion of our Republican Constitution.

Still, there seems to be a tension between the rise of the executive-administrative state and what I am calling the Democratic Constitution. Administrative agencies are made up of countless unelected anonymous bureaucrats, boards, and panels, all of which seem hopelessly impervious to the Democratic Constitution's demand for democratic accountability and control. In what way can the output of these institutions be characterized realistically as the collective "will of the people"?

But as I have already noted, this is to mistake the Democratic Constitution as the end being sought rather than merely the means to accomplishing whatever the progressive political agenda may be at any given time. When our Republican Constitution, based on individual popular sovereignty, was an obstacle to that agenda, the collective popular sovereignty of the Democratic Constitution was pitted against it.

As Madison predicted, the greatest danger to the liberties of the people lies where the greatest power resides, which in a republic is in the majority of the people. By harnessing the power of the majority, the progressives were able to overcome the barriers of the Republican Constitution.

Having breached those barriers, however, progressives then moved on to eliminate any "democratic" or majoritarian obstacles to *their* agenda. Indeed, at the very same time they were invoking the "will of the people" to undermine the constraints of the Republican Constitution being enforced by the Supreme Court, progressives were also advocating rule by an enlightened and dispassionate elite of public policy experts. Unlike the democratic "populists" who preceded them, the progressives' appeal to the Democratic Constitution in the courts was merely an opportunistic way to eliminate the obstacles to their progressive ends posed by our Republican Constitution.

We used to hear complaints from progressives like the late Arthur Schlesinger Jr. about the perils of "the imperial presidency."[29] Today we are witnessing the use of presidential prerogatives to obviate a Republican majority in control of a Congress that was elected to put a brake on aspects of today's progressive agenda. So now a progressive president is using unilateral "executive actions" to implement policies that are supported neither by a majority in Congress, nor by the citizenry. For our modern-day progressives, what matters is the end, not the means. Social justice, not democracy.

True, Congress retains powers it could use to resist these assertions of presidential power. But congressional action to reverse the actions of a progressive president requires the power to pass a bill out of both houses of Congress and then override a presidential veto. With a progressive minority in the Senate capable of filibustering any bill, or sustaining presidential vetoes, Congress cannot effectively negate presidential executive orders (assuming it was so inclined). So, once the president takes action, the separation of powers provided by our Republican Constitution can again be used to thwart any effort to reverse those policies legislatively.

That's assuming, of course, that Republicans in Congress have the will or desire to do so, which in many cases they do not. Modern-day Republicans can be just as opportunistic about republicanism as Democrats are about democracy. Many Republicans in Congress cannot wait to pass "tort reform" that would compel states to change their tort law on the ground that state tort law has a substantial effect on interstate commerce! And, like Democrats, Republicans support the war on drugs, which places what has historically been a matter for states into the hands of the federal government instead.

Just as the appeal to the Democratic Constitution was merely an opportunistic means to overcoming our Republican Constitution's hurdles to progressive ends, so also was the appeal to "judicial restraint" in the name of the will of the people. As we have seen, that too was qualified, opportunistically asserted, and then abandoned once progressives had control of the judiciary, only to be reasserted against a more conservative court.

In the next chapter, we examine in greater detail the demise of the judicial check on legislative power and what it would take to restore this vital dimension of the separation of powers.

CHAPTER 9

"IRRATIONAL AND ARBITRARY" LAWS

The Need for Judicial Skepticism

LEE OPTICAL OF Oklahoma was a subsidiary of a Texas company that owned a national chain of eyeglass retailers doing business the way Lenscrafters does today. Lee Optical was founded by Theodore Shanbaum, whose parents were Russian immigrants who had settled in Chicago.[1] After graduating from the University of Chicago, he earned his law degree from DePaul in the late 1930s.[2] Shanbaum got the idea of entering into the eyeglass industry after visiting his brother-in-law, an optometrist, at his home in Dallas.[3] To save money, he purchased a used business sign that said LEE OPTICAL. The name "Lee" had no other connection to the enterprise.[4]

It should come as no surprise that local ophthalmologists and optometrists were none too keen on this out-of-state competition advertising lower prices on glasses. Indeed, as we have seen, most of the famous economic liberty cases involved legislation siding with some firms in competition with others.

- In the *Slaughter-House Cases*, the statute gave special monopoly privileges to a single designated corporation at the expense of individual butchers.
- In *Lochner v. New York*, the statute promoted by the bakeshop union favored union-organized bakeries at the expense of small, ethnic, nonunion bakeshops.

- In *Muller v. Oregon*, white male union members were protected from competition from women.
- In *Nebbia v. New York*, the regulation raising the retail price of milk sought to protect big milk distributors from competition from small mom-and-pop retailers in poor neighborhoods.
- The statute in *U.S. v. Carolene Products* protected the powerful dairy constituency from competition from lower-priced and better-tasting "filled" milk.

And these are just the famous "landmark" cases.

So it is unsurprising that the Oklahoma legislature passed a law banning opticians from providing certain eyeglass services in competition with ophthalmologists and optometrists, effectively making Lee Optical's business plan illegal. What is surprising is that the federal district court upheld Lee Optical's Due Process Clause challenge to the statute, though it was 1954 and well after the New Deal revolution. A three-judge panel agreed that the statutory scheme was irrational and arbitrary, and that none of the restrictions enacted could realistically be justified as genuine health and safety measures.

In 1955, however, when the case reached the Warren Court, the justices reversed. In his opinion for the Court in *Williamson v. Lee Optical*, Justice William O. Douglas finally adopted the extreme deferential standard that had been urged by James Bradley Thayer and Oliver Wendell Holmes Jr.—the formalist approach that even Justice Brandeis and his New Deal Court colleagues had declined to expressly adopt.

In this chapter, I explain why the Supreme Court's approach to the due process of law is a sham. To illustrate how a Due Process Clause judicial inquiry ought to be conducted by a fair and impartial judiciary, I examine the lower court's opinion in *Lee Optical*.

THE VITAL ROLE OF AN IMPARTIAL JUDICIARY

Although the judiciary standing alone is not enough to secure the sovereignty of the people, the previous chapters make clear that, without judicial engagement, the veto gates of our Republican Constitution serve to block the repeal of laws and regulations that have expanded congressional power and overridden the separation of powers.

Obtaining the benefits of federalism requires federal courts to develop doctrines that identify the outer limits of Congress's enumerated powers, as the Supreme Court was attempting, however imperfectly, to do before 1937, and has tepidly done since 1995. And the Court must overcome its reluctance to enforce the separation of powers within the federal government—a reticence that has undermined the rights of the sovereign people by allowing the rise of an executive-administrative state with the prerogative powers of a sovereign king.[5]

That a judiciary is needed to secure the structural features of the Constitution should not be surprising. Recall John Locke's assessment that the state of nature is so "unsafe and uneasy," in part because it lacks "a known and indifferent judge, with authority to determine all differences according to the established law." This is because, when every person is "both judge and executioner of the law of nature," each "being partial to themselves, passion and revenge is very apt to carry them too far, and with too much heat, in their own cases."[6]

As with individuals, Congress should not be the judge in its own case about the extent of its powers, and the executive-administrative state has dangerously become the legislator, judge, and executioner of its own prerogative powers.[7] No one who views popular sovereignty as residing in the individual would confuse the people themselves with their representatives in the legislature—or with employees of administrative agencies—who are but men and women who may use their power to improperly restrain the liberties of the sovereign people.

So what should happen when some subset of the people, who are tasked with being "legislators" or "administrators," restrict the liberties of fellow citizens and joint sovereigns? As Madison explained in *Federalist* 10, "[n]o man is allowed to be a judge in his own cause, because his interest would certainly bias his judgment, and, not improbably, corrupt his integrity." But he then added that the same precept applies to legislatures: "With equal, nay with greater reason, *a body of men* are unfit to be both judges and parties at the same time."[8] Madison then observed that "many of the most important acts of legislation" function as "judicial determinations, not indeed concerning the rights of single persons, but concerning the rights of large bodies of citizens."[9]

According to Locke, the answer to this defect in the state of nature is the creation of an impartial judiciary. Or, as Madison put it in his speech to the House proposing a bill of rights, "independent tribunals of justice . . . will be an impenetrable bulwark against every assumption of power in the legislative or executive; they will be naturally led to resist every encroachment upon rights expressly stipulated for in the constitution. . . ."[10]

As it happens, the right to a fair and impartial adjudication has been "expressly stipulated for" in the Constitution, not once, but twice.

JUDICIAL ENGAGEMENT AND THE DUE PROCESS OF LAW

Among the express guarantees that were added to the Constitution is the Fifth Amendment, which says that no "person . . . shall . . . be deprived of life, liberty, or property, without due process of law." Likewise, the Fourteenth Amendment says that no state may "deprive any person of life, liberty, or property, without due process of law."

Since the New Deal, judges have employed these two Due Process Clauses to protect certain "preferred freedoms" or "fundamental rights." While some of these rights were enumerated in the text of the Constitution, others that were unenumerated have been selected by judges for special protection. This doctrine is called "substantive due process" because, rather than ensuring a fair *process* by which the law is applied to particular persons, the clause is being used to limit the scope of the legislature's power by protecting certain *substantive* rights, some of which are nowhere enumerated in the Constitution.

Judges and law professors today read this modern approach back into the Supreme Court's use of the Due Process Clause before 1937. Like modern courts, they say, in cases like *Lochner v. New York* the pre–New Deal Supreme Court improperly elevated the substantive right of the "liberty of contract" to the status of a fundamental right. While today's progressives on the left and "judicial conservatives" on the right all condemn this use of the Due Process Clause, they differ on why exactly it was wrong.

Like the New Deal justices who were dubbed "judicial activists" by Arthur Schlesinger Jr., modern progressives say the sin was not that the Court was using the Due Process Clause to protect "substantive" rights, but that it was protecting the *wrong* substantive rights. Like these old "activists," progressives today say the problem is "not that the old Court engaged in judicial legislation, for this is inevitable," but "that it engaged in *reactionary* judicial legislation."[11] Because "the Court cannot escape politics . . . let it use its political power for wholesome purposes,"[12] such as protecting a right of privacy.

On the other side of the aisle, like the New Deal justices whom Schlesinger dubbed "Champions of Self Restraint," modern judicial conservatives object to using the Due Process Clause to thwart the will of the majority by protecting *any* unenumerated right—whether the liberty of contract or a right of privacy. By protecting unenumerated rights at all, they say, courts are engaged in judicial lawmaking rather than confining themselves to ensuring a process in which laws are fairly applied to particular individuals.

In this way, both today's left and right are operating within the post–New Deal worldview. But this seriously distorts how the pre–New Deal Supreme Court was actually using the Due Process Clause. The pre–New Deal justices were not selecting certain "substantive" unenumerated rights and then elevating them for special protection. Instead, they viewed the Due Process Clause as providing a *procedure* by which a person who is deprived of his or her life, liberty, or property may challenge a law as outside the "just powers" of Congress or state legislators to enact.

In other words, before a sovereign individual can justly be deprived of his or her "life" (by capital punishment), "liberty" (by imprisonment), or "property" (by penalty or fine), the "due *process of law*" requires a judicial evaluation of whether a statute is within the power of Congress or state legislatures to enact. And the "due process *of law*" requires that a statute be a "law."

As Justice Chase wrote so movingly in *Calder v. Bull*, "[t]here are acts which the Federal, or State, Legislature cannot do, without exceeding their authority." This is because there are

> certain vital principles *in our free Republican* governments, which will determine and overrule an *apparent and flagrant* abuse of *legislative* power; as to authorize *manifest injustice by positive law*; or to take away that security for *personal liberty*, or *private property*, for the protection whereof of the government was established.[13]

Thus did Chase in 1798 identify the conformity of democratically enacted legislation with the just powers of governments as a first principle of "our Free Republican governments." Unless a statute is consistent with these principles for which republican governments are established, it is not truly "a law" that is binding in conscience on the sovereign individual. As Justice Chase explained:

> An ACT of the Legislature (for I cannot call it a law) contrary to the great first principles of the social compact, cannot be considered a rightful exercise of legislative authority. The obligation of a law in governments established on *express compact*, and *on republican principles*, must be determined by the *nature* of the power, on which it is founded.[14]

Such a statute that is not a rightful exercise of legislative authority does not carry with it "the obligation of a law" unless it is within the legislative power.

All of this is premised on the proposition that first come rights, and then comes government "to secure these rights." Although the sovereign people can consent to be governed, when their consent is not expressed but implied they cannot be presumed or supposed to have consented to a regime in which a legislature can act irrationally or arbitrarily. As was explained by Justice Chase when speaking of the power of state legislatures, "it is against all reason and justice, for a people to entrust a Legislature with SUCH powers; and, therefore, it cannot be presumed that they have done it."[15]

Under "the due *process of law*," then, the *process* of applying a law to a particular *person* includes a fair opportunity to contest whether a statute (or administrative regulation) is within the "proper" or "just power" of a legislature to enact and therefore carries the obligation of a *law*. And an irrational or arbitrary statute is not within the just powers of a republican legislature.

Crucially, the "due process of law" requires that the magistrate or judge hearing such a challenge be impartial. If the judge hearing a challenge simply "presumes" that the legislature is acting properly, or "defers" to the legislature's own assessment of its powers, then that judge is not acting impartially. Even worse, if the "presumption" in favor of legislation is irrebuttable, then the person dressed in a black robe is not acting as a judge at all.

When this happens, "fellow citizens and joint sovereigns" will be deprived of their "life, liberty, or property" without "the due process of law." And the benefits of federalism, separation of powers, the freedom of speech, and all the other structural and substantive protections afforded by our Republican Constitution will be severely weakened or altogether lost.

What about the states? As we have seen, the original Constitution placed very few limits on the scope of the legislative or "internal police" of the states. In *Calder*, Justice Chase was considering the proper scope of state legislative power because the case concerned one of these limits. Article I, Section 9 says: "No state shall pass any bill of attainder, ex post facto law, or law impairing the obligation of contracts, or grant any title of nobility." Nevertheless, for Chase, this express limitation on state power merely confirmed the fundamental Republican principle that the people "cannot be presumed" to have delegated to their state legislatures a power to impose arbitrary or irrational restrictions on their natural liberties.

Moreover, as we have seen, the Fourteenth Amendment provided a new republican check on state powers. Using wording deliberately mimicking Article I, Section 9, it commands: "No state shall make or enforce any law which shall abridge the privileges or immunities of citizens of the United States."

Of course, the scope of state legislative power differs from that of the national government. While Congress may legislate only to accomplish a specific list of objectives, state legislatures may pursue a much wider—and in important respects more fundamental—set of purposes. Unlike the federal government, the states are charged with securing *all* the individual rights of the people from being violated domestically by their fellow citizens. Actions that violate any of the rights of others are not rightful exercises of liberty and may justly be prohibited. For this reason, murder, rape, robbery, theft, and the like are punished by states rather than by the federal government.

The private rights retained by the people are threatened not only by such criminal acts as murder and theft, but by negligent and other risky conduct as well. Nor do states have to wait until after a rights violation has occurred to punish the offender. They can "regulate" conduct in advance to prevent the rights violation from occurring in the first place. The shorthand expression to summarize this aspect of the police power is that it includes the power to regulate for the "health and safety" of the public. Or, as John Marshall put it in *Gibbons v. Ogden*, "inspection laws, quarantine laws, health laws of every description, as well as laws for regulating the internal commerce of a State" are reserved to the states.[16]

Although the police powers of a state are more general than those of Congress, this does not mean that state legislative power is unlimited. The "due process of law" includes an assessment by an impartial judiciary that a particular statute was indeed a *law* within the powers that a people may be presumed to have delegated to their agents in state legislatures. Like the federal government, a state must be exercising its "just powers."

In the absence of a specific list of enumerated powers like the ones defining the scope of Congress's power, how are the "just powers" of states to be identified and protected? For one thing, the Due Process Clause of the Fourteenth Amendment only protects a person against being deprived of his life, liberty, or property. So when a government action is not depriving a person of any of these, he or she cannot object to that law in court, but must confine such objections to the political process. When this is the case, we say such a person lacks "standing" to sue. For example, a person cannot challenge the hours the postal service sets for its operation or myriad other regulations of government entities.

A Due Process Clause challenge, then, arises only if a government is restricting the life, liberty, or property of an individual. When (and only when) this has occurred, there is a two-part inquiry. First, is the purpose for the restriction within the "just powers" of a republican government in a free society? In the absence of an express delegation, is it the sort of power that a free people can be presumed to have delegated to their agents? For example, is the purpose of the measure to protect the health and safety of the public? Or is it, for example, "a law that destroys, or impairs, the lawful private contracts of citizens; a law that makes a man a Judge in his own cause; or a law that takes property from A. and gives it to B"?[17]

If the purpose is a proper one, we must next ask if the restriction on liberty is necessary to serve it. Strict logical necessity is not required, as that type of showing would undermine the purpose for which Republican "governments are instituted among men."[18] But some degree of means-ends fit must be shown.

A showing of means-ends fit helps ensure that the restrictions have truly been adopted as means to a proper end, and guards against the very real risk that they have been adopted for an improper motive. Such improper motives include (a) the desire to assist favored persons or groups at the expense of other citizens, (b) the desire to harm other individuals or groups, or (c) the desire to stigmatize or make more costly the exercise of a liberty of which some disapprove. In the absence of express consent, no citizen can be presumed to have consented to a lawmaking power with any of these as its purpose.

Everyone now agrees that the Court in *Plessy v. Ferguson* was wrong to accept a mere assertion of a public purpose. But we go wrong today by limiting our skepticism to a few exceptional circumstances. Whenever a law deprives a fellow citizen and joint sovereign of his or her life, liberty, or property, the "due process of law" requires that such laws be skeptically assessed by an impartial judge to ensure that they actually do serve a proper governmental purpose.

Requiring the government to identify its true purpose and then show that the means chosen are actually well suited to advance that purpose helps to smoke out illicit motives that the government is never presumed by a sovereign people to have authorized. If a law truly has an appropriate purpose, this should not be hard to establish. Such means-ends scrutiny is rather common in our constitutional history.

That this can be a very powerful way for courts to protect liberty is shown by Clark Neily. In his book, *Terms of Engagement*,[19] Neily relates case after case of special-interest legislation that was enacted not to advance the general welfare by protecting the health and safety of the public, but to benefit privileged existing economic interests at the expense of fledgling competition. Neily tells the stories of:

- The widow who was barred from arranging flowers for a grocery store because she lacked a license from the Louisiana Horticulture Commission, which was staffed by licensed florists and designed to limit competition. She died before her right to earn an honest living could be vindicated in court.[20]
- The licensed massage therapist who was ordered to desist from massaging horses because she was licensed only to provide human massage therapy.[21]
- The citizens who have been barred from African hair braiding without first obtaining a cosmetology license requiring two thousand hours of training on skills and knowledge that are entirely irrelevant to hair braiding.[22]

• Those in Florida and two other states, who must have a college
   degree from an accredited interior design school, serve a two-
   year apprenticeship with a state-licensed interior designer, and
   pass a three-day, thousand-dollar licensing exam before they
   can arrange furniture.[23]

He might also have included the story of the Benedictine monks
of St. Joseph Abbey in Louisiana who were barred by the Louisiana State Board of Embalmers & Funeral Directors from selling caskets without a funeral home director's license.

   In each of these cases, the citizens were represented by the
Institute for Justice, the public interest law firm for which Neily
works as a senior attorney, and in each of these cases, the Institute showed that the public health rationale for the restriction
was either sketchy or nonexistent.

   Further, in each of these cases, the prospect of vindicating
the rights of the sovereign individual through the "democratic"
political process—that is, by working to elect Democrats or
Republicans to office—was entirely fanciful. The very fact that
these cases are so obscure, and involved lone citizens of modest
means, prevented them from becoming any sort of political
issue in an election. How many actual elections will ever turn
on the fate of prospective flower arrangers, interior decorators,
hair braiders, horse massagers, or casket makers?

   Only by empowering the individual to bring suit before an
impartial judiciary that will require government regulators to
justify their restrictions on liberty as actually rational can these
rights be vindicated in practice. But these challenges require
that courts be realistic, not formalistic, in skeptically evaluating
the rationales proffered by the government for these restrictions.[24] In the next section, I explain how this can be done prac-
tically.

ASSESSING THE RATIONALITY AND ARBITRARINESS
OF STATUTES RESTRICTING LIBERTY

To get a sense of how this approach to the due process of law used to work in practice, we do not need to look to the Due Process Clause jurisprudence of the pre–New Deal Supreme Court. As I have mentioned, in the 1938 case of *U.S. v. Carolene Products*, the New Deal Court reiterated the traditional view "that a statute would deny due process which precluded the disproof in judicial proceedings of all facts which would show or tend to show that a statute depriving the suitor of life, liberty, or property had a rational basis."[25]

Of course, in *Carolene Products*, the Court proceeded to find that Congress did have a factually "rational basis" for prohibiting the interstate trade in filled milk. Justice Stone reached this conclusion by credulously reciting the junk science upon which Congress rested its piece of special interest legislation. For this, both Congress and the Court can be faulted. But that was not the end of the story.

The Realistic Evaluation of Rationality

Some three decades later, in a little-known development, the same Filled Milk Act the New Deal Supreme Court had found to be "rational" in *Carolene Products* was held to be irrational and unconstitutional by a federal court. The product at issue in *Carolene Products* was called "Milnut," after the coconut oil that was its distinctive ingredient. Later, when other lower-cost vegetable oils were used instead, the name was changed to "Milnot." But this change in formula in no way affected the rationality of the statute or figured in the reasoning of the court.

In his opinion invalidating the law, U.S. district court judge Robert Morgan provided the constitutional standard: "While

Congress may select a particular evil and regulate it to the exclusion of other possible evils in the same industry, any distinction drawn *must at least be rational.*"[26] On the basis of the evidence presented, Judge Morgan found it to be "crystal clear that certain imitation milk and dairy products are so similar to Milnot in composition, appearance, and use that different treatment as to interstate shipment caused by application of the Filled Milk Act to Milnot violates the due process of law to which Milnot Company is constitutionally entitled."[27] Whatever previous "dairy market conditions and dangers of confusion" had led to the passage and judicial upholding of the Filled Milk Act many years ago, Judge Morgan found that these had "long since ceased to exist."[28]

In short, Judge Morgan ruled that the Due Process Clause required that the Milnot Company be allowed to present evidence to an impartial judge to show the irrationality of the Filled Milk Act. Although his opinion was true to the New Deal Court's decision in *Carolene Products*, which it cited, he failed to acknowledge the more recent 1955 decision of *Williamson v. Lee Optical* that would have led to a different result. As I noted at the outset of this chapter, the *Lee Optical* case concerned an Oklahoma statute effectively banning the Lee Optical Company from providing eyeglass services the way that Lenscrafters does today. When Lee Optical challenged the law in federal court, however, it initially prevailed in the lower court.

Although the Warren Court eventually reversed this decision and upheld the statute by adopting the extreme deferential view that had been advocated by Thayer and Holmes, I want to focus on how the lower court realistically examined the "rationality" of Oklahoma's restriction of liberty. For the lower court's opinion provides a marvelous example of how impartial judges can critically assess whether a statute is truly justified as a health and safety measure.

In its lawsuit, Lee Optical challenged whether several restrictions on its business were a reasonable means to protect the health and safety of the public. For example, the statute barred anyone but a licensed optometrist or ophthalmologist "to fit, adjust, adapt or apply eyeglass lenses or frames to the face of a person or to duplicate any lenses" without a written prescription from an Oklahoma-licensed ophthalmologist or optometrist.[29] Second, the statute made it unlawful to advertise or solicit the sale of glasses to the public. Third, it barred any retailer from renting space to anyone to provide eye exams on its premises.

As was common practice when considering challenges to the constitutionality of legislation, the case was heard in federal district court by a three-judge panel. Lee Optical's challenge was heard by a circuit court judge, the chief judge of the district, and a district court judge.

In evaluating these three restrictions of liberty, the panel expressly accepted the version of the presumption of constitutionality that the Court adopted in 1931 in *O'Gorman*: "all legislative enactments are accompanied by a presumption of constitutionality; and . . . the court must not by decision invalidate an enactment merely because in the court's opinion the legislature acted unwisely." But it then followed the approach of *Carolene Products* that a "court only can annul legislative action where it appears certain that the attempted exercise of police power is arbitrary, unreasonable or discriminatory."[30]

Finally, here is how the panel expressed the traditional due process and equal protection clause standard: when "the public welfare is involved, the effect of the statute must bear a reasonable relation to the purpose to be accomplished and must not discriminate between two similarly circumstanced groups, regulating one group but exempting the other."[31] Although the terms "irrational" and "arbitrary" are not always clearly distinguished, a measure that lacks "a reasonable relation to the purpose" can be said to be *irrational*; a measure that "discriminate[s] between two similarly circumstanced groups" can be said to be *arbitrary*.

To see how this approach worked in practice—and could work again—let me describe how the panel assessed the restrictions on an optician's replacing broken lenses. According to the panel, the "unambiguous language" of the statute made it unlawful for an optician "to take old lenses and place them in new frames and then fit the completed spectacles to the face of the eyeglass wearer except upon written prescription from a qualified eye examiner."[32]

This served to prohibit consumers from exchanging their frames either to obtain more modern designs or because the former frames had broken, without first visiting an ophthalmologist or optometrist. As the panel noted, this "diverts from the optician a very substantial, as well as profitable, part of his business."[33]

The panel began its analysis of this restriction by noting that written prescriptions contain no instructions on how glasses are to be fitted to the face of the wearer. On the basis of the evidence, it concluded that the knowledge necessary to fit glasses to the face "can skillfully and accurately be performed without the professional knowledge and training essential to qualify as a licensed optometrist or ophthalmologist."[34] For this reason, although "the legislature can regulate the artisan, the merchant, or the professional where the regulated services embrace issues of public health and welfare, the services under consideration bear no real or rational relation to the actual vision of the public."[35]

After all, to make use of this service, a consumer must already have a pair of eyeglasses made according to a prescription from an ophthalmologist or optometrist. "The evidence establishes beyond controversy," wrote the court, "that a skilled artisan (such as an optician) can accurately ascertain the power of a lens, or fragment thereof, without the aid of a written prescription, and can thus duplicate or reproduce the original pair of spectacles without adversely affecting the visual ability of the eyeglass-wearing public."[36] This process "requires no unusual professional judgment, peculiar to the licensed professions of ophthalmology and optometry but is strictly artisan in character."[37]

My favorite part of the opinion is the panel's discussion of the "mechanical device known as the lensometer," a device that "scientifically measures the power of the existing lens and reduces it to prescriptive terms."[38] The panel found that the "operation of the lensometer does not rise to the need or dignity of exclusive professional supervision."[39] It heard testimony from a witness who demonstrated "that any reasonably intelligent person can be taught to operate the lensometer and become qualified to accurately learn the power of existing lenses, or fragments thereof, within several hours."

The evidence also showed that ophthalmologists usually do not require a patient to return to check the accuracy with which the original prescription has been filled. But when they do, "the lensometer is not operated by the physician but by a clerk in the office,"[40] just like at Lee Optical.

As a result of this evidence, the panel concluded that it "is absolutely unnecessary to delegate to professional men the control of and responsibility for the just-mentioned artisan tasks, where the opticians, as a group, possess adequate skill to fully protect the vision of the public in accurately duplicating existing lenses."[41] Therefore, it held that although "on this precise issue of duplication, the legislature in the instant regulation was dealing with a matter of public interest, the particular means chosen are neither reasonably necessary nor reasonably related to the end sought to be achieved."[42]

For these reasons, the "legislature has been guilty of undue oppression in failing to set up qualifying standards for the opticians, if such standards be necessary for the public protection," and at the same time it "arbitrarily" legislated the skilled opticians "out of a long recognized trade, by delegating the sole control of their skills and business to a professional group, when the public can be completely protected without taking from the optician this valuable property right."[43]

Having assessed the rationality and arbitrariness of the statute, the panel alluded in passing to the economic protectionism that no doubt had improperly motivated its enactment. In a footnote, the court noted that the effect of the restriction "is to place within the exclusive control of optometrists and ophthalmologists the power to choose just what individual opticians will be permitted to pursue their calling."[44] The "ophthalmologists will pointedly refer their business to a limited number of channels, thus denying all other opticians the opportunity to follow their trade regardless how competently the remaining opticians are qualified."[45]

Of course, this, and not the health and safety of the public, was the true motive for this restriction on liberty, as is the case for many economic regulations. But the requirement of a rationality review for means-ends fit avoided the need for the court to inquire directly into legislative motive.

Still, as with the segregation of streetcars in *Plessy v. Ferguson*, the regulation of labor contracts in *Bailey v. Alabama*, or the exclusionary zoning in *Buchanan v. Warley*, it is useful for the courts to at least be cognizant of what may lie behind an assertion of public interest. And the background here, as in these other cases, was discrimination. True, it was discrimination against opticians rather than against blacks. But opticians are persons, too, and their liberty may not be arbitrarily restrained.

So the panel was completely warranted to emphasize the discriminatory nature of this scheme. The "rule is clear that where the police power is ushered into play it must be exercised in an undiscriminating manner in relation to all persons falling within the same class or circumstance."[46] But here, "not only is the 'relation to the object of the legislation' questionable . . . but 'all persons similarly circumstanced' pointedly have not been treated alike."[47]

For this reason, we can see that laws that arbitrarily restrict the liberties of women or minorities would also fall under this approach to the due process of law, without any need for the express protection of these groups in, say, an "Equal Rights Amendment" to the Constitution. Unlike the Supreme Court in *Bradwell* and *Plessy*, which merely deferred to the legislature's exercise of discretion, a court must critically examine when one group is being treated differently from another to determine whether such differential treatment is warranted by the facts.

Note that the panel spent no time discussing the origin, scope, or fundamentality of the right at issue, as modern "substantive due process" doctrine requires. Indeed, the court never even specifically identified the right in question other than a passing reference to "a long recognized trade" and its characterization of the "skills and business" of the optician as a "valuable property right."[48] Given that the opticians were not acting wrongfully, the issue was not *whether* their liberty can reasonably be regulated, but *how*. Analyzing the right does none of the work in assessing the rationality of the restriction.

Nor did the court need to identify opticians as a "suspect class" deserving of enhanced protection. It was enough that opticians were citizens of the United States. Indeed, under the Due Process Clause it was enough that they were "persons."

Instead of identifying and defining the precise right being infringed, having adopted a presumption in the legislature's favor, the panel focused carefully on the practical operation of the statute to see if its discrimination against opticians was warranted. In this way, the court simply followed the New Deal Supreme

Court's injunction in *Carolene Products* that "no pronouncement of a legislature can forestall attack upon the constitutionality of the prohibition which it enacts by applying opprobrious epithets to the prohibited act,"[49] and that "a statute *would deny due process* which precluded the disproof in judicial proceedings of all facts which would show or tend to show that a statute depriving the suitor of life, liberty, or property had a rational basis."[50]

Then the Warren Court reversed.

The Formalist Hypothetical "Rational Basis" Scrutiny

By reversing the panel, the Warren Court for the first time repudiated the traditional conception of "the due process of law" that even the New Deal Court had reaffirmed. Justice Douglas's approach is easy to characterize. In place of the opportunity to present evidence showing that a particular restriction was irrational or arbitrary, legislation would now be upheld if the justices themselves could conceive of *any* hypothetical reason why the legislature *might* have enacted the restriction. Unless an exception applied, the Court would now implement the Democratic Constitution's deference to majoritarian rule, in the extreme form that had been urged by Thayer and Holmes.

Justice Douglas repeatedly made this clear. Although "in many cases the optician can easily supply the new frames or new lenses without reference to the old written prescription," the "legislature *might* have concluded that the frequency of occasions when a prescription is necessary was sufficient to justify this regulation of the fitting of eyeglasses."[51] Likewise, "when it is necessary to duplicate a lens, a written prescription may or may not be necessary. But the legislature *might* have concluded that one was needed often enough to require one in every case."[52] Or "the legislature *may* have concluded that eye examinations were so critical, not only for correction of vision but also for detection of latent ailments or diseases, that every change in frames and every duplication of a lens should be accompanied by a prescription from a medical expert."[53]

Justice Douglas conceded that "the present law does not require a new examination of the eyes every time the frames are changed or the lenses duplicated. For if the old prescription is on file with the optician, he can go ahead and make the new fitting or duplicate the lenses."[54] But to this he replied in what have now become canonical words, "*the law need not be in every respect logically consistent with its aims to be constitutional.* It is enough that there is an evil at hand for correction, and that it *might be thought* that the particular legislative measure was a rational way to correct it."[55]

Traditionally, a law that was not "logically consistent with its aims" was literally irrational and therefore unconstitutional. Now it was perfectly constitutional. In this way were courts deprived of the means by which they could assess whether a statute was within the just powers of a legislature to enact, and do so without needing to carefully identify and circumscribe a "fundamental right." Gone now was an enforceable requirement that a law be "rational."

Whereas the lower court looked to the unequal treatment of opticians as compared with ophthalmologists and optometrists, Justice Douglas did away with such scrutiny with more hypothetical justifications: "Evils in the same field may be of different dimensions and proportions, requiring different remedies. *Or so the legislature may think.*"[56] When it comes to the equal protection of the law, in a much-cited passage he insisted that reforms "may take one step at a time, addressing itself to the phase of the problem which seems most acute to the legislative mind. The legislature *may select one phase of one field and apply a remedy there, neglecting the others.*"[57]

Traditionally, treating similarly situated persons differently was the epitome of an arbitrary law. Now the differential treatment of one group as compared with another—a realistic tip-off that laws are rent-seeking and not serving the public interest—is to be disregarded. "The prohibition of the Equal Protection Clause," wrote Justice Douglas, "goes no further than the invidious discrimination."[58] Gone now was an enforceable requirement that a law not be "arbitrary."

In *Williamson v. Lee Optical*, the Court finally adopted the formalist approach that had long before been urged by Justice Holmes in his *Lochner* dissent, but that even Justice Brandeis in *O'Gorman* had not gone so far as to hold. Restrictions on liberty would now be upheld as long as a judge can imagine a possible reason why it *might* have been adopted. Never mind whether it was the actual reason, or whether the restriction on liberty could be shown to be irrational or arbitrary. The "presumption of constitutionality" would no longer be a true presumption that was rebuttable, but would henceforth be a rule of law irrebuttably favoring the servants of the people over their sovereign masters.

Whose Burden of Proof?

In *Restoring the Lost Constitution*, I proposed reversing the presumption of constitutionality in favor of a "presumption of liberty" that would place the burden on the government to justify its restriction of liberty. But the lower court opinions in the *Lee Optical* and *Milnot* cases show that who bears the formal burden of proof may be less important for preserving the sovereignty of the people than that courts *realistically* assess the rationality and arbitrariness of laws, even if the legislature is given the benefit of the doubt. While the burden of proof matters, what matters more is that an individual citizen or company be allowed to meet any burden of proof that may be imposed upon a challenger to a law.

Still, the individual conception of popular sovereignty

underlying our Republican Constitution supports a presumption in favor of the people. Not only does the Ninth Amendment say that the "rights . . . retained by the people" not be "denied *or disparaged*" by, for example, privileging certain liberties but not others, but the Tenth Amendment reserves "to the people" all powers not delegated to the federal or state governments. Both these textual affirmations of individual popular sovereignty suggest that it is "the people" as individuals who, as sovereigns, merit the benefit of the doubt when challenging the acts of their servants or agents.

The traditional approach to the due process of law differs from modern "substantive due process" and equal protection doctrines in important ways. The traditional approach protected all rightful exercises of liberty by everyone alike by examining the rationality and arbitrariness of a restriction on liberty. Modern due process and equal protection doctrine empowers judges to selectively identify "fundamental rights" or "suspect classes" of persons deserving of special protection.[59]

Ironically, "fundamental rights" in practice get judicial protection only when they are sufficiently popular, and "suspect classes" are recognized only when they become politically influential. In contrast, under the traditional approach to due process, a lower court judge can find any restriction of liberty to be unconstitutional if it is irrational or arbitrary without the need for the Supreme Court to bless a right as fundamental or decide that an identifiable group merits heightened protection.

Recall *Buchanan v. Warley*, in which racial exclusionary zoning was invalidated years before blacks were considered "worthy" of special legal protection. In this way, the separation of powers with its independent judiciary automatically protects the rights and liberties of "fellow citizens and joint sovereigns"—whether the rights of a majority are being restricted to benefit a privileged group, or the rights of a minority are being restricted at the behest of the majority.

∾

We can now see how the individual conception of popular sovereignty that underlies our Republican Constitution requires a skeptical judiciary to secure the liberties of the people. Because the people are sovereign, in the absence of their express consent there must be assurance that laws restricting their liberties are within the power of a legislature to enact. Laws that irrationally or arbitrarily restrict the rights retained by the people are not within the legislative power because no rational person can be presumed to have consented to their liberty being irrationally or arbitrarily restricted.

Legislators cannot be the judges in their own case when a citizen claims that a law restricting his or her liberty is irrational or arbitrary. The "due process of law" affords each person the opportunity to contest a deprivation of his or her life, liberty, or property as irrational or arbitrary before an independent tribunal of justice.

This is not the same as modern "substantive due process," which requires judges to identify certain preferred freedoms as fundamental, and then subject laws restricting these rights to so strict a scrutiny as to bar any reasonable regulation of their exercise. Nor is this the same as modern equal protection analysis that only protects groups that have become politically acceptable enough to demand special protections.

In sum, being able to challenge any restriction on the liberties of the people as irrational or arbitrary before an independent and impartial judge is a vital structural means to secure the sovereignty of the people, each and every one.

REDEEMING OUR REPUBLICAN CONSTITUTION

OUR REPUBLICAN CONSTITUTION is grounded on a profound and radical idea that was born in the American Revolution and matured in the great national struggle over slavery: that government is instituted by the people as individuals, that presidents and congressmen are the servants of the people as individuals, and that the just powers of government must protect the rights of each and every person.

Just as the Federalists organized to create our Republican Constitution and opponents of slavery organized the Republican Party, which improved it, we can today organize to redeem its original promise. That task may seem daunting. Partisans of the Democratic Constitution have won many victories, which they claim now to be irreversible.

- For the sake of their Democratic Constitution, the Supreme Court crippled the Reconstruction Amendments—the guarantees of liberty in the Thirteenth, Fourteenth, and Fifteenth Amendments.
- In the name of their Democratic Constitution, they adopted the Sixteenth and Seventeenth Amendments, which formally amended the text to weaken our federalist structure by providing for a power in Congress to impose an income tax—enabling it to bribe and extort each state to do its bidding with the money taken from its own taxpayers—and for the direct

election of senators, depriving state legislatures of a check on federal power.

- In the name of their Democratic Constitution, the New Deal Court overrode the scheme of limited and enumerated powers designed by the framers as a bulwark against an all-powerful national government.
- In the name of their Democratic Constitution, Congress and the president have time and time again violated the separation of powers and sabotaged the checks and balances that were designed to prevent tyranny—the concentration of legislative, executive, and judicial power in a single individual or institution.
- In the name of their Democratic Constitution, they have developed constitutional doctrines and presumptions that deny and disparage the rights retained by sovereign people.

Although this book has shown how Democrats and progressives took the lead in each of these developments, over the years many Republicans and conservatives have joined them in supporting the Democratic Constitution. Because their victories have been enshrined in the text of the Constitution and decisions of the Supreme Court—and are bipartisan to a significant degree—the restoration of our Republican Constitution will not be easy.

Not easy, but not impossible.

The visibility of our Obamacare challenge, and the way a Republican-nominated, conservative chief justice snatched defeat from the jaws of victory, may prove to be a political inflection point. More people are now open to the tenets of our Republican Constitution than have been in generations.

- There is a growing interest in reviving and renewing our Republican Constitution's commitment to the sovereignty of the people, considered as individuals.

- There is an increasing acceptance of the need to protect the liberties of the people by holding the federal government to its enumerated powers, thereby allowing federalism to provide a diversity of approaches to economic and social issues.
- There is an increasing appreciation of the need for a separation of powers to reduce the dangers of an increasingly powerful executive branch, which Congress has bestowed with the same sorts of prerogative powers that were possessed by the king of England.

Last to develop has been the recognition that an independent, engaged judiciary is needed to ensure that the structural constraints of our Republican Constitution are honored by the Congress and the president, as well as by the states. Increasingly, people are recognizing that

- under the separation of powers, judges too are servants of the people;
- as our servants, their most important responsibility is assessing the constitutionality of measures enacted by the more "popular" branches;
- no longer should the servants or agents of the people who are designated "legislators" be the exclusive judge of the scope of their own powers.

But how do we get a judiciary who will be more fully committed to these tenets of the Republican Constitution?

What Do We Do Now?

Overcoming the Democratic Constitution will not be easy, but because our Republican Constitution is in writing, there is still hope. Here are three things we need to revive it:

A Republican Narrative: Remembering Our Constitutional Heritage

The first thing we need to revive our Republican Constitution is to remember our constitutional heritage. This, frankly, is the principal purpose of this book. As we have seen, the story begins with the origins of our Republican Constitution on the day the country was founded, July 4, 1776, and in the swirl of events that led to the Constitutional Convention in Philadelphia in 1787.

- The Declaration of Independence concisely stated the republican premise on which the Constitution was based: *first come rights and then comes government*, and it is "to secure these rights" that governments are instituted among men.
- Eleven years later, to provide for "a more perfect union," the Philadelphia convention superseded the democratic forms of government then existing in the states by crafting an entirely new republican form of government to protect the sovereignty of We the People.
- To better secure the natural rights of the sovereign people, the power of the national government was limited to those "herein granted" in the written Constitution.
- Then, at the national level, power was divided further into three separate and coequal branches of government, each of which was to check and balance the others.
- Lawmaking power was to be separate from its enforcement, and an independent judiciary was empowered to ensure that all three branches played by the rules laid down in our Republican Constitution.

Unfortunately, the new Republican Constitution was incomplete. Eventually a new Republican Party arose to amend our Republican Constitution in significant ways.

- They began by enacting the Thirteenth Amendment, which eliminated the power of states to sanction the right of some to own the labor of another, and adding an enumerated power of Congress to end the practice within the states.
- After their Thirteenth Amendment proved inadequate to restore the freedmen to equal citizenship, their Fourteenth Amendment would protect the privileges and immunities of U.S. citizens by the legislative, judicial, and executive branches of their own states.
- Then, when its incentives for black suffrage proved inadequate to ensure black suffrage, the Republicans drafted and secured the ratification of the Fifteenth Amendment to ensure the rights of blacks to vote.

Together, these Republican-sponsored amendments, enacted over vociferous Democratic opposition, went a long way toward completing our Constitution. But the Twentieth Amendment protecting the right of women to vote was also needed. So too was judicial engagement by the Supreme Court in cases like *Bailey v. Alabama*, *Buchanan v. Warley*, and *Brown v. Board of Education* to see that these provisions of our Republican Constitution were finally enforced.

But, while it is essential, remembering our Republican Constitution is not enough. To get an engaged judiciary who will enforce it, we also need a republican politics.

A Republican Politics: Restoring a "Constitutional Republican" Party

For better or worse, our Republican Constitution provides that the process of selecting judges will be a political one. An elected president nominates judges, and an elected Senate confirms them. It was Democratic and Republican presidents such as Wilson,

Hoover, and the two Roosevelts who, together with the Senate, eventually gave us a Supreme Court committed to their Democratic Constitution. And it was Reagan and the two Bushes who gave us judges who were open to, if not restoring some semblance of the Republican Constitution, then at least arresting the progressive assault upon it. Yet most Republican-nominated judges remain a part of the post–New Deal consensus that the only legitimate constitution is a Democratic Constitution. And in this belief they are well within the mainstream of public opinion.

When it was founded, the Republican Party was also a constitutionalist party. That was why, even after all the slaves had been emancipated by war, they believed they needed to amend the Constitution, to ensure that the institution of slavery was finally abolished and that Congress was empowered to enforce this abolition. From its inception until the rise of progressivism, the Republicans were fastidious about adhering to our Republican Constitution's limits on federal power. They were gravely disappointed when the Supreme Court—dominated by justices nominated by Republican presidents—gutted their handiwork.

Our Republican Constitution will not be restored in our two-party system until one of the two major political parties embraces it as a central plank of its political platform. The natural home of the Republican Constitution is the modern Republican Party, the antecedent of which was responsible for completing the work that the founders only imperfectly began. This is not yet the Republican Party of today, though constituencies within the party have a passionate interest in what is called "constitutional conservatism," but which could also be called "constitutional republicanism."[1]

A Republican Party armed with an awareness of its noble republican history and how a Republican Constitution is the solution to the "majoritarian difficulty" can be the political agent of constitutional renewal. This will require that candidates for office are able to articulate the case for our Republican Constitution just as Teddy Roosevelt, Wilson, and FDR were able to do for their Democratic Constitution. Then the electorate will be faced with a true choice, rather than an echo of the Democratic Party.

Imagine if a Republican president described the Declaration of Independence this way:

> About the Declaration there is a finality that is exceedingly restful. It is often asserted that the world has made a great deal of progress since 1776, that we have had new thoughts and new experiences which have given us a great advance over the people of that day, and that we may therefore very well discard their conclusions for something more modern. But that reasoning can not be applied to this great charter. If all men are created equal, that is final. If they are endowed with inalienable rights, that is final. If governments derive their just powers from the consent of the governed, that is final. No advance, no progress can be made beyond these propositions. If anyone wishes to deny their truth or their soundness, the only direction in which he can proceed historically is not forward, but backward toward the time when there was no equality, no rights of the individual, no rule of the people. Those who wish to proceed in that direction can not lay claim to progress. They are reactionary. Their ideas are not more modern, but more ancient, than those of the Revolutionary fathers. . . .
>
> We live in an age of science and of abounding accumulation of material things. These did not create our Declaration. Our Declaration created them.[2]

Of course, this speech is not hypothetical. It was part of an address by Republican president Calvin Coolidge to commemorate the 150th anniversary of the Declaration. In it, he not-so-subtly responded to the progressives all around him, including those in his own party. We need a Republican Party that can say this, understand this, and truly believe this once again—and, if not the existing Republican Party, then a new one to replace it.

Until such a stance is taken by one of the two major parties, however, it will be impossible for the electoral process to produce the conditions needed to restore the judiciary as the guardians of the sovereignty of the people, each and every one. But even a judiciary committed to republican principles is not enough.

Republican Constitutional Amendments: State Legislatures Can Adopt a Bill of Federalism

Just as the newly formed Republican Party needed to complete the Constitution with constitutional amendments, so too do we need to amend the Constitution to restore and reinforce its original structural protections of the sovereignty of the people. Under Article V of the Constitution, state legislatures have the power to apply to Congress to "call a convention to propose amendments" to the Constitution.

Such amendments would not be necessary if we were just to follow the original Constitution as it has been amended. But amendments can be useful to reverse the Supreme Court's precedents that have gutted the enumerated power scheme, the separation of powers, and the textual safeguards for abuse of federal and state legislative power. Structural amendments can also obviate the courts, which are currently loaded with judges who ignore the original meaning of our Republican Constitution. They can also provide for a more perfect union by better implementing the tenets of our Republican Constitution. After all, in the long run, the existing Constitution was insufficient to prevent its own effective demise. It could use some bolstering.

To this end, I have proposed a Bill of Federalism consisting of ten new amendments that would undo the damage done both by judicial decisions as well as by the Sixteenth and Seventeenth Amendments, while addressing some other problems the founders did not anticipate or adequately address. In formulating the Bill of Federalism, I largely sought structural provisions that are self-enforcing, rather than substantive ones that require judicial enforcement (although it also instructs the courts that they are to adhere to the original meaning of the Constitution). For example, I propose

- establishing term limits for members of Congress, which the Founders decided against adding;
- repealing the income tax amendment (while empowering Congress to adopt a uniform consumption tax);
- replacing the now-defunct power of state legislatures to select senators with a new state check on federal power by giving a majority of state legislatures representing a majority of the population the power to repeal any federal law or regulation.[3]

I intended these proposals to provide the starting point for a discussion of what changes need to be made to the text of the Constitution to restore its original meaning and to address problems that have arisen since its enactment. We need not wait until Congress proposes such amendments to the states for ratification. Under Article V, "on the application of the legislatures of two thirds of the several states," Congress "*shall* call a convention for proposing amendments" to the Constitution.

The founders gave state legislatures this power precisely to preserve our Republican Constitution from abuses by the federal government. It was added to the Constitution in the waning days of the Philadelphia convention at the behest of George Mason to ensure that Congress alone did not have the power to propose amendments to the Constitution.

Responding to a draft that confined the power to propose amendments to Congress, James Madison reported Mason to have objected that such an amendment procedure would be "exceptional & dangerous" because "no amendments of the proper kind would ever be obtained by the people, *if the Government should become oppressive,* as he verily believed would be the case."[4] In response to Mason's concern, the states were given a concurrent power to propose amendments via a convention of the states.

Such a convention is not a "constitutional convention," but is more properly called an "amendments convention." It is a convention of the states, and subject to the rules established for its operation by the states themselves. There was a long history of such conventions in the United States before the Constitution, of which the framers were well aware when they inserted this express power of state legislatures.[5] And such conventions were almost always limited to specified subjects.[6]

The ultimate check on the power of a convention of the states is that the Constitution limits it to "proposing amendments." Whatever it proposes must then be ratified by the legislatures of three-quarters of the states, just like an amendment proposed by Congress. This means that one house in a mere thirteen states can block the ratification of any amendment proposed by a convention of the states. Such an assembly would provide the deliberation needed to craft a package of reforms that can obtain the approval of thirty-eight state legislatures.

As Mark Levin has concluded, the fact that three-quarters of the states must ratify any proposal emerging from an amendments convention "should extinguish anxiety that the state convention process could hijack the Constitution."[7] He views this process as essential to restoring "constitutional republicanism."[8] After all, the very same men who gave us our Republican Constitution gave us this means of defending it:

> The Framers anticipated this day might arrive, for they knew republics deteriorate at first from within. They provided

a lawful and civil way to repair what has transpired. We, the people, through our state legislatures—and the state legislatures, acting collectively—have enormous power to constrain the federal government, and secure individual sovereignty.[9]

REDEEMING OUR REPUBLICAN CONSTITUTION

Our Republican Constitution remains the law of the land, and its text has not been repealed. Proponents of a Democratic Constitution have never gathered enough political support to formally amend its fundamental guarantees of individual popular sovereignty, which are written in plain words in the text. Instead, they have adopted ingenious and insidious "interpretations" that render whole passages of our Republican Constitution inoperative.

Restoration of our Republican Constitution can be accomplished if a critical mass of We the People demand that our servants, in the halls of Congress and the offices of the executive, adhere to one simple principle: respect the original meaning of the constitutional text. The only "living constitution" is one that is followed; a constitution whose text is ignored is a dead one. Every justice appointed to the Supreme Court must publicly commit to the principle that judges have no power to amend or modify the Constitution of the United States by "interpretation."

Then, to reverse previous judicial decisions that have crippled our Republican Constitution, the legislatures of thirty-four states have the constitutional power under Article V to demand that Congress convene a convention of the states to amend the text of the Constitution in ways that cannot be evaded. This means favoring structural constraints that do not require judicial enforcement to operate effectively.

Only by recognizing the difference between our Republican Constitution and their Democratic Constitution can we ever hope to recapture the benefits of the principles and insights that distinguish the American form of constitutionalism from that of other countries. These include the principle that first come the rights of the people as individuals, and only then comes government as their servant. And the insight that the will of the majority is not the solution to the problem of constitutional legitimacy but is the problem a republican form of government is needed to solve.

For only a Republican Constitution like ours can, if followed, secure the liberty and sovereignty of We the People—each and every one.

ACKNOWLEDGMENTS

IN A BOOK that is the culmination of years of writing and speaking on the Constitution, it is impossible to credit all the persons who have helped me formulate the views I express here. But if I had to credit a single person with stimulating the thesis presented in this book, it would be my old friend Sandy Levinson. In the fall of 2012, he visited my Georgetown law seminar, Recent Books on the Constitution, to discuss his book, *Our Undemocratic Constitution: Where the Constitution Goes Wrong (and How We the People Can Correct It)*. In his book, Sandy comprehensively chronicled all the ways that the U.S. Constitution was "undemocratic." He objected to the electoral college and the various choke points in the legislative process, especially the presidential veto, pardon power, and life tenure for unelected federal judges. He was positively indignant about the equal representation in the Senate that the Constitution affords every state regardless of population, and also strongly objected to the fact that incompetent and unpopular presidents get to serve out their terms rather than being replaced (as in parliamentary systems) by their own party when public opinion turns.

When in the summer of 2013 I was asked to review Sandy's book for the *Claremont Review of Books*—to whom I am also grateful—the seed of *Our Republican Constitution* was born. There I wrote:

> In the founders' republican form of government, the people retain their sovereignty through numerous checks on

government power but do not themselves rule day to day. The founders' concern was somehow to empower an "energetic" government to advance the general welfare while preventing it from violating the rights of the majority or a minority, or even the rights of a single individual. So if democracy equals simple majority rule, as it did for the founders, then the Constitution is not only undemocratic, it is downright antidemocratic.

From there it was a short step to the realization that, with their new "undemocratic constitution," the founders had altered the very meaning of "republican." Sandy also provided very helpful feedback on an earlier draft of the book, when I presented the idea at Harvard Law School.

The other major contributor to my thesis was my dear friend Larry Solum. For it was he who admonished me to read *Chisholm v. Georgia*, which first exposed me to the individual conception of popular sovereignty that is at the core of this book. And he was, as always, an invaluable sounding board for all these ideas throughout their formative stages. I am also grateful to my friend Jack Balkin for his comments on an earlier draft at a talk I gave at Yale Law School. And I appreciate the feedback on the manuscript I received from the Georgetown Law students in my Recent Books seminar. The students at Georgetown Law make being a professor there so rewarding.

My editor, Adam Bellow, offered invaluable suggestions for how to make an earlier draft more accessible. As a result of his comments, the book was thoroughly revised and reorganized in ways that greatly improved it. I thank Alexa Gervasi for her research as well as her skillful edits of previous drafts. I am grateful as well for the summer and sabbatical research support provided by Georgetown Law and my dean, William Treanor, with additional support provided by Scott Banister.

Finally, I thank my loving wife, Beth, for her patience and encouragement as I wrote.

This book is dedicated to the memory of the man who had the greatest influence on my political convictions: my father and personal hero, Ronald Evan Barnett—who was a true "republican" as I am defining the term. Throughout its writing he was caught in the horrible downward spiral of Alzheimer's, and he was never far from my mind as I wrote, as he is in my thoughts now as I write this. I miss him dearly, but know he would proudly and justly have considered this book a part of his legacy as well as mine.

NOTES

INTRODUCTION: TRIUMPH AND TRAGEDY

1. Also in the group was a young lawyer named Josh Blackman, who went on to become a law professor and author of the definitive account of the Obamacare challenges. See Josh Blackman, *Unprecedented: The Constitutional Challenge to Obamacare* (New York: PublicAffairs, 2013).
2. *The Arena*, September 18, 2009, available at http://www.politico.com/arena/archive/healthcare-reform-constitutionality.html.
3. Ibid.
4. Congressional Budget Office, "The Budgetary Treatment of an Individual Mandate to Buy Health Insurance" (1994) (emphasis added), available at http://www.cbo.gov/ftpdocs/48xx/doc4816/doc38.pdf.
5. Randy E. Barnett, Nathaniel Stewart, and Todd F. Gaziano, "Why the Personal Mandate to Buy Health Insurance Is Unprecedented and Unconstitutional," Heritage Society Legal Memorandum #49, December 9, 2009, available at http://www.heritage.org/research/reports/2009/12/why-the-personal-mandate-to-buy-health-insurance-is-unprecedented-and-unconstitutional#_ftn1.
6. See Trevor Burrus, ed., *A Conspiracy Against Obamacare: The Volokh Conspiracy and the Health Care Case* (New York: Palgrave Macmillan, 2013).
7. National Federation of Independent Business v. Sebelius, 132 S. Ct. 2566, at 2608 (opinion of Roberts, C.J.).
8. *Id.* at 2587.
9. *Id.* at 2592.
10. *Id.* at 2588 (citations omitted).
11. *Id.* at 2589 (emphasis added). *Accord* Barnett, at 583 ("A newfound congressional power to impose economic mandates to facilitate the regulation of interstate commerce would *fundamentally alter the relationship of citizen and state* by unconstitutionally commandeering the people" [emphasis added]).
12. See *NFIB*, 132 S. Ct. at 2607 (opinion of Roberts, C.J.). ("[W]e determine . . . that §1396c is unconstitutional when applied to withdraw existing Medicaid funds from States that decline to comply with the expansion.")

13. Adam Aigner-Treworgy, "President Obama: Overturning Individual Mandate Would Be 'Unprecedented, Extraordinary Step,'" CNN, April 2, 2012, http://whitehouse.blogs.cnn.com/2012/04/02/president-obama-overturning-individual-mandate-would-be-unprecedented-extraordinary-step/.

14. Randy E. Barnett, "The Disdain Campaign: Responding to Pamela S. Karlan, *Democracy and Disdain*," *Harvard Law Review Forum* 126 (2012): 1.

15. Jeffrey Rosen, "Second Opinions: Obamacare Isn't the Only Target of Conservative Judges," *New Republic*, May 4, 2012.

16. Bill Mears, "Leahy Urges High Court to 'Do the Right Thing,' Keep Health Care Law," CNN, May 15, 2012.

17. See Jan Crawford, "Roberts Switched Views to Uphold Health Care Law," CBS News, July 1, 2012, http://www.cbsnews.com/8301-3460_162-57464549/roberts-switchedviews-to-uphold-health-care-law/.

18. *NFIB*, 132 S. Ct. at 2594 (emphasis added).

19. *Id.* at 2566.

20. *Id.* at 2579–80.

21. *Id.* at 2579.

22. Alexander Bickel, *The Least Dangerous Branch: The Supreme Court at the Bar of Politics* (Indianapolis: Bobbs-Merrill, 1962), 16.

23. See Sanford Levinson, *Our Undemocratic Constitution: Where the Constitution Goes Wrong (and How We the People Can Correct It)* (New York: Oxford University Press, 2008).

24. See Randy E. Barnett, "Constitutional Conventions," *Claremont Review of Books* 7 (Summer 2007), http://www.claremont.org/crb/article/constitutional-conventions/.

25. James Madison, *Notes of Debates in the Federal Convention of 1787* (New York: Norton, 1987), 42 (statement of E. Randolph).

26. Ibid. (emphasis added).

27. Ibid., 39 (statement of R. Sherman, advocating that House members be chosen by state legislatures) (emphasis added).

28. Madison *Notes of Debates*, 233 (statement of G. Morris).

29. Ibid., 39 (statement of G. Mason) (emphasis added).

30. Richard Beeman, *Plain Honest Men: The Making of the American Constitution* (New York: Random House, 2009), xi.

31. Ibid., 122.

CHAPTER 1: "TO SECURE THESE RIGHTS"

1. From the congressional vote of June 11, 1776, in Pauline Meier, *American Scripture: Making the Declaration of Independence* (New York: Vintage Press, 1977), 126.

2. Ibid.

3. For a detailed examination of the drafting of the Declaration, see ibid., 97–153.

4. Ibid., 104.

5. See Committee Approved Draft of Virginia Declaration of Rights (May 27, 1776), http://www.gunstonhall.org/georgemason/human_rights/vdr_first_draft.html.

6. Ibid. (emphasis added).

7. For another account of the centrality of the Declaration to the political and legal theory that underlies the Constitution, see Timothy Sandefur, *The Conscience of the Constitution: The Declaration of Independence and the Right to Liberty* (Washington, DC: Cato Institute, 2014).

8. Barry Alan Shain, ed., "Diary Entry by Silas Deane (October 3, 1774)," in *The Declaration of Independence in Historical Context: American State Papers, Petitions, Proclamations, and Letters of the Delegates to the First National Congresses* (New Haven, CT: Yale University Press, 2014), 244.

9. Elizur Goodrich, "The Principles of Civil Union and Happiness Considered and Recommended: A Sermon (1787)," reprinted in *Political Sermons of the American Founding Era: 1730–1805,* ed. Ellis Sandoz (Indianapolis: Liberty Press, 1991), 911, 914–15.

10. Ibid., 914.

11. Ibid.

12. Ibid., 914–15.

13. Ibid., 915 (emphasis added).

14. Ibid.

15. Randy E. Barnett, *The Structure of Liberty: Justice and the Rule of Law,* 2nd. ed. (New York: Oxford University Press, 2014), 77–82.

16. Avalon Project at Yale Law School, "Declaration and Resolves of the First Continental Congress, October 14, 1774," Documents Illustrative of the Formation of the Union of the American States, http://avalon.law.yale.edu/18th_century/resolves.asp (accessed September 11, 2014).

17. Ibid. (emphasis added).

18. John Locke, *Two Treatises of Government,* ed. Peter Laslett, rev. ed. (New York: Mentor, 1965), §6, 311 (emphasis added).

19. Avalon Project at Yale Law School, "Virginia Declaration of Rights" (emphases added), http://avalon.law.yale.edu/18th_century/virginia.asp (accessed September 11, 2014).

20. William Ewald, "The Committee of Detail," *Constitutional Commentary* 28 (2012): 240.

21. Maier, *American Scripture,* 193.

22. Corfield v. Coryell, 6 F. Cas. 546, 551–552 (1823) (emphasis added).

23. Dred Scott v. Sandford, 60 U.S. 393 (1856), superseded (1868).

24. Committee Approved Draft of Virginia Declaration of Rights (May 27,

1776), http://www.gunstonhall.org/georgemason/human_rights/vdr_first_draft.html.

25. Hugo Grotius, *2 De Jure Belli ac Pacis Libri Tres*, trans. Francis W. Kelsey (Oxford: Clarendon Press, 1925), 13.

26. 3 U.S. 386, 388 (1798).

CHAPTER 2: REVISING "REPUBLICANISM"

1. Jack Rakove, "James Madison and the Constitution," http://www.gilder lehrman.org/history-by-era/creating-new-government/essays/james-madison-and-constitution.

2. Ibid.

3. Ibid.

4. James Madison, "Vices of the Political System of the United States, April 1787," in *The Papers of James Madison*, ed. William T. Hutchinson et al., vol. 1 (Chicago and London: University of Chicago Press, 1962–77), http://press-pubs.uchicago.edu/founders/documents/v1ch5s16.html (accessed September 11, 2014).

5. Ibid.

6. Ibid.

7. Ibid.

8. Ibid.

9. "Constitution of Delaware, 1776," http://avalon.law.yale.edu/18th_century/de02.asp#1; Commonwealth of Pennsylvania Constitution, 1776, Pennsylvania Archives, vol. 10, 1896, http://avalon.law.yale.edu/18th_century/de02.asp#1; "Constitution of New Jersey, 1776," http://avalon .law.yale.edu/18th_century/nj15.asp#1; "Constitution of Georgia, February 5, 1777," http://avalon.law.yale.edu/18th_century/ga02.asp; "Fundamental Orders of 1639," http://avalon.law.yale.edu/17th_century/order.asp; Oscar Handlin and Mary Handlin, eds., *The Popular Sources of Political Authority: Documents on the Massachusetts Constitution of 1780* (Cambridge, MA: Belknap Press of Harvard University Press, 1966); "Constitution of Maryland, November 11, 1776," http://avalon.law.yale .edu/17th_century/ma02.asp#1; "Constitution of South Carolina, March 19, 1778," http://avalon.law.yale.edu/18th_century/sc02.asp; "Constitution of New Hampshire, 1776," http://avalon.law.yale.edu/18th_century/nh09.asp; "Constitution of Virginia, June 29, 1776," http://www.law .gmu.edu/assets/files/academics/founders/VA-Constitution.pdf; "Constitution of New York, April 20, 1777," http://avalon.law.yale.edu/18th_century/ny01.asp; "Constitution of North Carolina, December 18, 1776," http://avalon.law.yale.edu/18th_century/nc07.asp#2; "Charter of Rhode Island and Providence Plantations, July 15, 1663," http://avalon.law.yale .edu/17th_century/ri04.asp.

10. James Madison, "Federalist #10," in *The Federalist Papers*, ed. Clinton Rossiter (New York: New American Library, 1961), 77.
11. Ibid. (emphasis added).
12. Ibid.
13. Ibid., 78.
14. Ibid., 80 (emphasis added).
15. Ibid. (emphasis added).
16. Ibid.
17. James Madison, *Notes of Debates in the Federal Convention of 1787* (New York: Norton, 1987), 39–41 (statement of E. Gerry).
18. Ibid., 39 (statement of R. Sherman, advocating that House members be chosen by state legislatures).
19. Ibid., 42 (statement of E. Randolph).
20. Ibid.
21. The central importance of Morris's role at the conference is examined in William Michael Treanor, "Gouverneur Morris's Constitution" (work in progress).
22. Madison, *Notes of Debates*, 233 (statement of G. Morris).
23. Ibid., 39 (statement of G. Mason).
24. Madison, "Federalist #10," in *The Federalist Papers*, 82 (emphasis added).
25. Ibid., 84.
26. James Madison, "Federalist #51," in *The Federalist*, ed. J. R. Pole (Indianapolis: Hackett, 2005), 282.
27. Ibid.
28. Ibid.
29. James Madison, "Federalist #45," in *The Federalist*, ed. J. R. Pole (Indianapolis: Hackett, 2005), 253.
30. Ibid.
31. Ibid.
32. Alexander Hamilton, "Federalist #78," in *The Federalist*, ed. J. R. Pole (Indianapolis: Hackett, 2005), 414.
33. Ibid. 415 (emphasis added).
34. Ibid. 414 (emphasis added).
35. Ibid. (emphasis added).
36. On the important difference between a power of judicial review and a judicial duty to follow the law, see Philip Hamburger, *Law and Judicial Duty* (Cambridge, MA: Harvard University Press, 2008).
37. Marbury v. Madison, 5 U.S. 137, 177 (1803).

CHAPTER 3: "WE THE PEOPLE" AS INDIVIDUALS

1. Randy E. Barnett, "Squaring Undisclosed Agency Law with Contract Theory," *California Law Review* 75 (1987): 1981.

2. U.S. Const. amend. IX.
3. Randy E. Barnett, "The Ninth Amendment: It Means What It Says," *Texas Law Review* 85 (2006): 1; Randy E. Barnett, "Kurt Lash's Majoritarian Difficulty: A Response to 'A Textual-Historical Theory of the Ninth Amendment,'" *Stanford Law Review* 60 (2008): 937.
4. "Roger Sherman's Draft of the Bill of Rights," in *The Rights Retained by the People*, ed. Randy E. Barnett (Fairfax, VA: George Mason University Press, 1989), 351.
5. Ibid.
6. Ibid.
7. Mass. Const. art. I (amended by art. CVI).
8. N.H. Const. art. II.
9. N.Y. Const. of 1777.
10. Pa. Const. of 1776, art. I, § 1.
11. Vt. Const. of 1777, ch. I, art. I.
12. *The Debates in the Several State Conventions, on the Adoption of the Federal Constitution, as Recommended by the General Convention at Philadelphia, in 1787*, ed. Jonathan Elliot, vol. 3 (1830), 657, http://memory.loc.gov/cgi-bin/ampage (accessed September 11, 2014).
13. *Register of Debates in Congress*, vol. 6 (Washington, DC: Gales & Seaton, 1838), 320 (emphasis added).
14. 32 U.S. 243, 250 (1833).
15. Chisholm v. Georgia, 2 U.S. 419 (1793).
16. *Id.*
17. *Id.*
18. *Id.* at 454 (Wilson, J.).
19. *Id.*
20. *Id.*
21. *Id.* at 458 (Wilson, J.) (emphasis added).
22. *Id.* at 456 (Wilson, J.).
23. *Id.* (emphasis added).
24. *Id.* at 477 (Jay, J.).
25. *Id.* at 479 (emphasis added).
26. *Id.* at 473 (emphasis added).
27. *Id.* at 448 (Iredell, J.).
28. *Calder*, 3 U.S. at 398 (Iredell, J.)
29. Lysander Spooner, *The Unconstitutionality of Slavery*, rev. ed. (1860), reprinted in *The Collected Works of Lysander Spooner*, vol. 4, ed. Charles Shively (Weston, MA: M&S Press, 1971), 225.
30. Ibid., 143 (emphasis added).
31. Locke, *Two Treatises of Government*, §131, 398 (emphasis added).
32. Edmund Randolph, "Opinion of Edmund Randolph, Attorney General of the United States, to President Washington," in *Legislative and*

Documentary History of the Bank of the United States, ed. M. St. Clair Clarke and D.A. Hall (New York, 1832), 86.

33. Ibid. (emphasis added).

34. 3 U.S. at 388 (Chase, J.)

35. *Id.*

36. *Id.* (emphases added).

37. See Randy E. Barnett, *Restoring the Lost Constitution: The Presumption of Liberty*, 2nd. ed. (Princeton, NJ: Princeton University Press, 2014), 369.

38. U.S. Const. amend. XI.

39. Bruce Ackerman, "De-Schooling Constitutional Law," *Yale Law Journal* 123 (2014): 3106.

40. Hans v. Louisiana, 134 U.S. 1, 14 (1890).

41. *Id.* at 14.

42. 10 U.S. 87 (1810). (Cranch, W.)

43. *Id.* at 139 (emphases added).

44. *Id.* (emphasis added).

45. See, e.g., Martha A. Field, "The Eleventh Amendment and Other Sovereign Immunity Doctrines: Part One," *University of Pennsylvania Law Review* 126 (1978): 515 (arguing that sovereign immunity is a common law doctrine and not constitutionally compelled); William A. Fletcher, "A Historical Interpretation of the Eleventh Amendment: A Narrow Construction of an Affirmative Grant of Jurisdiction Rather Than a Prohibition Against Jurisdiction," *Stanford Law Review* 35 (1983): 1033 (arguing that the amendment does not cover federal question or admiralty jurisdiction); John J. Gibbons, "The Eleventh Amendment and State Sovereign Immunity: A Reinterpretation," *Columbia Law Review* 83 (1983): 1889 (arguing from a historical standpoint that the amendment's passage was primarily secured as part of a bargain to enforce the peace treaty); Vicki C. Jackson, "Principle and Compromise in Constitutional Adjudication: The Eleventh Amendment and State Sovereign Immunity," *Notre Dame Law Review* 75 (2000): 1010 (arguing that "sovereign immunity is in some respects unjust" and "the Eleventh Amendment need not be understood to have endorsed that injustice as a general proposition"); James E. Pfander, "History and State Suability: An 'Explanatory' Account of the Eleventh Amendment," *Cornell Law Review* 83 (1998): 1269 (arguing that the amendment represented a compromise on fiscal policy between the states and the federal government).

CHAPTER 4: HOW SLAVERY LED
TO A MORE REPUBLICAN CONSTITUTION

1. Joseph J. Ellis, *Founding Brothers: The Revolutionary Generation* (New York: Knopf, 2002), 196.

2. Alexander Hamilton, "Opinion of Alexander Hamilton, on the

Constitutionality of a National Bank," February 23, 1794, in M. St. Clair Clarke and D. A. Hall, eds., *Legislative and Documentary History of the Bank of the United States* (1832) (New York: August M. Kelley Publishers, 1967), 98.

3. See Gerald Leonard, *The Invention of Party Politics: Federalism, Popular Sovereignty, and Constitutional Development in Jacksonian Illinois* (Chapel Hill: University of North Carolina Press, 2002).

4. Ibid., 5.

5. Ibid.

6. Gerald Leonard, "Jefferson's Constitutions," in *Constitutions and the Classics: Patterns of Constitutional Thought from John Fortescue to Jeremy Bentham*, ed. D. J. Galligan (Oxford: Oxford University Press, 2014), 369.

7. Leonard, *Invention of Party Politics*, 39.

8. George Fitzhugh, "Centralization and Socialism," *University of Michigan: Humanities Text Initiative* 20 (1985): 692.

9. Ibid.

10. Leonard, "Jefferson's Constitutions," 370.

11. William Lloyd Garrison to Rev. Samuel J. May, July 17, 1845, in *The Letters of William Lloyd Garrison*, ed. Walter M. Merrill, vol. 3 (Cambridge, MA: Harvard University Press, 1973), 303.

12. Lewis Perry, *Radical Abolitionism: Anarchy and the Government of God in Antislavery Thought* (Knoxville: University of Tennessee Press, 1995), 167.

13. James Oakes, *Freedom National: The Destruction of Slavery* (New York: Norton, 2012), 14.

14. Doris Kearns Goodwin, *Team of Rivals: The Political Genius of Abraham Lincoln* (New York: Simon & Schuster, 2005), 109.

15. Randy E. Barnett, "From Antislavery Lawyer to Chief Justice: The Forgotten Career of Salmon P. Chase," *Case Western Reserve Law Review* 63 (2013): 653–702; Frederick J. Blue, *Salmon Chase: A Life in Politics* (Kent, OH: Kent State University Press, 1987), 31–32.

16. U.S. Const. art. IV, §2.

17. See Spooner, *The Unconstitutionality of Slavery*.

18. *Speech of Salmon P. Chase, in the Case of the Colored Woman, Matilda* (Cincinnati: Pugh & Dodd, 1837), https://archive.org/details/speechofsalmon pc00chas (accessed September 11, 2014).

19. Richard H. Sewell, *Ballots for Freedom: Antislavery Politics in the United States, 1837–1860* (Oxford: Oxford University Press, 1980), viii.

20. Salmon P. Chase, *An Argument for the Defendant, Submitted to the Supreme Court of the United States, at the December Term, 1846: In the Case of Wharton Jones v. Vanzandt* (1847), 89. (In the title of this pamphlet, the defendant's name is spelled "Vanzandt," unlike the Supreme Court reporter, which spells it "Van Zandt.")

21. Ibid.

22. Ibid., 93–94.

23. Ibid., 94.
24. See In re Booth, 3 Wis. 1 (1854) (decision by Justice Smith); 3 Wis. 54 (1854) (decision by full court).
25. Ableman v. Booth, 62 U.S. 506 (1859).
26. Sewell, *Ballots for Freedom*, 300.
27. Willard Carl Klunder, *Lewis Cass and the Politics of Moderation* (Kent, OH: Kent State University Press, 1996), 267–68.
28. James Huston, *The Lincoln-Douglas Debates of 1858*, ed. Robert W. Johannsen (New York: Oxford University Press, 1965), 48.
29. Speech of the Hon. S. P. Chase, of Ohio, in the Senate, Feb. 3, 1854, "Maintained Plighted Faith," Appendix to the *Congressional Globe*, 33rd Congress, 1st Sess., 133–40.
30. Eric Foner, *Free Soil, Free Labor, Free Men: The Ideology of the Republican Party Before the Civil War* (New York: Oxford University Press, 1970), 87.
31. Oakes, *Freedom National*, 144.
32. Ibid., 386.
33. Ibid., 360.
34. 60 U.S. 393 (1856).
35. United States Department of State, "Opinion of Mr. Attorney-General Bates, Dated November 29, 1862," in *Foreign Relations of the United States, Part 2* (Washington, DC: U.S. Government Printing Office, 1873), 1370.
36. Ibid., 1371.
37. Ibid., 1372.
38. Ibid., 1370.
39. Ibid.
40. U.S. Const. amend. XIII, §2.
41. Civil Rights Act of 1866, 14 Stat. 27 (1866).
42. President Andrew Johnson, Veto of the Civil Rights Bill, March 27, 1866, http://wps.prenhall.com/wps/media/objects/107/109768/ch16_a2_d1.pdf (accessed September 11, 2014).
43. Ibid.
44. Ibid.
45. Ibid.
46. Garrett Epps, *Democracy Reborn: The Fourteenth Amendment and the Fight for Equal Rights in Post–Civil War America* (New York: Henry Holt, 2006).
47. Corfield v. Coryell, 6 F. Cas. 546, 551–552 (1823) (emphasis added).
48. *Congressional Globe*, 39th Cong., 1st Sess., 2765.
49. Ibid., 1265–66.
50. Ibid., 2765.
51. Although he accepts the importance of Howard's explanation of "privileges or immunities," Kurt Lash has claimed that because Article IV rights described in *Corfield* only protected out-of-state citizens from discrimination when residing in another state, the rights that Senator

Howard quoted from Justice Washington's opinion in *Corfield* were only to receive equal protection from discriminatory state laws. See Kurt T. Lash, *The Fourteenth Amendment and the Privileges and Immunities of American Citizenship* (New York: Cambridge University Press, 2014), 155–60. But Howard makes no such distinction in his speech. Instead, he combines both sets of rights together as an undifferentiated "mass of privileges, immunities, and rights" that are derived from the first eight amendments and from Article IV. Nor does Lash produce anyone who contemporaneously articulated his theory that the Privileges or Immunities Clause referred to two differentially enforceable classes of rights. For other problems with Lash's account, see Christopher R. Green, "Incorporation, Total Incorporation, and Nothing but Incorporation?," *William & Mary Bill of Rights Journal* 24 (2015). This is not the place to debate this highly complex issue of original meaning. However, even if Lash was correct that the protection of these civil rights is limited to nondiscrimination, my proposal in Chapter 9 that the "due process of law" requires judges to fairly adjudicate a citizen's challenge to irrational or arbitrary restrictions of liberty would still be warranted.

52. U.S. Const. amend. XIV, §2.
53. *Congressional Globe*, 30th Congress, 1st Sess. (1847, Appendix: 45), Speech of Thomas Clingman on December 22, 1847.

CHAPTER 5: LOSING OUR REPUBLICAN CONSTITUTION

1. The details of the massacre and the subsequent prosecution are taken from the excellent book by Charles Lane, *The Day That Freedom Died: The Colfax Massacre, the Supreme Court, and the Betrayal of Reconstruction* (New York: Henry Holt, 2009).
2. Stephen P. Halbrook, *Freedom, the Fourteenth Amendment, and the Right to Bear Arms, 1866–1876* (Westport, CT: Greenwood, 1998), 160.
3. Lane, *The Day That Freedom Died*, 137.
4. United States v. Cruikshank, 92 U.S. 542, 548 (1875).
5. Lane, *The Day That Freedom Died*, 204.
6. 83 U.S. 36 (1873).
7. 83 U.S. 130 (1872).
8. *Id*. at 139 (Miller, J.).
9. *Cruikshank*, 92 U.S. at 554.
10. Francisco M. Ugarte, "Reconstruction Redux: Rehnquist, Morrison, and the *Civil Rights Cases*," *Harvard Civil Rights–Civil Liberties Law Review* 40 (2006): 507.
11. *The Civil Rights Cases*, 109 U.S. 3, 35 (Harlan, J., dissenting).
12. See C. Vann Woodward, *Reunion and Reaction: The Compromise of 1877 and the End of Reconstruction* (Boston: Little, Brown, 1951), 8; Allan

Peskin, "Was There a Compromise of 1877?," *Journal of American History* 60 (1973): 63–75; C. Vann Woodward, "Yes, There Was a Compromise of 1877," *Journal of American History* 60 (1973): 215–23 (1973). One argument against the existence of a secret deal is the claim that Hayes had already promised during the campaign to withdraw the remaining federal troops and other aspects of the alleged compromise were never carried out.

13. Pamela Brandwein, *Rethinking the Judicial Settlement of Reconstruction* (New York: Cambridge University Press, 2011), 9.

14. Ibid., 184–205. See also ibid., 18. ("Scholars have gotten right the idea that the definitive abandonment of blacks followed and consolidated the Republican Party's definitive political abandonment of them. But scholars have gotten wrong the timing and vehicles of definitive abandonment.") With this talk of Republican "abandonment," it perhaps bears noting that, only because the Democrats were unremitting in their efforts to subordinate blacks, Democrats cannot be said to have abandoned them.

15. Ibid., 9.

16. Plessy v. Ferguson, 163 U.S. 537, 540–41 (1896).

17. *Id.* at 550–51.

18. *Id.*

19. *Id.* at 543.

20. *Id.* at 550–51.

21. Jennifer Roback, "The Political Economy of Segregation: The Case of Segregated Streetcars," *Journal of Economic History* 56, no. 4 (December 1986).

22. *Plessy*, 163 U.S. at 555.

23. *Id.* at 557.

24. *Id.*

25. *Id.*

26. *The Columbia Encyclopedia*, 6th ed., s.v. "progressive era."

27. Ronald Hamowy, "Preventive Medicine and the Criminalization of Sexual Immorality in Nineteenth Century America," in *Assessing the Criminal: Restitution, Retribution, and the Legal Process*, eds. Randy E. Barnett and John Hagel III (Pensacola, FL: Ballinger, 1977), 33–95.

28. See, e.g., Lochner v. New York, 198 U.S. 45 (1905).

29. James B. Thayer, "The Origin and Scope of the American Doctrine of Constitutional Law," *Harvard Law Review* 7 (1893): 129.

30. Ibid. (emphasis added).

31. Ibid.

32. Ibid., 130 (emphasis added).

33. Ibid., 131–32.

34. Ibid., 132.

35. Barnett, *Restoring the Lost Constitution*, 139.

36. Thayer, "The Origin and Scope of the American Doctrine," 136.

37. Ibid.
38. Barnett, *Restoring the Lost Constitution*, 136.
39. Thayer, "The Origin and Scope of the American Doctrine," 144 (emphasis added).
40. Ibid.
41. Ibid.
42. Ibid (emphasis added).
43. *Plessy*, 163 U.S. at 550–51 (emphasis added).
44. Thayer, "The Origin and Scope of the American Doctrine," 156.
45. *NFIB*, 132 S. Ct., at 2579.
46. *Lochner*, 198 U.S. at 76 (1905) (emphasis added).
47. *Id.*
48. Thomas Healy, *The Great Dissent: How Oliver Wendell Holmes Changed His Mind—and Changed the History of Free Speech in America* (New York: Henry Holt, 2013), 61.
49. Ibid., 60.
50. Ibid., 61–62.
51. Letter of Franklin D. Roosevelt to Oliver Wendell Holmes Jr., February 23, 1935, in Brad Snyder, *The House of Truth* (manuscript).
52. Theodore Roosevelt, "The Right of the People to Rule, March 20, 1912," in *New Outlook*, ed. Alfred Emanuel Smith and Francis Walton (New York: Outlook, 1912), 618.
53. Ibid., 619.
54. Michael A. Cohen, "Theodore Roosevelt Defines His New Nationalism Platform, Osawatomie, Kansas, August 31, 1910," in *Live from the Campaign Trail: The Greatest Campaign Speeches of the Twentieth Century and How They Shaped Modern America* (New York: Bloomsbury, 2011), 49.
55. Roosevelt, "The Right of the People to Rule," 618.
56. Ibid.
57. Ibid.
58. Ibid., 619.
59. Ibid., 620.
60. Ibid., 622.
61. Ibid.
62. Ibid., 624.
63. Ibid., 623.
64. "Roosevelt Hits at Taft Again," *New York Times*, March 21, 1912, http://query.nytimes.com/mem/archive-free/pdf?res=9801E3D9143CE633A-25752C2A9659C946396D6CF.
65. Theodore Roosevelt, "Address by Theodore Roosevelt before the National Convention of the Progressive Party in Chicago, August 6th, 1912," in *Theodore Roosevelt's Confession of Faith before the Progressive National Convention* (New York: Allied Printing, 1912).

66. Ibid., 5–6.
67. Ibid., 8.
68. W. W. Spooner et al., *National Political Parties with Their Platforms* (Syracuse, NY: Syracuse University Press, 1922), 406.
69. Donald G. Lett, *Phoenix Rising: The Rise and Fall of the American Republic* (Bloomington, IN: AuthorHouse, 2008), 81
70. Christopher Caldwell, "Schoolmaster to the World," *Claremont Review of Books* 14, no. 1 (Winter 2013–14), http://www.claremont.org/article/schoolmaster-to-the-world/#.VRGVevnF_Ro.
71. Ibid.
72. Woodrow Wilson, "From Wilson's Shorthand Diary," in *The Papers of Woodrow Wilson*, 69 vols., ed. Arthur S. Link (Princeton, NJ: Princeton University Press, 1966–93), 5:65–68.
73. Ibid.
74. A. Scott Berg, *Wilson* (New York: Penguin Group, 2013), 71.
75. Ibid., 110.
76. "Conversation, January, 1915, Mr. Trotter and Mr. Wilson," in *New Crisis* 107, no. 4 (July–August 2000): 60.
77. William M. Tuttle Jr., *Race Riot: Chicago in the Red Summer of 1919* (Urbana and Chicago: University of Illinois Press, 1996), 230.
78. William Keylor, "The Long-Forgotten Racial Attitudes and Policies of Woodrow Wilson," *Professor Voices*, March 4, 2013, http://www.bu.edu/professorvoices/2013/03/04/the-long-forgotten-racial-attitudes-and-policies-of-woodrow-wilson/.
79. "The Crisis," January 1915, 119–20, reprinted in William Loren Katz, *Eyewitness: The Negro in American History* (New York: Pitman, 1967), 389–90.
80. Letter of Oliver Wendell Holmes Jr. to Lewis Einstein, August 14, 1927, in Snyder, *The House of Truth*, 65.
81. Bailey v. State of Alabama, 219 U.S. 219, 230 (1911).
82. *Id.* at 244.
83. *Id.* at 247 (Holmes, J., dissenting).
84. *Id.* at 248.
85. *Buchanan v. Warley*, 245 U.S. 60 (1917).
86. Christopher Alan Bracey, *Saviors or Sellouts: The Promise and Peril of Black Conservatism, from Booker T. Washington to Condoleezza Rice* (Boston: Beacon Press, 2008), 36.
87. Ibid.
88. *Harris v. City of Louisville*, 177 S.W. 472, 476 (Ky. 1915).
89. David E. Bernstein and Ilya Somin, "Judicial Power and Civil Rights Reconsidered," *Yale Law Journal* 114 (2004): 591.
90. *Buchanan*, 245 U.S., 73–74.
91. *Id.* at 78.
92. *Id.*

93. *Id.* at 79.
94. *Id.*
95. *Id.* at 81.
96. Bernstein and Somin, "Judicial Power and Civil Rights Reconsidered," 629.
97. Ibid.
98. Ibid.
99. Ibid.
100. Ibid., 629–30.
101. Holmes Draft Dissent, in *Oliver Wendell Holmes Jr. Papers*, Harvard Law School, Series XX, Box 80, Folder 12.
102. Ibid.
103. Ibid.
104. Ibid.
105. Ibid.
106. Ibid.
107. Berg, *Wilson*, 240.
108. Ibid., 400.
109. 208 U.S. 412 (1908).
110. Brief for the *State of Oregon, Curt Muller, Plaintiff in Error, v. The State of Oregon, Defendant in Error*, WL 27605 *18 (U.S. January 31, 1908).
111. Ibid., 22.
112. 83 U.S. 130, 139–42 (1872) (Bradley, J., concurring).
113. *Id.* at 139 (Miller, J.).
114. *Id.* at 141 (Bradley, J., concurring).
115. *Id.*
116. *Id.* at 142 (emphasis added). See Richard L. Aynes, "*Bradwell v. Illinois*: Chief Justice Chase's Dissent and the 'Sphere of Women's Work,'" *Louisiana Law Review* 59 (1999): 520. Available at http://digitalcommons.law .lsu.edu/lalrev/vol59/iss2/7.
117. *Muller*, 208 U.S., at 421.
118. 261 U.S. 525 (1923).
119. *Id.* at 567 (Holmes, J., dissenting).
120. *Id.* at 568.
121. David M. Kennedy, "The Dilemma of Difference in Democratic Society," *Tanner Lectures on Human Values* (May 13, 2003): 642.
122. *Letter from Susan B. Anthony to Myra Bradwell* (April 28, 1873), in Jane M. Friedman, "Myra Bradwell: On Defying the Creator and Becoming a Lawyer," *Valparaiso Law Review* 28 (1994): 1287, 1300.
123. See ibid., 1301.
124. 282 U.S. 251 (1931).
125. *Id.* at 257–58.
126. *Id.* at 258.

127. Walton H. Hamilton, "The Jurist's Art," *Columbia Law Review* 31 (1931): 1073, 1074–75.

128. Walter White, *A Man Called White: The Autobiography of Walter White* (Athens: University of Georgia Press, 1995), 106.

129. Letter of Felix Frankfurter to Henry Stimson, February 9, 1932, in Snyder, *House of Truth.*

130. Snyder, *House of Truth.*

131. Letter from Willis Van Devanter to Mrs. John W. Lacey, February 29, 1932, in ibid, 4.

132. Letter from Willis Van Devanter to Frank B. Kellogg, March 10, 1932, in ibid., 2.

133. Letter of Felix Frankfurter to Herbert Hoover, February 16, 1932, in ibid., 2.

134. Joan Hoff-Wilson, *Herbert Hoover: Forgotten Progressive* (Boston: Little, Brown, 1975).

135. *New York World*, July 21, 1920, 10, in Snyder, *House of Truth*, 118.

136. Ibid.

137. Leonard Baker, "History of the Court: Depression and Rise of Legal Realism," in *The Oxford Companion to the Supreme Court of the United States*, ed. Kermit Hall, 2nd ed. (New York: Oxford University Press, 2005), 450, 452.

138. 304 U.S. 144 (1938).

139. *Id.* at 152 (emphasis added).

140. *Id.* at 153 (emphasis added).

141. *Id.* at 153–54 (emphasis added).

142. 348 U.S. 483 (1955).

143. See Geoffrey P. Miller, "The True Story of Carolene Products," *Supreme Court Review* 1987 (1987): 397.

144. Ibid., 419.

145. Ibid., 404.

146. United States v. Carolene Prods. Co., 304 U.S. 144, 152 n.4 (1938).

147. *Id.*

148. John Hart Ely, *Democracy and Distrust: A Theory of Judicial Review* (Cambridge, MA: Harvard University Press, 1980).

149. Arthur M. Schlesinger Jr., "The Supreme Court: 1947," *Fortune*, January 1947, 73.

150. Ibid.

151. Ibid., 74.

152. Ibid., 73.

153. Ibid., 76.

154. Ibid., 77.

155. Ibid., 78.

156. Ibid., 201.

157. Ibid., 75–76.
158. Ibid., 202.
159. Ibid.
160. Ibid., 204.
161. Ibid., 202.
162. Ibid., 210.
163. Ibid., 206.
164. Ibid., 208.
165. Ibid.
166. Michael W. McConnell, "The Originalist Case for *Brown v. Board of Education*," *Harvard Journal of Law and Public Policy* 19 (1995–96): 457.
167. Bickel, *The Least Dangerous Branch*, 16.
168. Ibid.
169. Madison, "Federalist #10," 78.

CHAPTER 6: WHY FEDERALISM MATTERS

1. U.S. Const. amend. IX (emphasis added).
2. U.S. Const. amend. X (emphasis added).
3. "Letter from James Madison to George Washington, December 5, 1789," in *Documentary History of the Constitution of the United States of America, 1786–1870*, vol. 5 (Washington, DC: U.S. Department of State, 1905), 221–22 (emphasis added).
4. Sanford Levinson, *Our Undemocratic Constitution: Where the Constitution Goes Wrong (and How We the People Can Correct It)* (New York: Oxford University Press, 2008) (harshly criticizing the Senate and other undemocratic elements of the Constitution, without denying these elements exist).
5. 22 U.S. 1, 203 (1824).
6. *Id.*
7. *Id.*
8. *Id.* at 203–4 (emphases added).
9. 285 U.S. 262, 311 (1932) (Brandeis, J., dissenting).
10. *Id.*
11. *Id.* at 271.
12. *Id.* at 273.
13. *Id.* at 278.
14. *Id.* (internal citations omitted).
15. *Id.* at 279.
16. *Id.* at 280.
17. *Id.* at 280.
18. F. A. Hayek, *The Fatal Conceit: The Errors of Socialism* (Chicago: University of Chicago Press, 1988).

19. Ilya Somin, *Democracy and Political Ignorance* (Stanford, CA: Stanford University Press, 2013), 119–54.

20. Clint Bolick, *Grassroots Tyranny: The Limits of Federalism* (Washington, DC: Cato Institute, 1993).

21. Michael S. Greve, *The Upside-Down Constitution* (Cambridge, MA: Harvard University Press, 2012).

22. U.S. Const. art. 1, §8 (emphasis added).

23. See Randy E. Barnett and David G. Oedel, "ObamaCare and the General Welfare Clause," *Wall Street Journal*, December 27, 2010, A17.

CHAPTER 7: PROTECTING RIGHTS BY LIMITING FEDERAL POWER

1. Declaration of Diane Monson in Support of Motion for Preliminary Injunction (October 29, 2002): 4.

2. Declaration of Angel Raich in Support of Preliminary Injunction (October 25, 2002): 1.

3. For an explanation of how and why this challenge failed, see Randy E. Barnett, "Scrutiny Land," *Michigan Law Review* 106 (2008): 1479.

4. U.S. Const. art. 1, §1 (emphasis added).

5. U.S. Const. amend. X.

6. *The Papers of James Madison*, http://press-pubs.uchicago.edu/founders/documents/v1ch14s50.html.

7. Ibid.

8. Ibid.

9. James Madison, "Speech in Congress Proposing Constitutional Amendments," June 8, 1789, in *James Madison, Writings*, ed. Jack N. Rakove (New York: Library of America, 1999), 437, 447.

10. Collins Denny Jr., "The Growth and Development of the Police Power of the State," *Michigan Law Review* 20 (1921): 173.

11. *The Records of the Federal Convention of 1787*, ed. Max Farrand, vol. 2 (New Haven, CT: Yale University Press, 1911), 21 (July 17, 1787; from resolution proposed to the convention).

12. Alexander Hamilton, "Federalist #17," in *The Federalist Papers*, ed. Clinton Rossiter (New York: New American Library, 1961), 118 ("The resolution of the mere domestic police of a State appears to me to hold out slender allurements to ambition"); Hamilton, "The Federalist #34," *The Federalist*, 309 (referring to "expenses arising from those institutions which are relative to the mere domestic police of a state").

13. 41 U.S. 539 (1842).

14. U.S. Const. art. IV, §2.

15. U.S. Const. art. IV, §1.

16. U.S. Const. art. 1, §8.

17. *Prigg*, 41 U.S. at 619 (emphasis added).

18. That this expansion relied mainly on the Necessary and Proper Clause is explained in Randy E. Barnett, "Commandeering the People: Why the Individual Health Insurance Mandate Is Unconstitutional," *New York University Journal of Law and Liberty* 5 (2010): 589–95.
19. 488 U.S. 1041 (1992).
20. 501 U.S. 452 (1991).
21. 521 U.S. 898 (1997).
22. 517 U.S. 44 (1996).
23. 527 U.S. 706 (1999).
24. 514 U.S. 549 (1995).
25. 529 U.S. 598 (2000).
26. U.S. Const. amend. II.
27. 529 U.S. at 613.

CHAPTER 8: A GOVERNMENT OF MEN AND NOT OF LAWS

1. Transcript, "Univision Interview with President Obama after State of the Union Address," January 26, 2012, http://latinalista.com/media-2/transcripts/transcript-univision-interview-with-president-obama-after-state-of-the-union-address.
2. U.S. Const. art. II, §3.
3. Locke, *Two Treatises of Government*, §123, 395.
4. Ibid.
5. Ibid.
6. Ibid., §124, 396.
7. Ibid., §125, 396.
8. Ibid.
9. Ibid., §126, 396.
10. Ibid., §126, 397.
11. Montesquieu, *The Spirit of the Laws*, vol. 1, trans. Thomas Nugent (London: J. Nourse, 1777), 138.
12. Ibid.
13. Ibid.
14. Mass. Const. art. XXX (1780) (emphasis added).
15. J. W. Hampton, Jr., & Co. v. United States, 276 U.S. 394, 409 (1928).
16. Department of Transportation v. Association of American Railroads, 575 U.S. ____ (2015) (Thomas, J., concurring), slip opinion at 19.
17. *Id.* slip opinion at 27.
18. *Id.* slip opinion at 12.
19. See Gary Lawson, "The Rise and Rise of the Administrative State," *Harvard Law Review* 107 (1994): 1231–54.
20. Perez v. Mortgage Bankers Association, 575 U. S. ____ (2015) (Thomas, J., concurring), slip opinion at 8.

21. *Id.* slip opinion at 5.
22. Chevron U.S.A., Inc. v. Natural Resources Defense Council, Inc., 467 U.S. 837 (1984).
23. *Perez*, 575 U.S. ____ (Thomas, J., concurring), slip opinion at 13.
24. *Id.*
25. *Id.* slip opinion at 11.
26. *Id.* slip opinion at 13.
27. *Id.* slip opinion at 11.
28. *Id.* slip opinion at 23.
29. See Arthur M. Schlesinger Jr., *The Imperial Presidency* (New York: Houghton Mifflin, 1973).

CHAPTER 9: "IRRATIONAL AND ARBITRARY" LAWS

1. Obituary of Theodore Shanbaum, *Dallas Morning News*, October 6, 1999.
2. Ibid.
3. Ibid.
4. Ibid.
5. F. H. Buckley, *The Once and Future King: The Rise of Crown Government in America* (New York: Encounter Books, 2014).
6. Locke, *Two Treatises of Government*, §124, 396.
7. See Philip Hamburger, *Is Administrative Law Unlawful?* (Chicago: University of Chicago Press, 2014).
8. Madison, "Federalist #10."
9. Ibid.
10. *The Papers of James Madison*, http://press-pubs.uchicago.edu/founders/documents/v1ch14s50.html.
11. Schlesinger, "The Supreme Court: 1947," 202.
12. Ibid.
13. 3 U.S. at 388 (Chase, J.) (emphases in original).
14. *Id.* (emphases in original).
15. *Calder*, 3 U.S. at 388.
16. 22 U.S. 1, 203 (1824).
17. *Id.*
18. Declaration of Independence para. 2 (U.S. 1776).
19. Clark M. Neily III, *Terms of Engagement: How Our Courts Should Enforce the Constitution's Promise of Limited Government* (New York: Encounter Books, 2013).
20. Ibid., 1–2, 59–60.
21. Ibid., 20.
22. Ibid., 159–60.
23. Ibid., 57–58.
24. For more on why "the due process of law" requires general laws that are

not irrational or arbitrary, see Sandefur, *The Conscience of the Constitution*, 71–155.

25. 304 U.S. at 152.
26. Milnot Company v. Richardson, 350 F. Supp. 221, 224 (N.D. Ill. 1972).
27. *Id.*
28. *Id.*
29. *Lee Optical*, 120 F. Supp. 128, 135 (W.D. Okla. 1954).
30. *Id.* at 132.
31. *Id.* at 134.
32. *Id.*
33. *Id.* at 135.
34. *Id.*
35. *Id.*
36. *Id.* at 136.
37. *Id.*
38. *Id.*
39. *Id.* at 137.
40. *Id.*
41. *Id.*
42. *Id.*
43. *Id.* at 137–38.
44. *Id.* at 137 n. 20.
45. *Id.*
46. *Id.* at 138.
47. *Id.* at 139.
48. *Id.* at 137.
49. *Carolene Products*, 304 U.S. at 152.
50. *Id.* (emphasis added).
51. *Id.* at 487.
52. *Id.*
53. *Id.*
54. *Id.*
55. *Id.* at 488 (emphasis added).
56. *Id.* at 489 (emphasis added).
57. *Id.* (emphasis added).
58. *Id.*
59. See Barnett, "Scrutiny Land."

CONCLUSION : REDEEMING OUR REPUBLICAN CONSTITUTION

1. Mark A. Levin, *The Liberty Amendments: Restoring the American Republic* (New York: Threshold Editions, 2013), 1.

2. Calvin Coolidge, *Address at the Celebration of the 150th Anniversary of the Declaration of Independence*, July 5, 1926, http://www.presidency.ucsb.edu/ ws/?pid=408.

3. See Barnett, *Restoring the Lost Constitution*, 412–19. For another set of thoughtful proposals aimed at the same restorative end, see Levin, *The Liberty Amendments*.

4. *The Records of the Federal Convention of 1787*, ed. Max Farrand, vol. 2 (New Haven, CT: Yale University Press, 1937), 629 (statement by George Mason, September 15, 1787) (emphasis added).

5. See Robert G. Natelson, "Founding-Era Conventions and the Meaning of the Constitution's 'Convention for Proposing Amendments,'" *Florida Law Review* 65 (2013): 615. See also Robert G. Natelson, "The Article V Convention Process and the Restoration of Federalism," *Harvard Journal of Law and Public Policy* 36 (2013): 955.

6. See Michael B. Rappaport, "The Constitutionality of a Limited Convention: An Originalist Analysis," *Constitutional Commentary* 81 (2012): 53. See also Michael Stern, "Reopening the Constitutional Road to Reform: Toward a Safeguarded Article V Convention," *Tennessee Law Review* 78 (2011): 765.

7. Levin, *The Liberty Amendments*, 15.

8. Ibid., 1.

9. Ibid., 18.

INDEX

ABOUT THE AUTHOR

RANDY E. BARNETT is the author of eleven books, including *Restoring the Lost Constitution* and *The Structure of Liberty*. He is the Carmack Waterhouse Professor of Legal Theory at the Georgetown University Law Center, where he teaches constitutional law and contracts, and is the director of the Georgetown Center for the Constitution. He is also a recipient of a Guggenheim Fellowship in Constitutional Studies and the Bradley Prize.